OWL

# THE POLITICS OF SOCIAL RESEARCH

MARTYN HAMMERSLEY

SAGE Publications
London • Thousand Oaks • New Delhi

First Published 1995. Reprinted 2000

 SAGE Publications Ltd
6 Bonhill Street
London EC2A 4PU

SAGE Publications Inc
2455 Teller Road
Thousand Oaks, California 91320

SAGE Publications India Pvt Ltd
32, M-Block Market
Greater Kailash – I
New Delhi 110 048

**British Library Cataloguing in Publication data**

A catalogue record for this book is
available from the British Library

ISBN 0 8039 7718 2
ISBN 0 8039 7719 0 (pbk)    1003497315

**Library of Congress catalog card number 94-74901**

Typeset by M Rules
Printed and Bound by Selwood Printing Ltd. West Sussex

# Contents

# Acknowledgements

Many debts have been incurred in the course of writing this book, and I am not able to record them all. Chapters have been presented, in various forms, at conferences and seminars in several institutions during the past three years. My thanks go to all the participants for their questions and comments. In addition, I would like to express my appreciation to David Hamilton for organising the ESRC-sponsored seminars on Methodology and Epistemology in Educational Research, at which Chapters 1 and 6 were presented.

There are also some more persistent and diffuse debts, to a whole range of people. In particular, though, I am grateful to Barry Cooper, Peter Foster, Roger Gomm, Donald Mackinnon and John Scarth for providing the sort of colleagueship which I find indispensable.

Finally, and as usual, my family has had to put up with much, not least with piles of books and papers all over the house, and with someone whose mind has often been elsewhere. My love and thanks go to Joan, Rachel and Paul.

Chapters 3, 4 and 8 are slightly revised versions of articles which first appeared in *Sociology* (1992, vol. 26, 2, pp. 187–206), the *British Journal of Sociology* (1993, vol. 44, 3, pp. 429–48) and *International Studies in the Sociology of Education* (1992, vol. 2, 2, pp. 165–83), respectively. An earlier and substantially different version of Chapter 7 is to be published in B. Troyna and D. Halpin (eds), *Researching Education Policy: methodological and ethical issues*, London, Falmer.

# Introduction

During the first half of the twentieth century social research became institutionalised in Western societies, in both universities and independent research organisations. A central element of the case made for it was that it was scientific, more or less on the model of the natural sciences. And a crucial corollary was that it promised, and was expected to deliver, much the same sort of contribution to practical affairs as other sciences had done. As we approach the end of the century, the social sciences remain institutionally well established, even though they are by no means free from threat. However, the rationale for their position has started to disintegrate. Not only have expectations about their practical payoff been frustrated to a substantial degree, but a growing number of social scientists have themselves lost faith in the original mission: a broad consensus about the character and function of social research has been replaced by a plethora of competing proposals. As part of this, increasingly, there have been denials that social research can be scientific, declarations that it is political, and debates about its role in relation to social and political practice. Its nature and function have become highly contested.

An important aspect of this shift in attitude towards social research has been a move away from the model of the natural sciences, towards the view that it has more in common with the humanities. An early sign, perhaps, was the return to influence of political philosophy, despite supposedly having been made obsolete by political science in the 1950s. More recently, there has been the revival of 'grand theorising' within sociology, largely under the influence of continental European philosophy, after a period in which such theorising was dismissed in favour of a more routine scientific concern with empirical research, whose goal extended to 'middle range theory' at most. Finally, in more specifically methodological terms, there is the growing popularity of qualitative methods in social research. These had long been employed, but until the second half of the century they were largely subordinated to quantitative work. From the 1960s onwards, however, they started to be seen by many as a self-contained alternative to quantitative method, even as a replacement for it. Furthermore, where initially qualitative researchers were keen to stress the scientific character of their work, and to distinguish it from journalism and literature, appeals to science have recently become much less usual. Correspondingly, there has been increasing emphasis on qualitative research as a form of writing, one which has much in common even with fictional prose and poetry.

Equally important has been a weakening of the boundaries between social research, on the one hand, and politics and other forms of practice, on the other. Previously, the fact that social research was scientific marked it off from politics and practice, while at the same time providing for the distinctive character of the contribution it could make to them. Its most enthusiastic supporters saw it as replacing politics with some form of scientific administration, but even more moderate advocates regarded it as capable of curbing political excess by demonstrating what could and could not be achieved, and what the costs of different courses of action would be. Increasingly today, though, it is argued that social research cannot but be political, so that there are calls for partisan and openly ideological research. There has also been growing pressure to gear research directly to political goals: for it to meet national needs as defined by governments, to serve the practical requirements of industry and the professions, or to support the political struggles of subordinate groups.

To a large extent, these political demands stem from disappointment at the actual practical contribution which it is felt social research has made. The complaint is both that this has been smaller than hoped, if not virtually non-existent, and that it has been by no means always progressive: thus the radical Left has accused it of serving capitalism, the radical Right of being anti-capitalist. Furthermore, that social research has the capacity to produce knowledge of the same kind as natural science, and thereby to have the same sort of technological impact as the latter, is denied by growing numbers of social scientists.[1]

This book addresses some of these changes in ideas about the nature of social research, focusing particularly on the fields of sociology and applied social research, where the most fundamental challenges to earlier ideas have taken place. Its central preoccupation is with views that see social research as a political enterprise, which claim that it is and should be motivated by political concerns, and that it should be carried out in such a way as to realise certain political ideals or to lead directly to desirable practical results. As I have already noted, such views are to be found on both the Left and the Right, in government circles and among those alienated from governments. In my view, this

[1] Indeed, natural science has itself lost some of its earlier prestige: because expectations of its technological contribution have sometimes outstripped what could be achieved; as a result of growing recognition that technology has negative as well as positive effects; and because of the escalating costs of 'big science'.

politicisation of research is founded on arguments which are defective and which serve to undermine research as a distinctive form of activity. To the extent that they become widely accepted, they negate social researchers' attempts to preserve some autonomy from the state and from other powerful social interests, thereby destroying the conditions in which research can flourish, perhaps even threatening its survival.

At the same time, the problems, both practical and theoretical, which have given rise to these developments are genuine, and they point to important weaknesses in the way that social scientists have previously conceptualised and carried out their work. In many respects, these problems reflect the failings of some of the Enlightenment presuppositions which have long guided social research. There is an urgent need to re-examine these presuppositions, and much of my argument in this book represents an attempt to do this, and thereby to rethink the philosophical rationale for social inquiry.

Some of the chapters which follow focus specifically on the arguments presented in support of forms of social inquiry which have explicit and direct political commitments, notably 'critical', feminist, 'anti-racist' and postmodernist approaches. While critical of these positions, I have sought to take their arguments seriously and to think in a sustained way about their implications. Other chapters address the underlying issues more directly, considering the senses in which social research is scientific or political, and what its relationship should be to social and political practice. While each chapter stands alone, much the same point of view underlies them all.[2]

In the first chapter I look at changes in the philosophical ideas that have informed social research over the past few decades. These changes have legitimised, and to some degree led to, the growing tendency to see research as political. Until the 1960s and 1970s, an important influence on social science methodology was positivist philosophy of science, along with associated trends of thought like operationalism and behaviourism. From this point of view, natural science method, interpreted in a particular way, was taken to be the model that social research should follow. After the collapse of positivism in the 1950s, and the emergence of competing approaches within the philosophy of science, social research methodology became open to diverse philosophical influences. Previously internalised but subordinated traditions like Marxism and

---

[2] Inevitably, the same issues are sometimes discussed in different places, though usually from different angles. The most obvious example of repetition is of the argument that relativism is self-refuting. A variety of formulations of this will be found in the pages that follow. This may be desirable, however, given that there are many who still do not see its force.

pragmatism resurfaced, and continental European ideas became influential, initially phenomenology and structuralism, later philosophical hermeneutics, poststructuralism and postmodernism. And one of the most important effects of this has been to undermine the basis for seeing social research as scientific. In this chapter, I examine positivist philosophy of science and its decline, and also what has followed it, arguing that the conclusions drawn by social scientists from developments in this field do not always reflect accurately what has happened there. I conclude that positive lessons can still be learned from positivism, as well as a very important negative one.

Chapter 2 examines the meaning of an influential umbrella term under which advocates of politically committed research often gather. It is now very common for approaches in many fields to be labelled as 'critical', largely on the model of 'critical theory'. In many ways, this reflects the continuing reverberations of New Left politics within the social sciences. Of course, the 'critical' tradition is by no means internally homogeneous: there are conflicting conceptions of 'critical theory'; and competing lines of thought as well, not least poststructuralism and postmodernism. And all of these make substantial philosophical claims which raise serious problems. Yet this seems to be systematically ignored by many critical social researchers. They often present their approach as if it were a coherent and relatively unproblematic one whose superiority is obvious. Furthermore, in my view, the criticisms they direct against other kinds of inquiry are inaccurate and misconceived. Indeed, I believe their proposal that research should serve political goals directly represents an abandonment of the obligations of the researcher. I conclude that there are no grounds for labelling any sort of inquiry as distinctively 'critical'.

As the example of 'critical research' makes clear, it is by no means just philosophical ideas which have led to increasing emphasis on the politics of social research. Equally important has been the impact of political movements. And it is not just the New Left which is of significance here. One of the most influential movements in the social sciences today is feminism. This has led to important theoretical developments and has also affected methodological thinking. Many feminists have argued for a specifically feminist methodology: one which emphasises the omni-relevance of gender, a respect for personal experience as against scientific method, a rejection of 'hierarchical' forms of research, and the emancipation of women as the goal of inquiry. I examine the arguments for a distinctively feminist methodology in Chapter 3, suggesting that, for the most part, they are neither new nor convincing. I conclude that while feminism has played, and continues to play, an important role in stimulating research in neglected areas and in correcting bias, there is no justification for the idea that research carried out by feminists should be guided by different method-ological canons to those of non-feminists.[3]

Similar developments can be found in the study of inter-ethnic and 'race' relations. Here there has been a growing tendency to require research to be devoted to combating racism, under the influence of the 'anti-racist' movement. Chapter 4 looks in depth at a dispute which has taken place in the field of research on racism among teachers in British schools. This raises some fundamental methodological issues. In par-ticular, there is the question of the standards by which research should be judged; and, ultimately, of the purposes of research in this field. Is the aim to generate knowledge about school processes or to serve a political cause? An important element of this debate is criticism of research which is not directly committed to 'anti-racism' as empiricist, and the employment of alternative epistemological positions like rela-tivism, standpoint theory and instrumentalism. This criticism and the grounds for it are examined, and the implications of social scientists abandoning a foundationalist epistemology are considered. It is argued that this does not necessarily, and should not, lead us to adopt those extreme epistemological alternatives. Instead, a less radical non-foun-dationalism is defended, and its implications explored. It is also suggested that, even from an 'anti-racist' point of view, relinquishing the relative autonomy of research from practical politics is unwise.

Chapter 5 reviews the growing attention given to the nature of aca-demic writing, largely under the influence of structuralism, poststructuralism and postmodernism. The specific focus is a promi-nent feature of these discussions which might be called 'textual radicalism'. This is founded on a critique of conventional modes of reporting research, not just those characteristic of quantitative method but also those typical of much qualitative research as well. Indeed, one of the main targets of attack has been realist forms of ethnographic writing in anthropology and sociology. It is claimed that these present a particular perspective, usually a white, Western, bourgeois, male view-point, as if it were reality itself. The critics call for alternative forms of writing which will draw attention to the constructed character of accounts, give space to the perspectives of those on the political mar-gins, and counter the discursive closure characteristic of conventional research reports. I consider the epistemological and political arguments underlying this textual radicalism, suggesting that they are of doubtful value; and I outline what I believe to be a more appropriate rhetorical policy for social research.

---

[3] See Gelsthorpe (1992), Ramazanoglu (1992) and Williams (1993) for responses to the publication of an earlier version of this chapter; and Hammersley (1994a) for a reply to them.

Chapter 6 adopts a wider focus, examining the whole issue of the senses in which social research may reasonably be described as political. It points out that if we interpret this term in a broad way, as implying involvement in power relations or reliance on value judgments, then there are various respects in which research is indeed political, although much the same is true of other human activities. However, I argue that there is another, narrower, sense in which social research should not be political: it should not be directed to any other immediate goal than the pursuit of knowledge. This does not mean that researchers must be apolitical, or that they can or should work in a manner which ensures that their research has no political consequences. Rather, it is to insist that, in the activity of research, concerns other than the production of knowledge must generally be subordinated to that goal.

Chapter 7 looks at prevailing ideas about the relationship between social research, on the one hand, and policy-making and practice, on the other. It argues that these are typically based on Enlightenment assumptions which require a strong, scientifically based body of knowledge about the social world, and a relatively simple and powerful relationship between it and progressive social change. Three models of the relationship between research and practice, which build on these assumptions, are examined: the disciplinary, engineering and critical models. In the second half of the chapter, arguments throwing doubt on the viability and desirability of the Enlightenment paradigm are reviewed. It is concluded that a re-assessment of the value of research and of its potential contribution to political and social practice is required.

The final chapter is concerned with the institution in which social research has been most successfully established: the university. It explores conflicting conceptions of this institution, looking in detail at what might be called the liberal model, and at two competitors to it which have gained increasing influence in recent years: the economic and ideological models. I examine the main criticisms of the liberal university coming from advocates of these other positions. Some of these criticisms represent a political challenge, claiming that the knowledge and education that the liberal university offers is of little practical value, or that what is offered is not politically neutral, that it serves to reinforce (or to subvert) the status quo, contrary to its claims. Other criticisms challenge the cognitive presuppositions of the liberal university. Here it is denied that contemplative knowledge of the social world is possible, or it is proposed that access to knowledge depends on social location, or that the validity of all claims to knowledge is culture-relative or paradigm-dependent. In the conclusion, I outline what I believe to be the strengths of the liberal university in comparison with its competitors.

Social research has been in crisis, recurrently, ever since it became institutionalised in the late nineteenth and early twentieth centuries. It has flourished despite this. But the level of disagreement about its purpose and justification is now greater than ever before. Moreover, there are currently changes taking place, both outside universities and within them, which threaten its existence. Attention to the issues with which this book is concerned has never been required so urgently.

# 1

# Paradigm Lost? Positivism and its Afterlife in the Philosophy of Social Research

Positivism, while long since pronounced dead, has not been buried and forgotten. In a recently published set of conference proceedings dealing with research methodology in the field of education, entitled *The Paradigm Dialog* (Guba 1990), there are at least 70 references to positivism and positivists; that is, on average, around one reference for every five pages of the book. And this is despite the fact that positivism is not one of the three paradigms around which the book is organised. This may be an extreme example, but it makes the point that positivism remains a significant feature on the intellectual landscape of social research methodology.[1] However, it occupies a peculiar place in that landscape. What is striking is not just the *frequency* of references to positivism, but also the *character* of those references.

First, the references are typically directed at others. No one today, or hardly anyone, refers to themselves or their own work as positivist.[2] Instead, references to positivism are primarily used as a device for promoting other positions. Secondly, and this follows from the previous point, most of the references are negative: they are disparaging if not dismissive. Moreover, positivism is rejected not just in intellectual but in moral and political terms, for instance on the grounds that it involves the disguising of value biases as objective knowledge and/or implies support for the socio-political status quo.

A consequence of this usage is that the terms 'positivism' and 'positivist' are applied to diverse targets; for example, not just to quantitative research but also to naturalistic ethnography.[3] Their meaning has thereby become so wide-ranging as frequently to be obscure. It

---

[1] There is a problem of terminology here, with other terms (such as 'empiricism', 'empirical-analytical approach', 'scientific paradigm') sometimes being used as synonyms for 'positivism'. There is also variation in the meaning of 'positivism' (see Halfpenny 1982; Phillips 1983).

[2] For a qualified exception, see Silverman (1989).

[3] See, for instance, Roman and Apple (1990). This is not entirely new, Leach criticised Malinowski's approach to ethnography as empiricist in the 1950s (Leach 1957). At the same time, see Marsh (1982) for the argument that quantitative research is not necessarily positivist.

is only a slight exaggeration to say that all one can reasonably infer from unexplicated usage of the term 'positivism' in the social research literature is that the writer disapproves of whatever he or she is referring to.

Usage of 'positivism' in this way is fairly recent, and it reflects in large part a growing tendency to think about social research methodology not in terms of a single, scientific approach in which a variety of methods are used more or less appropriately for different purposes, but rather as consisting of competing paradigms based on quite different conceptions of the purposes and nature of social research, many of them rejecting not just positivism but the natural science model as well. Guba's book *The Paradigm Dialog* (1990) is organised around such a view, as its title indicates. There, positivism is portrayed as the deposed paradigm, with a conflict now taking place among postpositivism, critical research and constructivism to replace it. This is an exemplification of what have been called 'the paradigm wars' (Gage 1989).

From this paradigmatic point of view, positivism is a mode of social research whose essential feature is that it is founded on certain distinctive philosophical assumptions which the new paradigms reject. These assumptions typically include some or all of the following:

- that what is taken to be the method of the natural sciences is the only rational source of knowledge;
- that this method should be applied in social research irrespective of any supposedly distinctive features of social reality;
- that quantitative measurement and experimental or statistical manipulation of variables are essential, or at least ideal, features of scientific research;
- that research can and should be concerned with producing accounts which correspond to an independent reality;
- that scientific knowledge consists of universal laws;
- that research must be objective, with subjective biases being overcome through commitment to the principle of value neutrality.

Of course, the paradigm view of social research is in one way itself a reaction against positivism. In extreme form, the latter appears as an anti-philosophy rather than a philosophy: it denies the role of philosophical assumptions in scientific research. Such a denial is, of course, misguided, since it fails to recognise that even this denial is a philosophical claim. There is no escaping philosophical presuppositions, as advocates of the paradigm view have emphasised. At the same time, it seems to me that looking at social research methodology in terms of competing paradigms is also unhelpful. It exaggerates the depth of empirical differences in view among social researchers and the scale of the impact of these on the practice of research. It also leads to far too restricted a characterisation of the difficult methodological issues that face social research, and of the positions which can be taken towards them. Moreover, it gives the impression that these issues can and should be resolved simply by a choice among paradigms.

The treatment of positivism as a paradigm illustrates these dangers; indeed, in many ways it may be taken as a test case. It implies that all the features listed above, or some subset of them, belong together. But this is true neither philosophically nor empirically. One may be committed to the natural science model but not to the primacy of quantitative method, and to both without believing that they should be applied irrespective of the distinctive features of social reality. And none of these commitments necessarily goes with realism (that is, with the assumption that objects in the world exist independently of our beliefs about them), with the idea that scientific knowledge consists of universal laws, or with the principle of value neutrality. Neither does realism logically imply that scientific knowledge consists of laws or that inquiry can or should be value neutral. Furthermore, if one looks at the history of social research, one finds representatives of various combinations of these and other commitments, not a well-defined group of philosophers and social scientists adhering to 'positivism' which is faced by another group that rejects it. Of course, advocates of the paradigm model sometimes recognise this, but when they do the normative character of their position usually comes into play: they argue that those who do not sign up wholeheartedly for one side or the other are confused or have been insufficiently reflexive about their foundational assumptions (see, for example, Smith and Heshusius 1986). For these reasons, thinking about social research methodology in terms of paradigms obscures both potential and actual diversity in orientation, and it can lead us into making simplistic methodological decisions.[4]

Closely associated with the idea that social research is governed by competing methodological paradigms is a distinctive account of its recent history. According to this view, the philosophy of science was until recently dominated by positivism and it determined the methodological orientations of social scientists (albeit without them always being aware of this). But, so the story continues, positivism was overthrown in the philosophy of science some time ago, bringing to light the socially constructed and culturally relative character even of natural science; though news of this has not yet reached many

---

[4] For an application of this argument to the distinction between qualitative and quantitative method, see Hammersley (1992a: ch. 9).

natural scientists and social researchers, who continue to adopt an outdated positivist orientation.

In significant respects this history is a myth. As with most myths there is some truth in it, but it is very misleading.[5] In this chapter I will look briefly at the development of positivist philosophy in the twentieth century, and at the arguments against and alternatives to it which can be found in recent philosophy of science and elsewhere. I will end by considering what conclusions social researchers should draw from this history of changing philosophical ideas.

## The rise of positivist philosophy of science

The history of the philosophy of science as a distinct subdiscipline is largely restricted to the twentieth century. Of course, philosophical writing about knowledge, science and the process of inquiry is much older than this. But it was only in this century that some philosophers began to write for fellow philosophers of science and started to teach the philosophy of science to students.

To a large extent, what has come to be called 'logical positivism' was the driving force behind the establishment of the philosophy of science as a separate subdiscipline. Indeed, at the beginning it seemed as though positivism was destined to turn the whole of philosophy into the philosophy of science. A central role in the promotion of logical positivism was played by the Vienna Circle, a group of philosophers, scientists and mathematicians who worked together in the 1920s, issuing in 1929 what amounted to their manifesto, entitled *The Scientific Conception of the World* (Hahn et al. 1929). This title makes clear the centrality for them of the natural sciences. Science was crucial in two ways: as a methodological model for, and as the main focus of, philosophical work.

The logical positivists took science to represent the model for all human inquiry and knowledge, and it was in terms of this model that they rejected much previous philosophy as metaphysical, as literally nonsense. A key task, then, was the development of a philosophy modelled on the methodology of natural science. As part of this, they were concerned to restrict philosophy to questions that were answerable. They were keen to abandon what they saw as confusing and inconclu-

---

[5] Needless to say, by talking about myths and their truth and falsehood I automatically position myself within the field of discourse I am describing; and for many this will reveal me to be a positivist! I could say that this is an inaccurate description of my position, but of course in some eyes that claim would itself confirm my positivism. To treat all who are not relativists as if they were positivists is precisely the sort of obscuring of important distinctions which the paradigm model encourages.

sive discussions of pseudo-problems, for example about whether there is a world beyond our perceptions, about whether there are other minds besides our own etc.; questions which had greatly preoccupied previous philosophers.

They developed what came to be called the verifiability principle. According to this principle, science, philosophy, and indeed all rational discourse, consist of only two sorts of statement:

1 Logical statements that are true by definition, with mathematics included under this heading.
2 Empirical statements, that is, statements whose validity can be determined, at least in principle, on the basis of empirical evidence, the latter interpreted as consisting ultimately of observable givens.

According to the verifiability principle, no other sorts of statement are meaningful; so that these two types of statement are the only legitimate components of science and are to be the sole components of a scientific philosophy. The logical positivists believed that by applying this principle they could rule out much that claimed falsely to be knowledge, especially in the fields of theology, ethics and politics; and in this way avoid philosophical pseudo-problems and so pave the way for sustained philosophical progress.

However, science was also central to the thinking of the logical positivists because there were philosophical problems surrounding recent developments in the natural sciences, which they believed required resolution if further progress was not to be impeded. For instance, it was argued that some of the concepts that physicists had inherited from Newton, notably absolute space and time, were metaphysical and were not reconcilable with the latest findings. (This point was highlighted by Einstein's theories of relativity.) In response to this, the positivists sought to reconstruct physics on the basis of logical inference from perceptual givens or observables, thereby avoiding reliance in the future on assumptions not open to, or that had not been subjected to, direct scientific investigation.

Of course, positivism did not begin in the 1920s with the logical positivists. The term 'positivism' had been invented in the nineteenth century by Auguste Comte, and the ideas associated with it were very influential in that century, especially as formulated by John Stuart Mill.[6] Furthermore, the belief that natural science provides a model for all inquiry, and that it requires reliance only on what can be observed, goes back well beyond the nineteenth century. In particular, twentieth-century positivists have drawn heavily on the radical empiricism of

---

[6] For a history of positivism, see Kolakowski (1972). See also Giddens (1979).

David Hume. Taking the spirit of the seventeenth-century revolution in science to what seemed to be its logical conclusion, Hume had denied that we can have knowledge of any natural order of the universe, insisting that our knowledge is restricted to immediate experience and what can be logically derived from this.

In broad terms we must see Hume and his successors as exemplifying a central strand of Enlightenment thinking. Hume's arguments were an attack on natural theology, on the idea that inquiry must presuppose some view of the nature of reality as a whole, such as that represented by the Aristotelianism which had dominated philosophy and science up to the seventeenth century, and whose influence persisted long after that. This natural law tradition was rejected by Hume and others because it made claims which went beyond the evidence.

Another significant feature of Aristotelianism was its teleological character, seeing everything as having a goal or purpose, so that rational conclusions could be drawn about values as well as about facts. By contrast, Hume drew a sharp distinction between facts and values, insisted that value conclusions could not be derived from factual premises alone, and that true knowledge about values was not available to us. This doctrine, the central component of the principle of value neutrality, was taken over by many, though not by all, nineteenth- and twentieth-century positivists.[7]

Where the logical positivists differed most significantly from Hume, Comte and Mill, as their name implies, was in their emphasis on the role of logic and mathematics in science. This reflected developments within the study of logic in the latter part of the nineteenth-century, notably the shift from Aristotelian to symbolic logic principally associated with the names of Frege and Russell. One of the effects of this concern with logic was to lead twentieth-century positivists to give great attention to language, focusing their epistemological arguments on propositions rather than on ideas (the terms in which earlier empiricists had operated). It also led them to emphasise the importance of clarity of expression, often using logical symbolism to facilitate this. They regarded natural language expressions as frequently confused

---

[7] Some, for example Comte, believed that science was capable of answering value questions. See Keat (1981: ch. 2) for a useful discussion of this. It is perhaps worth pointing out that the natural law tradition is by no means dead: it is preserved, for example, within Catholic scholarship (see, for example, Midgley's 1983 critique of Weber). And outside of Catholicism strong traces of it are to be found in the writings of Leo Strauss and his students (Strauss 1953; Storing 1962). It is also central to MacIntyre's recent work (MacIntyre 1990). Incidentally, it is not *too* far fetched to see the Hegelian-Marxist-critical tradition as a historicised version of natural law theory.

and confusing. Indeed, the fruitless metaphysical debates which had preoccupied previous philosophers were regarded by them as deriving in large part from linguistic confusions.

Let me summarise the character of twentieth-century positivist philosophy in terms of three main elements:

1. The primacy of natural science as the model for inquiry and knowledge. In shorthand terms, what is sometimes called 'methodological monism'.

2. A conception of the nature of science which emphasises method and conceives of this as involving logical argument, the testing of ideas against what is observable, and the rejection as meaningless of claims to knowledge that go beyond what is logically derivable or observable. This is sometimes referred to as 'empiricism', though the term is not entirely satisfactory because it is often used to cover a broader range of positions than this.

3. The idea that science, and rigorous inquiry generally, can only produce factual knowledge, they cannot generate evaluative or prescriptive conclusions. For the sake of convenience, we might call this 'objectivism'.

Now, it may look as if this summary represents a candidate definition of the positivist paradigm in the philosophy of science. It does capture assumptions that, by and large, the Vienna Circle philosophers all held. However, it does not constitute a set of necessary and sufficient conditions for the identification even of a *logical* positivist, both because there were disagreements over the interpretation of these matters among the core members of the Circle, and because there were many outside it who shared one or more of these assumptions but did not see themselves (and were not seen) as positivists.

As regards internal disagreement, the second component, the empiricist conception of scientific knowledge, was subject to considerable debate by logical positivists. And, over the course of time, there was a general trend away from extreme empiricism or phenomenalism towards physicalism, towards treating physical objects that could be observed, and whose features were open to intersubjective agreement, as existing independently of our perceptions of them; though agnosticism remained about the existence of real entities corresponding to *theoretical* concepts.

Similar complexities in view are to be found as regards objectivism. I have already noted that some positivists have believed that science could resolve value disagreements, seeing the possibility of a scientific politics. And, indeed, the principle of value neutrality owes its most influential formulation to Max Weber who was not a positivist, and whose work predated that of the logical positivists.[8] Nevertheless, in the twentieth century positivist philosophy has tended to be associated with that principle.

Equally, we need to take note of the areas where positivism, defined in this way, overlaps with other approaches. For example, it shares much with some versions of pragmatism: the verifiability principle is similar in many respects to Peirce's pragmatic maxim; and the writings of Charles Morris and others before the Second World War exploited this similarity (see, for example, Morris 1946). Perhaps more surprisingly, positivism overlaps significantly with the phenomenology of Edmund Husserl. Both positivism and phenomenology were committed to a scientific philosophy, and both attempted to base knowledge on subjective givens.[9] Positivism and structuralism also have something in common, notably commitment to a scientific approach to the study of the social world. Thus, the work of the anthropologist Levi-Strauss owes much to Durkheim, who is often taken to have been a positivist. Finally, it is worth emphasising how close logical positivism comes to relativism, especially as developed by Carnap. He drew a sharp distinction between problems internal to a particular framework of rules, and those external to that framework. The former are simple 'in principle', though perhaps technically difficult to solve; the latter are practical questions which concern whether we should accept particular frameworks, not theoretical questions that are open to judgment in terms of truth or falsity (Wick 1951: 53). And, as Toulmin has argued, the position of the early Wittgenstein, who was on the margins of the Vienna Circle and influenced their thinking, was even more radical in this respect, implying that no system of symbols could be *logically* anchored to the world (Toulmin 1969). We see here the germ of Kuhn's concept of paradigm, and it is an argument which has been pursued, still largely within a logical empiricist framework, by Quine (see, for example, Quine 1984).

Even in the case of positivist philosophy of science, then, it is not possible to produce a definition consisting of an unambiguous and agreed set of paradigmatic assumptions that are necessary and sufficient to distinguish it. Rather, we have a collection of ideas subject to some variation in interpretation and combination. Furthermore, not

[8] Weber is probably best thought of as a neo-Kantian, drawing heavily on the work of Rickert (Burger 1976; Oakes 1988). And what distinguished him from Rickert was in large part the influence of Nietzsche.

[9] On Husserl and phenomenology, see Kolakowski (1975a) and Hammond et al. (1991). Also, see the work of Kaufmann (1958), who draws on both positivism and phenomenology, and whose book seems to have had an important impact on Garfinkel's ethnomethodology.

only was there considerable disagreement among logical positivists, and change in their views over time, but also these views blur into and even overlap with those of other philosophical traditions. In short, where the paradigm model encourages us to see sharp differences, when we look more closely we find more subtle ones as well as significant interrelationships.

Before I turn to the criticisms of logical positivism and its subsequent demise, I think it is worth emphasising something about it which is sometimes forgotten today. It is often seen as essentially conservative in character: this was very much the view of Frankfurt School critical theorists, for example, and it has become widely accepted among social researchers today. Yet this is a long way from the truth. Philosophically speaking, it was very radical in its time. As I noted, it involved a turning against much that had previously passed for philosophy. Michael Scriven captures this nicely by means of a vivid metaphor, commenting that 'it performed a tracheotomy that made it possible for philosophy to breathe again', this being necessary because philosophy had become 'pompously verbose' (Scriven 1969: 165).[10]

The positivists also saw their work as progressive in a broader political sense, much as had their forerunners in the eighteenth-century Enlightenment. 'Theirs was a radical, liberating, apocalyptic movement which thought of itself as a kind of International Liberation Front – *for* scientific enlightenment and *against* the conservative obscurantism of idealist philosophy' (Toulmin 1969: 50). They were generally of the Left in political terms, albeit usually not communist; though Otto Neurath, the prime mover of the Vienna Circle, regarded himself as a Marxist and had been involved in the Spartacist movement in Munich before the First World War (Ayer 1956; Cohen 1967). Neurath and most other Austrian and German positivists were forced to emigrate in the 1930s when the Nazis came to power. Some of their opponents, by contrast, stayed and even gave support to the new regime: as is now well known, Heidegger became a National Socialist for a short while, and never publicly renounced that association.[11]

I have concentrated on the twentieth-century history of positivist philosophy, and of course this is not the same as the history of positivism in the social sciences. In fact, I suspect that the relationship was

---

[10] Scriven goes on to point out, though, that infection from such radical surgery can 'prove just as fatal as choking to death on a mess of verbiage'. It is worth mentioning that one of those whose work was subjected to surgery by the logical positivists was Martin Heidegger, whose subsequent influence on European continental philosophy was considerable, especially on philosophical hermeneutics and poststructuralism.

[11] See Wolin (1990, 1991). I hasten to add that this is not a reason to dismiss his work, but neither is the supposed conservatism of the positivists a reason to reject theirs.

a lot more tenuous than the paradigm model would lead us to believe. Social research as it developed in the first half of this century was strongly influenced by the model of natural science, but for a long time primarily by nineteenth-century conceptions of scientific method (Hamilton 1980). Furthermore, in the way in which it was pursued, it reflected the contingencies of its practical context, as much as philosophical assumptions. We need to remember that in research, as elsewhere, there is often a considerable gap between theory and practice.[12]

### The demise of positivist philosophy and its aftermath

I want to consider now what has happened in the philosophy of science since 1950. Where once that subdiscipline had been almost completely identified with positivism, in the 1950s the positivist consensus collapsed and a variety of alternative positions started to appear (Suppe 1974). We can identify three main problems on which positivism foundered. One was the formulation and status of the verifiability principle. In particular, it seemed to render itself meaningless, being neither a matter of logic nor open to empirical confirmation. The second problem centred on the assumption that hypotheses could be tested one by one against data. It was pointed out that hypotheses rely on the theory from which they derive, so that if the evidence goes against them we cannot know whether it is the hypothesis itself or one of the assumptions built into the theory which is false. The implication of this is that theories can only be tested as wholes, and this makes the drawing of conclusions about the validity of hypotheses much more uncertain.[13] The third problem was the reliance of the positivist account of science on the idea of given, observable knowledge whose validity is certain, and against which hypotheses can be tested. All attempts to provide philosophical grounds for such knowledge failed, and it came to be generally accepted that all observation is assumption laden.[14]

These problems, or rather the failure to find solutions to them, led in

[12] On positivism in sociology, see Bryant (1985).

[13] This argument had in fact been developed before the emergence of logical positivism by the conventionalist philosopher of science Pierre Duhem, and was familiar to the positivists (see Gillies 1993). The most systematic exploration of the implications of this argument for positivism is to be found in the work of Quine (see, for example, Quine 1953, 1960).

[14] See Hanson (1958). It is worth noting that this too was by no means a new idea. For instance, it was crucial to the view of science of Charles Peirce, and provided the foundation for his critical commonsensism. It was also recognised by the ancient Greek sceptics in the form of the problem of the criterion, on which see below.

the early 1950s to the disappearance of what had been a substantial positivist consensus in the philosophy of science. In Bas van Fraassen's words, 'positivism had a rather spectacular crash' (van Fraassen 1980: 2). This is not to say, however, that positivist ideas were totally abandoned by philosophers of science and have no influence today. This is worth emphasising because some appeals to the philosophy of science by social researchers give this impression (for example, Smith 1989). Most contemporary Anglo-American philosophers of science retain substantial assumptions in common with positivism, treating natural science as the primary model for rational inquiry, adopting some form of empiricism, and/or retaining the value-neutrality principle. This applies not just to the older generation who were instrumental in undermining positivism from within and without, such as Quine and Popper, but also to more recently influential writers such as Hesse, van Fraassen, Hacking and Cartwright. There are, of course, those who have made a much more radical break with positivism, such as Paul Feyerabend and Richard Rorty, but they are not representative of the field. For this reason, there is no simple answer to the question of whether positivism is dead, even within the philosophy of science; and this despite Popper's confession to murder and the reports of many witnesses who claim to have seen the corpse (Cohen 1980; Phillips 1983; Popper 1992).

An important aspect of the arguments against positivism which I have not mentioned up to now, and which Feyerabend's and Kuhn's work exemplifies, is the challenge to the empirical account of the work of scientists which underpins the positivist philosophy of science. The positivists' prescriptions for future progress were based on what they took to have been successful practice in the past. But it is argued by Feyerabend and others that in fact even the successful science that the positivists treated as a model did not operate in the way that they supposed.

Especially influential in challenging the history of science implicit in positivism was, of course, Thomas Kuhn's book *The Structure of Scientific Revolutions*, first published in 1962 (Kuhn 1970). There are some good reasons for treating Kuhn's book as a symbol of significant change in views about the character of natural science. It had and continues to have an extraordinary influence, and it does capture many features of much new thinking about science. At the same time, there are dangers in giving it such prominence. One obvious one is that it is now quite old, and so it does not represent the most recent developments. There are other dangers too. Kuhn is a historian rather than a philosopher of science, and his work is much more significant for what it tells us about how scientists go about their work than for any specifically philosophical claims it makes. And, of course, the aim of the logical positivists was not to produce an empirical account of scientific work but rather a logical reconstruction of it (Feigl 1969). Also important to remember is the fact that many of the ideas which have since come to be associated with Kuhn's name were not original to him.[15]

Kuhn's analyses of various episodes in the history of science seem to show that the positivists' assumptions about how their scientific heroes of the past did their work were in error in several respects. For instance, rather than disavowing metaphysics, these successful scientists often operated on the basis of metaphysical presuppositions and indeed sometimes on presuppositions that seem to us today to be not just wrong but bizarre. Furthermore, these assumptions were not kept logically separate from their scientific beliefs; they often formed an integral part of them, playing a key role in bringing about the discoveries for which these scientists became famous.

Kuhn went on from this to question the view of scientific development as a gradual cumulation of knowledge, an idea built into positivism. He argued that the history of scientific fields seems to be punctuated by what he calls scientific revolutions, in which the metaphysical assumptions that had previously guided work in the field are replaced by new ones. And he argued that at the very least this complicates our notion of scientific progress. This is because the prevailing paradigm, consisting of metaphysical and other assumptions embodied in exemplary studies, does not operate on some neutral bed of data but rather guides scientists' selection and interpretation of data in such a way that there is a sense in which those working in different paradigms see the world differently. He summarised this point by claiming that scientific paradigms are incommensurable.

If Kuhn's interpretation of the history of natural science is accepted, it can lead to the abandonment of many of the central features of positivism as an empirical model of successful science: the verifiability criterion of meaning as well as the idea of observational givens, and perhaps even objectivism too. Also, it reduces the scope for the unity of scientific method, since it suggests that there is not even unity within the same science over time. However, there has been much debate about what Kuhn meant, as well as about whether his account of natural scientific work is accurate.[16]

Kuhn's work has stimulated a considerable amount of research in both the history and sociology of science. In part, this has simply extended the sort of analysis he had provided to new fields and to new

[15] It is to Kuhn's credit that he makes this clear at the beginning of his book.

[16] See Kuhn's (1970) appendix to the second edition of his book, and also Hacking (1981) and the references included in the latter.

time periods, including the present. However, there has also been a tendency to radicalise Kuhn's position. This is to be seen in the so-called 'strong programme' in the sociology of science (Barnes 1974, 1982; Bloor 1976), and even more so in the work of those who have turned to discourse analysis of scientific communications (Gilbert and Mulkay 1984; Woolgar 1988; Ashmore 1989). Here there has been a move towards adopting explicitly relativistic positions which are committed to treating natural science, and the social study of science itself, as distinctive forms of life or discursive practices that require reflexive explication.

This drift towards relativism has been paralleled in the reception of Kuhn's work among social scientists generally, where it has been an influential resource in thinking about methodology. His work was the major stimulus for the paradigm model of social research that I mentioned at the beginning of this chapter. This influence is ironic because Kuhn makes a point of denying the relevance of his analysis to social science, on the grounds that the latter is pre-paradigmatic, not yet having reached an initial scientific consensus. Nevertheless, social scientists have sometimes drawn the conclusion from his work that all knowledge is founded on assumptions which are arbitrary from a rational point of view, and that ultimately it is a matter of taste or politics which paradigm one adopts.

## Other philosophical influences

A variety of influences outside the philosophy of science have fuelled the popularity of relativistic ideas in thinking about social research methodology over the past few decades. Within the Anglo-American tradition the impact of linguistic philosophy has been important, especially the later writings of Wittgenstein. As I noted earlier, his early work had been very influential for logical positivism. While he was not himself a positivist, his view of the nature of scientific knowledge conformed quite closely to theirs, though he regarded what could *not* be known in this way as more important than what could. In his later work, however, Wittgenstein abandoned the idea that scientific knowledge, encapsulated in a logically perfected language, represents the model for all knowledge. Instead, he came to the conclusion that everyday language use is the basis of all thinking, and is diverse in character. From this point of view, science is just one form of 'language game' among others, having its own distinctive rules but not being in any general sense superior.

Some of those influenced by Wittgenstein, notably Peter Winch, have applied his ideas to the social sciences. In doing so, Winch criticised anthropologists for their tendency to treat primitive cultures as rationally defective by comparison with Western science. He argued that all cultures, that of the West included, are founded on forms of practice and presuppositions which are not open to rational appraisal; and that the West and the societies studied by anthropologists differ in their foundational practices (Winch 1958, 1964). In Kuhn's terms they are incommensurable.

The growing influence of continental European philosophy has also been important in encouraging relativism on the part of many social researchers. Phenomenology was influential in the 1960s and 1970s, and the main conclusion drawn by social scientists from the writings of the phenomenologists was that our understanding of the world is constructed on the basis of assumptions, rather than being a reflection of how the world actually is. However, whereas Husserl had viewed those assumptions as universal givens, social scientists have tended to treat them as culturally relative, implying that different cultures produce different realities (Berger and Luckmann 1967).

More recently, two other continental European movements, philosophical hermeneutics and poststructuralism, have had a similar effect. Hermeneutics is concerned with the problems surrounding the process of understanding cultural products. In the eighteenth and early nineteenth centuries it developed as a methodological concern on the part of scholars in the humanities with problems involved in the interpretation of historical texts, especially those of ancient Greece and Rome and, of course, the Bible. Later, it came to focus on the more general historical problem of understanding the past. It represented a counter to the influence of positivism in the human sciences, since it emphasised the distinctive requirements and possibilities of understanding human behaviour as compared to the study of physical phenomena. In its most influential twentieth-century form, in the work of Hans Georg Gadamer, it promotes the argument that all understanding is based on an interaction between the prior assumptions of the interpreter, reflecting his or her cultural and historical circumstances, and the phenomenon being interpreted. The implication of this is that there is no method by which universally valid knowledge can be produced because all knowledge reflects the sociohistorical context of its production (Warnke 1987).

Poststructuralism is much more difficult to characterise because it has taken diverse forms and many of its representatives deny the very possibility of any clear and fixed characterisation of it (or of anything else). However, it can be defined negatively in terms of what it rejects. It denies the possibility of any kind of universally valid knowledge of the kind proposed by advocates of the scientific model. It insists not just on the relativity of all knowledge claims, but also that knowledge is a product of desire or power. Witness Lyotard's comment that 'in truth, there is no such thing as a lie, except as measured by the standard of the desire for truth, but this desire is no truer than any other desire' (quoted in Dews 1987: 210). Any claim on the part of researchers to be in pursuit of the truth, or to be in possession of knowledge, is treated by poststructuralists as hiding the work of other interests. Thus, Foucault portrays knowledge as necessarily intertwined with power: what is taken to be knowledge at any particular time depends on which 'regime of truth' is dominant; and, while these regimes change, they do not do so in any predetermined direction, and certainly not in a way that implies scientific progress.[17]

Foucault's work highlights one of the conclusions often drawn from relativism: that the previously assumed distinction between science and politics no longer holds. If research is always based on presuppositions that are socio-historical products, it is argued, this means that it represents the views of a particular culture, or of a particular group, rather than constituting universally valid knowledge. Indeed, given that knowledge can no longer be seen as a matter of disinterested inquiry, all knowledge must be treated as interested: as serving the interests of those who produce or sponsor it. This has led to calls for social research to be explicitly reorientated towards emancipatory political goals, in other words for openly partisan or ideological research (see, for example, Lather 1986, 1991; Gitlin et al. 1989). There are, however, good reasons not to accept the relativist epistemology on which such calls are based.

## The fallacy of relativism

Recent developments in the philosophy of science are often appealed to by those promoting relativist positions. However, as I noted earlier, most contemporary work in that field is not relativistic. Thus, in the past few decades, one influential strand in the philosophy of science has been scientific realism.[18] The goal of science from this point of view is to find a true description of unobservable processes that explain observable ones. The truth of descriptions is taken to be universal not relative, though knowledge of their validity is necessarily less than certain. Of course, scientific realism has by no means gone unchallenged, but much of that challenge has come from empiricists like van Fraassen, who draw on logical positivism even though they also depart from it in significant ways (van Fraassen 1980;

[17] On Foucault's work, see, for example, Sheridan (1980), Merquior (1985) and Dews (1987). For an interesting, and sympathetic, attempt to work out the implications of Foucault's work for the philosophy of science, see Rouse (1987).

[18] There are many versions of realism. See, for example, Keat and Urry (1975), Bhaskar (1978), Trigg (1980), Harré (1986), and Vision (1988).

Churchland and Hooker 1985). And while some of the non-positivist philosophical sources on which writers dealing with social research methodology now draw seem close to relativism, notably philosophical hermeneutics and poststructuralism, others are not. Neither Wittgenstein nor Husserl was a relativist in any straightforward sense of that term. Indeed, ironically, Husserl's original motivation was to counter what he saw as the drift towards relativism within German philosophy.

It is important to recognise that the trend towards relativism in social research methodology is due to internal as much as to external factors. A major complaint about positivist research on the part of social scientists has been its alleged failure to take account of the fact that people *make* sense of the world, drawing on cultural resources rather than simply responding to external stimuli in a mechanical fashion. Furthermore, the sense people make of this world differs; in effect, they construct 'multiple realities'. Thus, if one is to describe and explain their behaviour accurately, one must understand the cultures or perspectives which structure what they see, think and do. This is, of course, the central insight of social and cultural anthropology, as well as of symbolic interactionist sociology. Such a view is not necessarily relativist as it stands. However, it can become so if it is applied to social research itself. Then, researchers must be regarded as actually constructing the phenomena which they describe, on the basis of the cultural resources available to them. In other words, their descriptions and explanations reflect their own perspectives rather than, or as much as, the nature of the phenomena they claim to be describing. In this way, what is sometimes referred to as social constructionism has led to the adoption of relativistic positions of various kinds (for examples, see Holstein and Miller 1993).

One of the problems with debates about relativism is that, like positivism, the term does not have a standard, well-defined meaning. Thus, while there are some who declare themselves to be relativists (for instance, Smith 1989; Guba 1992), often arguments about relativism amount to accusations and denials (for example, Eisner 1983; Phillips 1983). This indicates that the term is used to cover a variety of positions.[19] However, what seems to be central to discussions of relativism in social research methodology is the idea that knowledge is paradigm-dependent, in other words that its validity is relative to a set of assumptions about what the world is like and how it can be understood, those assumptions being beyond rational justification (and perhaps forming part of one or another political philosophy).

Most of the arguments used by relativists to establish their position

---

[19] Quine (1984) provides a good demonstration of how complex this position is.

are very old. This is not a criticism of them, it is merely to point out that they are old enough to have been subjected to a considerable amount of scrutiny by philosophers. They were developed by the Greek sceptics, though we know of their ideas for the most part only through the writings of Sextus Empiricus, produced around 200 AD (see Sextus Empiricus 1985). The sceptics constructed a whole battery of arguments against 'dogmatists', one of the central ones being the problem of the criterion. This problem takes the following form. When someone makes a knowledge claim we can always ask by what criteria he or she judges that claim to be true. And, when the criteria are presented, we can ask about the basis on which this set of criteria is believed to be valid. Then, when this basis is provided, we can ask why *that* is believed to be true. This process is open to no definitive termination which is not logically circular.[20]

There is no doubt about the power of sceptical arguments; in fact they are so powerful that they are self-devouring. To the extent that sceptics or relativists seek to claim on the basis of them that there is no universal truth or no reality, they are hoist by their own petard. Like the positivist principle of verifiability, the argument undermines itself. If it is true that the validity of all valid claims is not universal but relative to some framework of assumptions, then for relativists this is true of relativism as well. And this means that they must recognise that their position is false when viewed from other points of view: it is not just that representatives of those other positions *think* relativism is false but that it truly is false within the framework of their assumptions. Moreover, there is no larger framework within which relativism can be presented as true, and therefore as superior to non-relativist positions (Scheffler 1967; Siegel 1987). This problem was recognised by the Pyrrhonian sceptics, who sought to avoid all such metaphysical claims.[21] They abandoned philosophy, and indeed reflective thought generally, in the interests of a rather conservative conception of personal contentment. However, in my view, one cannot escape the dilemma even in this way, and such an attitude hardly provides a satisfactory basis for social research. Nor can it support the radical political stance that some relativists among social researchers want to adopt (for example, Lather 1991).

We must recognise that absolute certainty is not available about anything, and that attempts to produce absolutely certain knowledge by appeal to sense data, or to anything else, are doomed to failure. However, accepting this does not mean concluding that any view is as

---

[20] On the history of scepticism, see Popkin (1979) and Popkin and Schmidt (1987).

[21] The parallel with positivists should be obvious, and it is not surprising since Hume drew heavily on Sextus Empiricus. On the parallel, see Chisholm (1941).

likely to be true as any other, or that anything can be true in some other framework if not in ours. In my view, the best basis for a resolution to the problem is Peirce's critical commonsensism, where assumptions are relied on until subject to genuine doubt.[22]

### Conclusion: some lessons from positivism

There is little doubt that the positivists were dramatically wrong about many things, for example about the verifiability principle and about the theory neutrality of observation; and that their views have had some negative consequences for social research. However, this does not render their work of no value. Indeed, they still have much to teach us.

One feature that is striking about the work of the Vienna Circle and their successors is the degree to which they were prepared to address the difficulties which their work raised, and to clarify and seek to resolve those difficulties; indeed substantially to change their position if this proved necessary. There are few if any of the currently standard criticisms of positivism which were not recognised by positivists and addressed by them. There was an openness to discussion, and a belief that issues could be resolved, that we would do well to emulate in thinking about social research methodology; though we probably ought to be less sanguine about the prospects of resolving our problems and reaching agreement.

A second point is that we should not conclude from the collapse of positivism that natural science has no relevance to our work as social researchers. It is certainly right that it must not be copied slavishly, but in my view it should remain the primary model, even though we can also learn much from the humanities. In part, of course, anti-positivism in social research methodology involves an attempt to move away from the model of science, drawing on hermeneutics, poststructuralism etc. But those positions have themselves been affected by ideas about science, negatively but also in some respects positively. We must not confuse the adoption of natural science as a methodological model with positivism (see Keat and Urry 1975).

Similarly, I do not believe that we should abandon the principle of value neutrality. I accept the criticism made of Weber's formulation of that principle by Habermas and others: that it abandons ethics and politics to irrationalism, and that this is unnecessary and undesirable (Habermas 1971). But, at the same time, there is a danger, exemplified in the case of some versions of action research and critical ethnography,

---

[22] On Peirce, see Reilly (1970) and Rescher (1978). For an attempt to identify standards in terms of which research should be assessed on this basis, see Hammersley (1990, 1992a: ch. 4).

of re-importing the excessive ambition of a scientific politics into social research (see Hammersley 1992a: chs 6 and 8). And it is possible to retain the principle of value neutrality without assuming that value judgments are irrational (see Chapter 8).

A fourth lesson from positivism is the importance of clarity of expression: a concern to define terms where this is necessary, and to make relevant distinctions. It seems to me that this is particularly necessary given the complexity and difficulty of the methodological issues we currently face. This applies, for example, when someone declares that all social research is necessarily political. We need to ask which of the several senses of the word 'political' is intended, because this can have major implications for what is being claimed, and what conclusion we should draw about that claim (see Chapter 6). It is all too easy for such statements to operate as little more than slogans. This may seem banal: after all who could be against clarity? The answer is that some currently influential voices are. Take, for example, Barthes' celebration of 'writerly' texts (Barthes 1975), or the character of Adorno's or Derrida's writings.[23] What all this neglects is the dialogical form of reading that is possible with clearly formulated texts, as against the individualistic character of free interpretation.

A fifth lesson is that philosophy must not be seen as superordinate to empirical research. As I mentioned at the start of this chapter, there is an increasing tendency for social researchers who write about methodology to see philosophical assumptions as providing the foundation on which social research is built. This contrasts with what is in my view the much more appropriate 'underlabourer' role conceived for philosophy by positivists from John Locke onwards. Research is a practical activity and cannot be governed in any strict way by methodological theory. Furthermore, such theory must be open to correction and modification in the light of what we learn in practice.

Of course, I am not suggesting that these lessons are exclusive to positivism. Indeed, it follows from my rejection of the paradigm model that they are unlikely to be. I do believe that they are of great importance, however. Moreover, there is also an important negative lesson to be learned from positivism. This is that those who dismiss the work of their predecessors are likely to repeat previous errors. As Adorno remarks, commenting on the 'positivist dispute' in German sociology, 'the past usually takes its revenge' (Adorno et al. 1976: 4). Earlier, I noted the radical way in which logical positivism rejected most previous

---

[23] On Adorno's style, see Rose (1978). We can trace this preference for elusive forms of writing back to Nietzsche's concern to write in a way which would only be understood by the elect. It is worth noting one effect of this: that any failure to understand is automatically laid at the door of the reader.

philosophy as nonsense. In effect, the decline and death of positivism charts a process in which many of the problems which the positivists thought they had abolished came back to haunt them. We should not simply dismiss positivism, lest we suffer the same fate.

# 2
# A Critique of 'Critical' Research

The adjective 'critical' is frequently used in the social sciences as a way of characterising a particular sort of approach, and it is a usage which seems to be growing ever more popular. Thus, we have not only 'critical theory', 'critical sociology' and 'critical anthropology', but also 'critical criminology', 'critical policy research', 'critical hermeneutics', 'critical discourse analysis', 'critical ethnography', 'critical action research', to mention just a few examples.[1] However, while widely used in this way, the meaning of 'critical' in such contexts is often not clear. Rarely addressed is the fact that the term is open to alternative, indeed to fundamentally conflicting, interpretations. Yet, if we are to be in a position to assess 'critical' approaches to social research, we need to understand what is being claimed for them, and why. In this chapter I will explore the meanings of the term, and assess its usefulness as a way of distinguishing some forms of inquiry from others.

According to common-sense usage, to be critical of something is to believe that it has defects that are worthy of attention. As it relates to the critic, the word carries a neutral, or perhaps an ambivalent, evaluative loading. The *Oxford English Dictionary* includes meanings with both positive and negative connotations:

1  Given to judging, especially given to adverse or unfavourable criticism; fault finding, censorious.
2  Involving or exercising careful judgment or observation; nice, exact, accurate, precise, punctual.

In common-sense terms, then, it is in principle neither good nor bad to be critical. Of course, in particular cases criticism (and particular criticisms) may be judged to be justified or unjustified. There is also scope for evaluation of a critic as, on the one hand, hyper-critical, too ready to criticise or excessive in criticism, or as, on the other hand, justifiably critical, for example as willing to state unwelcome truths.

By contrast, in the context of social research, 'critical' is for the most

---

[1] There are many others. Here are three mentioned in just one source: 'critical psychological anthropology', 'critical psychiatry' and 'critical medical anthropology' (Scheper-Hughes 1992: 222).

sed as an applauding adjective: to be critical is generally taken to sirable. Thus, a critical approach to reading the research literature quently recommended; and researchers are expected to adopt a critical attitude towards the data they collect and the interpretations they develop. Such methodological criticism is central to what Popper and others have labelled 'critical rationalism'. This is a version of the philosophy of science which rejects the foundationalism of traditional rationalism and empiricism, concluding that only knowledge claims which are falsifiable are legitimate, that only falsification not verification of hypotheses is possible, and that the status of scientific knowledge is always fallible and never proven (see, for example, Bunge 1964; Popper 1976; Albert 1985). However, this critical rationalism is not the model for 'critical' approaches in the social sciences. Instead, this is generally provided by the 'critical theory' of the Frankfurt School, a very different philosophical approach with which the critical rationalists were at odds in the 'positivist dispute' of the 1960s (Adorno et al. 1976).[2]

Nevertheless, 'critical' approaches following the critical theory model are sometimes presented as constituting a necessary extension of methodological criticism. For instance, conventional forms of research, whether empirical quantitative investigations or interpretive qualitative work, are often accused by 'critical' researchers of taking appearances for reality: of not subjecting the data and interpretative resources on which they rely to sufficient critical scrutiny, of failing to recognise that these are social products, and the implications of this for their validity. Thus, it is claimed that while the methodological orientation of conventional social research purports to be merely formal and neutral, it is actually based on implicit social theories which are ideological. Furthermore, the accounts produced are not simply false, they both reflect and serve to reproduce the status quo.

The major source for this argument is, of course, Marxism. But the critical theorists were by no means orthodox Marxists, and while they drew heavily on the concept of critique built into that tradition they made use of other sources as well.

## Critical theory

Connerton traces the origins of the concept of critique to the Enlightenment; though he notes that the term predates this, being used

---

[2] There is also, of course, an old and internally diverse tradition of criticism in the field of literary studies (Watson 1962: ch. 1). However, literary criticism has not generally been a significant model for critical approaches within the social sciences, unless one counts Derrida's deconstruction under this heading.

to refer to the interpretation of biblical and classical texts in the Renaissance and the Reformation, in which it came to be identified as 'the essential activity of reason' (Connerton 1976: 16). What was characteristic of the Enlightenment was the extension of this process of criticism to the political sphere. Critique in this sense contrasted with reliance on religious revelation and tradition, ecclesiastical or other authority etc. All beliefs and social practices are to be brought before the court of reason, and condemned if found wanting. Society is to be reorganised in a more rational, and (it was taken to follow automatically) a more just, fashion. Furthermore, because reason is available to all, and because it gives conclusive results, everyone should be able to see the falsity and injustice of the old regime, and the rightness of the new one that is to replace it.

This Enlightenment concept of critique is at the core of Marx's work, but his thinking was also shaped by subsequent reinterpretation of the concept by Kant, and even more by Hegel's critical 'overcoming' of Kant's philosophy. The later Kant saw his whole philosophical task as critique, by which he meant the project of identifying the conditions of possible knowledge. His aim was to use reason to scrutinise itself, an act of reflexivity that became enormously influential. He took Newtonian science as the paradigm of rational knowledge, but argued that despite its validity and power it can only inform us about things as they appear to us, not as they are in themselves. This conclusion followed, he suggested, from the fact that there are features of everyday and scientific knowledge which could not have come from the senses, and which therefore must be *a priori*; that is, they are constitutive of the very apparatus by which human beings understand the world. Moreover, he argued that this constitutive framework includes features that we normally think of as part of the world, such as spatial, temporal and causal relations.

In this way, Kant's investigation of the conditions of possible knowledge served at the same time to determine its limits, to indicate what sorts of knowledge rational inquiry is and is not capable of producing. This had implications for the rationalist metaphysics to which he had previously been committed. He believed that his arguments showed why investigations in this area had been so inconclusive by comparison with the physical inquiries on which they were supposedly modelled. He argued that this sort of 'uncritical' philosophy made excessive claims about the scope of rational knowledge, and that it also threatened to undermine human freedom and morality by extending the determinism of science into the sphere of ethics and religion.

Hegel built on the work of Kant, but at the same time he returned to rationalist metaphysics. He did this by using Kant's own philosophical investigation of the powers of reason as the model for rational inquiry, rather than Newtonian physics, and by denying the validity of Kant's conclusions about the limits of knowledge. He claimed to show that Kant had underestimated the power of reason, and that rational knowledge of reality as a whole is possible, incorporating morality and religion. Indeed, such knowledge is essential, he believed, for *any* of our knowledge to be valid. If these realms were excluded, our knowledge would be incomplete and therefore distorted. The other side of this is his rejection of the limit which Kant had placed on our understanding of the empirical world: he denies that we can only have rational knowledge of reality as it appears to us, not as it is in itself. For Hegel, knowledge of appearances could not be true knowledge. Most important of all, he departed from Kant in treating knowledge as a historical product, as a product of the development of Mind (or the World Spirit) towards self-knowledge over the course of history. So, where Kant had identified universal *a priori* elements of human cognition, Hegel saw human beings as forming part of a developmental process that was itself rational, but which would only produce a fully comprehensive and valid system of knowledge at its completion. Each epoch of human history represented a stage in the development of Mind, involving values, beliefs and institutions that were initially appropriate to that stage but which subsequently became reified and served as constraints on its further development. However, Hegel believed that the development of Mind was nearing its completion, and that the Prussian society in which he lived approximated to the final stage of social development, while his own philosophy represented the completed system of knowledge, realising absolute truth.

The concept of critique does not play the same central role in Hegel as it does in Kant. However, what is usually referred to as his dialectical method provided the basis for Marx's version of critique. By this method, Hegel set out to show the logic of historical development. He argues that contradictions latent within the partial and abstract views characteristic of any particular epoch lead to the emergence of new ideas, and new forms of social organisation based upon them, which overcome those contradictions; though, of course, this process generally produces new contradictions which need to be overcome through further development. For Hegel, the role of the philosopher was to reveal the rationality of past historical development; but also, as the end of history approached, to criticise what was discrepant with the new age, and thereby to facilitate reconciliation with it.

Of course, Marx rejected the idea that history had realised its *telos* in early nineteenth-century Prussian society and Hegelian philosophy. He was convinced that it had not yet finished its work. Furthermore, he did not see the task of rational inquiry as solely retrospective. He believed that it was possible, on the basis of an understanding of the logic of history and the structure of contemporary society, to prepare the way for future progress. So, for him the task was not to encourage reconciliation with the status quo. Quite the reverse, what was needed was a critique designed to bring about change. Marx modified Hegel's approach in other important respects too. Where Hegel saw the progression of reason in terms of the development of ideas which determined forms of social organisation, for Marx ideas were a reflection of the material organisation of society, and it was the latter which had to be changed. Thus, while the dominant ideas needed to be criticised, the real target of critique was the forms of social organisation from which they derived. Also, where Hegel had accepted a certain level of economic and political inequality as inevitable and desirable, and viewed the state as essential, for Marx historical development pointed to an egalitarian society in which the state would wither away, no longer having any function.

So, Marx saw critique as concerned with understanding and attacking the constraints that are hindering the emergence of more rational forms of society. The nature of the knowledge produced by such critique has been a matter of some dispute within Marxism (see McCarney 1990). However, from the point of view of critical theorists, it must be seen not as the speculative knowledge characteristic of philosophy, nor as the empirical knowledge typical of the sciences, nor even as the practical knowledge we use in everyday life. It is a form of theoretical understanding which transcends the functions of all of these.

Marx's work was the most important influence on the Frankfurt theorists, but their thinking was also shaped by the philosophies of Kant and Hegel. Furthermore, to varying degrees, critical theory was informed by another and very different nineteenth-century version of critique: the anti-Hegelian, and indeed anti-Enlightenment, views of Nietzsche. Like Marx, Nietzsche rejected Hegel's project of bringing about reconciliation with the world as it is. He produced an uncompromising cultural critique of the decadence of modernity, its loss of creative drive and its resulting mediocrity. However, where Marx saw the prospect of a more truly human and rational society emerging out of existing social arrangements, completing a history of dialectical progress, Nietzsche rejected the concept of progress and the Enlightenment celebration of reason. The ideal underlying his critique was an aesthetic and ethical one. He attacked any notion of the truth as a cognitive representation of reality, interpreting it instead in instrumentalist and relativist terms: what is true is what serves ethical purposes, and all truths are relative to points of view. For his ethics, Nietzsche looked back to the ideals of pre-Socratic Greece, seeing subsequent changes as decline, exemplified by the baneful influence of

Christianity; but he also held a cyclical view of history as eternal recurrence, and this allowed the prospect of a transvaluation of values following 'the death of God'. He saw himself as heralding the emergence in the future of a more heroic form of man.[3] Nietzsche hated bourgeois society and liberalism, but not because they were exploitative. Rather, he deplored the form of humanity which they promoted. And he rejected egalitarianism, democracy and socialism for the same reason. He believed that hierarchy was essential to the achievement of human greatness, at one point even presenting a justification for slavery on this basis (Dannhauser 1982).

Of course, the Frankfurt theorists lived in social conditions different from these earlier writers; and in the case of Marx this was especially significant because events since his death had posed major problems for Marxian theory: the failure of capitalism to be overthrown in advanced capitalist societies, the distortion of socialism in Russia, the rise of fascism, and the holocaust. As a result, the critical theorists were generally more pessimistic than Marx about the prospects for social transformation. Indeed, some of them came to the conclusion that the most that could be done was to keep critical thinking alive in an inhospitable climate: there was little scope for effective political action. History had taken a wrong turning, so that a reformulation of Marx's analysis was now essential. They explained the absence of the changes he had expected, and the occurrence of many which he had not, in terms of the cultural features of advanced capitalism; some of which, like consumerism and mass culture, were open to criticism from a Nietzschean point of view. However, Frankfurt theorists differed among themselves somewhat in their approaches to critical theory. I will look briefly at three of the key figures: Horkheimer, Adorno and Habermas.

Horkheimer's account, in his essay 'Traditional and critical theory', is fairly close to the concept of critique embodied in the work of Marx, though it is interpreted through the influence of Hegel and Lukacs. He portrays 'traditional theory', including under this category both the natural sciences and most forms of social theory and research, as reflecting the development of, and in large part functioning to serve, capitalism; however, he sees natural science as not directly related to class conflict and as ultimately progressive in effect. By contrast, while critical theory arises out of society, 'its purpose is not, either in its conscious intention or in its objective significance, the better functioning of any element in the structure' (Horkheimer 1972: 207). The focus of critical theory is the social totality; it is concerned with the way in which current social arrangements fail to meet human needs and ideals. And

---

[3] On the debates about Nietzsche's views of women, see Ansell-Pearson (1992) and Gane (1992).

an important task of critique is to show that the cultural categories in terms of which bourgeois society understands itself do not truly comprehend the character of that society; indeed, that they block understanding of how it needs to be changed.

What was required, Horkheimer believed, was a reintegration of philosophy with empirical social research, the links between these having been broken by positivism. In his address on becoming director of the Frankfurt Institute of Social Research, he argued that:

> philosophy as a theoretical intention focused on the universal, the 'essential', is in a position to give inspiring impulses to the specialist disciplines and, at the same time, is open enough to the world in order to allow itself to be impressed and changed by the advance of concrete studies. (quoted in Honneth 1987: 352)

Much further work was required in concrete terms. In political economy, there was a need to document and theorise the changes that had taken place since Marx had written *Capital*. Also necessary, Horkheimer believed, was the development of a social psychology (modelled on the work of Freud) and a theory of culture, these being required to explain how capitalism had managed to survive (Honneth 1987).

Critical theory is not merely about understanding the world, however. It is 'motivated by the effort really to transcend the tension and to abolish the opposition between the individual's purposefulness, spontaneity, and rationality, and those work-process relationships on which society is built' (Horkheimer 1972: 210). And, indeed, bringing about social change is seen as an intrinsic feature of critical theory, not a matter of its subsequent application: 'in genuinely critical thought explanation signifies not only a logical process but a concrete historical one as well. In the course of it both the social structure as a whole and the relation of the theoretician to society are altered' (1972: 211).

Adorno's position was more complex and ambivalent than Horkheimer's in the 1930s, though they moved closer together later (see Habermas 1993). Most of the Frankfurt theorists shared concerns to be found throughout the German academic world in the late nineteenth and early twentieth centuries: about the effects of the growth of science, modern technology and commercialisation on intellectual and artistic values (Jay 1984). For Adorno, the deformation of culture which these developments produced made essential the discovery of new aesthetic forms appropriate to the future; and he saw this as necessitating social change. In exploring the possibilities for this, he drew as much on non-Marxist as on Marxist sources, including the pre-Marxist writings of Lukacs and Benjamin. The position he developed rejected all philosophies of history, including those of Hegel and Marx. He believed that because of its very nature current society cannot be represented in systematic and unambiguous terms. As Jay (1984: 97–8) comments, summarising Adorno's views: 'In a world still dominated by the exchange principle and the division of labour, it would be ideological to assume that society was intrinsically meaningful, a text to be read by those with the proper hermeneutic empathy.' The aim was not to try to encapsulate reality in a theory or comprehensive interpretation, but to decipher its contradictory manifestations. There is a rejection here of contemporary forms of social science, and even of Marx's political economy, both of which looked for causal laws which would make possible prediction and manipulation of the future. Instead, Adorno, like Benjamin, aimed at a kind of 'secular revelation' based on close examination of the details of particular socio-cultural phenomena (Buck-Morss 1977; but see Rose 1979).

More than this, Adorno believed that totalizing theories themselves constituted a form of domination. They are products of the Enlightenment reason which is characteristic of the 'administered society'. This had promised to free humanity from myth, yet had become a myth itself, forcing the qualitatively different forms of human activity into a single mould; homogenising individuals in the same way that the exchange principle homogenised the products of labour. Adorno's aim was to undermine all closed ways of thinking since they encouraged the unreflective affirmation of society as it is.

These ideas had implications for Adorno's practice of critique and for the form in which it was expressed (see Rose 1978: ch. 1). His position ruled out not just any appeal to transcendental standards as a basis for socio-cultural critique, but even the Hegelian idea that human ideals are progressively realised through the historical process. A very particular form of immanent critique was required: the task was to discover the transcendent within the specifics of current reality. This involved pitting the ambiguous implications of bourgeois concepts against one another and against their referents, in order to show not only that they are inadequate representations of the world but also that the world as it is presently constituted is an inadequate realisation of those concepts. The task was empirical not speculative, then; but the goal was not simply to reproduce empirical reality as it is. Rather, the aim was, through what he called 'exact fantasy', to 'over-shoot' reality, to show the unrealised possibilities within it, yet at the same time to stay close to the phenomenon, thereby not lapsing into metaphysical speculation. Exact fantasy was to reveal traces or pre-figurations, in the ruins of a decadent society, of material possibilities which had escaped the dominating power of the prevailing reality: it worked against the grain of what existed, in the hope thereby of opening up different and better possibilities. In this respect, Adorno's orientation represented an oscillation between empiricism, on the one hand, with its passive acceptance of the contemporary world as the only reality, and idealism, on the other, with its emphasis on the active transformation of reality, but only in the subjective realm. He adopted a style of writing designed to achieve this which 'gives an impression of confusion, but in fact amounts to a set of parallaxes, apparent displacements of an object due to changes of observation point' (Rose 1978: 12–13). Adorno's goal, like that of Marx, was the objective transformation of society, though his concept of what was involved in bringing this about was rather different (Buck-Morss 1977; Jay 1984).

Habermas's orientation diverges in several important respects from that of Horkheimer, and even more from that of Adorno. Although his work builds on theirs in various ways, it reflects a distinctive pattern of influence. Nietzsche becomes much less, and Kant rather more, important. But, in addition, he draws on a wide range of other resources in recent philosophy and social theory. He retains a strong commitment to the ideals of the Enlightenment and seeks to reconstruct Marxism in such a way as to provide a systematic account of the nature of advanced capitalism, and of how it might be transformed to achieve a more rational form of society. At the same time, his account of the nature of such a society differs from Marx's. He criticises the latter for his exclusive focus on labour, treating this as a reflection of the distorting over-emphasis on instrumental reason which dominates modern society. One of the most significant results of this instrumentalism in Western thinking, according to Habermas, is that values come to be rendered a matter of irrational decision, since instrumental reason can only specify means not ends. In fact, the latter become reduced to the former, so that strategic action and manipulation determine social relations, as exemplified in the bureaucratic domination of both Western capitalism and East European socialism.

Habermas does not deny the value of instrumental reason, or that of the natural sciences which he believes embody it. But he insists on the fundamental importance of language-based social interaction, and of the communicative rationality intrinsic to it. He argues that though the control of nature is essential to human life, it depends on the communicative coordination of human behaviour; so that in this sense interaction is more fundamental than labour. Furthermore, he believes that political life should be governed by rules based on agreement, where 'coming to agreement' arises from a process of critical reflection whose character ensures that the agreement is free and therefore rational. And he seeks to justify this rational and democratic ideal by showing that human communication embodies a set of norms which presuppose it. He argues that critical reflection can specify the conditions of possibility of rational agreement, and can use these as a standard for assessing current social arrangements.

It should be obvious from this brief, and necessarily crude, summary that there is considerable variation in the views of critical theorists about the nature of critique. Moreover, these views involve ambitious philosophical claims and raise fundamental questions which have generated a very substantial literature of commentary and discussion.

## Questioning the grounds of critique

As Bubner (1982) has pointed out, Marxism and critical approaches generally have sought to combine two senses of the word 'critical': that implying reflection on the presuppositions and conditions of knowledge, and that referring to political criticism of prevailing social forms. In fact, they have not just combined these but attempted to fuse them on the basis of a radically social epistemology, derived from Hegel, according to which the validity of ideas is determined by their social origins and functions (see Geuss 1981). On this view, understanding ideas and institutions requires a process of ideology critique designed to uncover their socio-historical significance; and this, in turn, opens the way to their social transformation. As Connerton (1976: 20) comments, 'Criticism . . . renders transparent what had previously been hidden, and in doing so it initiates a process of self-reflection, in individuals or in groups, designed to achieve a liberation from the domination of past constraints. Here a change in practice is a constituent element of a change in theory.' What distinguishes critical from traditional theorists, it is argued, is that the latter do not incorporate in their work an analysis of their own social function, whereas critical research reflexively accounts for itself and is directed thereby towards emancipatory goals. In this way, critical approaches are often presented not just as politically and ethically superior to traditional forms of inquiry, but also as more thoroughly critical in a methodological sense.

This reflexivity, and the fusion of epistemological and political critique to which it leads, are appealing in many respects; not least in portraying intellectual work as serving a direct practical function without turning it into propaganda. However, they require an epistemological theory which can justify the claim that critical researchers are able to gain genuine knowledge of social reality rather than being deceived by appearances like everyone else. Critical theory relies on a conception of the social totality as generating, but as obscure to, common-sense understanding and conventional inquiry, and this raises the question: from what vantage point can critical theorists view this totality? How can they escape from the grip of ideology; and, having escaped, what cognitive resources are available for them to produce a true account?

There are various attempted solutions to this problem within the crit-

ical tradition. In Hegelian Marxist versions, appeal is made to a teleological meta-narrative in terms of which true knowledge is gradually
realised. Thus, in his early writings at least, Marx builds on Hegel's
attempt to ground his position in a meta-narrative about the rational
unfolding of history. But this necessarily leaves open the question of the
nature of the validity of that meta-narrative. What sort of knowledge is
being claimed? We need to know this in order to decide what kinds of
evidence would be sufficient to support it. But the answer which is given
makes any such judgment virtually impossible. It is supposed to be a
form of knowledge that transcends the distinctions between cognitive,
moral and aesthetic truths, along with those between theory and practice, knowledge and reality. Thus, what is discovered through critique is
believed to be necessary in some sense, rather than being an empirically
contingent matter (this is what distinguishes it from utopian thought);
but at the same time it does not provide the basis for 'mechanical' predictions about the future. This position is obscure, to say the least, and
has produced a major fault-line in Marxism: between deterministic and
voluntaristic interpretations of historical development.

Another set of problems arises from the fact that, on Marx's view, it
is not he himself whom history has placed in a position which provides
privileged access to knowledge of the totality but rather a whole social
class. Inverting Hegel, he proposed a picture of history as the dialectical overcoming of alienation, with humanity's estrangement from
nature being superseded through development of the forces of production, but only at the expense of increased alienation of human beings
from one another. This process reaches its most intense form in capitalism, where the material resources for human liberation from nature
are available but the relations of production represent the most extreme
level of social alienation. Marx argues that the position of the working
class under capitalism, which experiences the brunt of this alienation,
gives it potential access to a form of understanding which is not available to the other social classes. This is certainly a less egocentric
position than Hegel's, but it means that Marx's philosophy does not
even validate itself in its own terms; after all, his own social position
was hardly typical of the working class. From this point of view, too,
the problem of epistemological grounding remains unresolved, as it
does with later versions of standpoint epistemology in feminism and
'anti-racism' (see Chapters 3 and 4).[4]

---

[4] There is, of course, an alternative form of epistemological grounding to be found in
Marx's work: the appeal to scientific method. However, this is currently not very influential for critical social research because appeals to science are widely regarded as
positivist. There is also considerable disagreement among those who regard Marxism as
scientific, see, for instance, Sayer (1979), Collier (1979) and McCarney (1990).

The Frankfurt theorists initially adopted Marx's meta-narrative, but over time a rather different one emerged, in which human domination of nature is the problem not the basis for a solution. Thus, the source of human alienation is no longer simply capitalism, and the overthrow of capitalism will not in itself overcome alienation. Honneth (1987: 360) claims that for Adorno and the later Horkheimer 'humanity's freedom is defined as the ability to submit properly to nature.' This change in meta-narrative has the effect both of making the social transformation required even more radical than in the case of Marx, and at the same time of undercutting completely the ground for seeing the proletariat as an epistemologically privileged and emancipatory agent. The impact of this is revealed most clearly in the work of Adorno, who seems to propose reliance on a sort of secular faith modelled on religious mysticism. He provides no reason to believe that critique can produce the objective realisation of the possibilities that are excluded by present reality, nor any indication of why this would be desirable. There are, after all, always many unrealised possibilities whose realisation would not be desirable, even in principle. And, in fact, Adorno himself distrusts the process of realisation, so that in a sense only unrealised possibilities can offer hope.[5]

By contrast with this, Habermas provides a much more direct and systematic attempt to solve the problem. He sets out to found critique on the logical implications of communicative acts, on what he calls a universal pragmatics. He argues that communications involve implicit norms which require people to try to ensure that their communications are truthful, comprehensible, sincere and justifiable. However, there are difficult questions to be answered here about whether all communications are guided by these norms, given the diversity of language games, and about the philosophical justification for seeking to derive a universal critical standard, the ideal speech situation, from them. Indeed, one might argue that Habermas's project is itself disconfirmed by the demonstrable fact that Adorno's work is capable of being read and written about! Critics of Habermas have also pointed out that his procedural concept of the ideal speech situation cannot itself be justified through reflective discourse, at least not without circularity: either the transcendental critical reflection he engages in takes place in the ideal speech situation, in which case it presupposes what it is supposed to validate, or if it does not this implies that rational agreement in the ideal speech situation is not the ultimate arbiter of validity. Finally, there are good reasons to suppose that even without structured inequalities discourse would not necessarily produce a rational

[5] Buck-Morss (1977). See McCarney (1990: 30) for a useful account of how this impasse arises in Adorno's thought.

consensus (see Lobkowicz 1972; McCarthy 1978: ch. 4; Lukes 1982; Thompson 1982). Among the strongest critics of critical theory have been poststructuralists and postmodernists. They offer a radical challenge to critical theorists' attempts to ground critique. Needless to say, we are not faced here with a single and coherent body, or even with two distinct bodies, of argument, but rather with a complex array of interpretations and proposals (see Sturrock 1979; Dews 1987; Best and Kellner 1991; Docherty 1992). Nevertheless, we can identify one of the central themes of this work as opposition to what is taken to be the philosophical project of modernity: the goal of producing a corpus of universal and absolutely valid knowledge about the world, and about humanity itself, on the basis of the self-reflection of a subject (individual or collective). This goal is seen as characteristic not just of Cartesian rationalism and of empiricism and positivism, but also of Kantianism, Hegelianism and Marxism. And it is rejected on the grounds both that it is not achievable and that the attempt to realise it involves the enforcement of a single point of view, and the persecution of those who refuse to accept it. The conclusion of many of these writers, radicalising Adorno, is that reason is inherently totalitarian.

To a large extent this critique of modernity is inspired by Nietzsche, but interpreted now through Heidegger. Whereas the critical theorists had used Nietzsche to develop the Marxist critique of bourgeois society, Nietzsche is now deployed increasingly to condemn Marx and Marxism as themselves symptoms of a corrupt and oppressive modernity, as constituting part of the problem not the solution. This is a development which is most explicit in the case of the *nouveaux philosophes* (Dews 1986).

While poststructuralist and postmodernist writing has had a considerable impact on those advocating critical approaches in the social sciences, it does not provide a more effective epistemological grounding for critique than critical theory. Indeed, while often retaining a 'critical' commitment, it generally denies any possibility of grounding, or the need to ground, critique epistemologically. On the contrary, the focus of critical attention becomes precisely such attempts at epistemological grounding, which are seen as the source of modern political repression. In this sense, poststructuralism is an even more negative approach than critical theory. Where the latter typically seeks to found critique on an epistemology which reveals truths obscured from conventional viewpoints, and which promises a social transformation that realises human values, poststructuralism rejects the possibility of this and the desirability of behaving as if it were possible. Thus, writing about deconstruction, Culler comments:

> It is . . . continuing engagement with the hierarchical oppositions which
> structure Western thought, and the recognition that the belief that one has
> overcome them once and for all is likely to be a facile delusion, that give
> deconstruction a critical edge, a critical role. These hierarchical oppositions
> structure concepts of identity and the fabric of social and political life, and
> to believe one has gone beyond them is to risk complacently abandoning the
> enterprise of critique, including the critique of ideology. (Culler 1992: 121–2)

What is involved here is a sustained scepticism and distrust of all
claims to knowledge. And it leads some poststructuralists and postmodernists to adopt an even more pessimistic meta-narrative than that
of the critical theorists; though, as with Nietzsche, the distinction
between optimism and pessimism may be seen as itself in need of
deconstruction. Foucault's genealogies present an account of Western
post-Enlightenment history which undermines any sense of the progression of civilisation, and one which leaves the prospects for
emancipation obscure and uncertain. He comments at one point that
to imagine another system is to extend our participation in the present
one (Foucault 1977: 230). While he sometimes seems to believe that it
is possible to dismantle the system, it is not clear whether he expects
anything to be left. Even less clear is whether something could replace
it that would be better, or indeed whether such an evaluative judgment
can be intelligible (Walzer 1983). Lyotard's position is similar in some
respects, but he also rejects all meta-narratives, dismissing them as
totalitarian. And at one point he switches from critique to affirmation
of contemporary capitalism: on the grounds that any critique assumes
an unjustifiable claim to superiority over what it criticises (Dews
1987).[6] Correspondingly, Baudrillard's work implies a current 'reality'
from which there is no escape, since all attempts at resistance are incorporated, if not generated, by what they seek to resist. He argues that
hyperconformity, or 'positive' indifference, may be the best strategy to
hasten the implosion of the 'social'; in fact, this may be the only form
of 'resistance' open to us (Bogard 1990).

From the point of view of poststructuralism and postmodernism,
critical theory is not critical enough. It is regarded as relying on the
Enlightenment assumption that the exercise of reason can produce
demonstrable moral truths about how society should be organised and
how change can be brought about. And, indeed, one does not have to
embrace relativism to recognise that, in relation to most value issues,
there are conflicting arguments of varying degrees of reasonableness,
the cogency of none of which is absolute, so that disagreement is not
simply a product of prejudice, ulterior motives, etc. At the same time,

---

[6] In their later work, Foucault and Lyotard pull back from these positions (see Dews
1987: 220).

the permanent revolution of critique which is proposed by poststructuralists and postmodernists seems to leave little scope either for knowledge of the world or for political commitments beyond simple negation or affirmation. Epistemological critique has swallowed up its political counterpart, preserving appearances only through impersonation.

## Where does critical social research stand?

One obvious conclusion to be drawn from the above discussion is that contemporary critical social research does not inherit a single, well-defined approach. Rather, there is a range of conceptions of the 'critical', and none of them is without serious problems. The implication of this is also clear. Focusing just on critical theory, Honneth, by no means an unsympathetic commentator, argues that 'only with the awareness of all its deficiencies can one today productively continue the theoretical tradition originated by Horkheimer' (Honneth 1987: 348). Yet, when one looks at the writings of critical social researchers, even in those places where they are explicating their approach, there is little discussion of the fundamental questions surrounding it. Indeed, they often proceed as if its foundations were beyond doubt.[7] Rather than any concerted attempt to think through the problem of epistemological grounding, or to face squarely the implications of poststructuralism and postmodernism, we find instead that Marxism, critical theory, poststructuralism and postmodernism are drawn on *selectively* in order to define and legitimate what is seen, more or less unproblematically, as 'the critical approach'. Aspects of those positions which threaten this are ignored or simply rejected.

Some writers adopt a fairly abstract definition of what critical social research is. Thus, Harvey (1990) defines it as integrating knowledge and critique, as producing an analysis which digs beneath 'ostensive and dominant conceptual frames, in order to reveal the underlying practices, their historical specificity and structural manifestations' (Harvey 1990: 4). This necessarily involves a critique of 'the "scientific" knowledge which sustains [oppressive social structures]' (p. 6), and leads the researcher to engage in praxis aimed at changing those structures (p. 22). Harvey's book is explicitly concerned with the methodology of

[7] This is not to suggest that there have been no recent attempts to address these questions. There is a considerable literature, much of it of a high quality. However, almost all of it is by philosophers, and it is given surprisingly little attention by social scientists. For instance, there are no references in Harvey's book *Critical Social Research* (1990) to Fay (1975, 1987), Geuss (1981) and Keat (1981), books which on any judgment must be ranked among the foremost discussions in English of the nature of critical research from a philosophical point of view.

critical research, and with making explicit 'the presuppositions that inform the knowledge that is generated' (p. 1). Yet the problem of the epistemological grounding of this kind of research is given no attention at all. Instead, the book is designed 'to reaffirm and endorse a major social research tradition' (p. 212).

Others writing in this field stay close to one particular version of critical theory. Thus, Carr and Kemmis's advocacy of critical action research relies almost exclusively on the work of Habermas (Carr and Kemmis 1986; Kemmis 1988). They present such research as democratic and empowering, and as directed towards improving 'the rationality and justice' of participants' own social practices, of their understanding of those practices, and of the situations in which they live and work. However, while these authors note that there have been criticisms of Habermas's position, they give no indication of how these have been, or can be, responded to (Carr and Kemmis 1986: 150–2). The only problem they address is the form that critical action research should take in practice. Indeed, they present critical action research as, in the words of one reviewer, 'a messianic path to righteousness' (Lewis 1987: 101).

Many 'critical' writers adopt a much wider base, of course. Thus, Kincheloe and McLaren list the genealogical writings of Foucault, the deconstruction of Derrida, and the postmodernism of Lyotard and others, along with critical theory, as 'critical' schools of thought. However, they draw a line between what they call 'resistance' and 'ludic' postmodernism, accepting the former but rejecting the latter on the grounds that it is 'decidedly limited in its ability to transform oppressive social and political regimes of power' (Kincheloe and McLaren 1994: 143). What is striking about this criticism is not just that no evidence is offered for it and that it could equally apply to much critical theory, but even more that it employs an entirely instrumental criterion. The starting point seems to be a set of political views about oppression and exploitation in contemporary society; rather than any inquiry into what constitutes oppression, why it occurs, and how it can be overcome, of the kind to be found in the work of Marx and the critical theorists.[8] This is paralleled in other accounts. For example, Carspecken and Apple (1992: 512) write 'the critical approach to field research is distinguished first of all in terms of the motivation of the researcher and the questions that are posed. Critical researchers are usually politically minded people who wish, through their research, to aid struggles against inequality and domination.'

What is involved here is a reduction of the concept of critique, as

---

[8] Not that the conclusions of these inquiries are unproblematic, of course, see Hammersley (1992a: ch. 6).

found in critical theory, to political criticism of society. The values guiding critical research are no longer explicitly located in a philosophy of history. While the epistemological dimension may not be completely lost, it now seems to be lodged in some sort of relativism, whereby values are a matter of sheer commitment rather than being open to rational justification. This probably reflects the influence of poststructuralism and other contemporary trends like constructivism (Guba 1990); though it may also indicate the continuing subterranean influence of existentialism and even of the old enemy positivism.[9]

It is rare, however, for accounts of critical social research to display an explicit and wholehearted commitment to relativism. Traces of the epistemology of critical theory usually remain. Indeed, there often seems to be a systematic ambiguity, an oscillation between these two positions, along with frequent appeals to more traditional methodological ideas which imply some sort of realism. And this is understandable: while resort to relativism avoids the epistemological problems raised by critical theory, it does so only at enormous cost. The very possibility of knowledge is undermined, and so too is the ground for justifying particular political judgments and ideals against others (Dews 1987).

The tendency to treat political commitments as the starting point for critical social research may also be an adaptation to the practical challenge posed by the virtual disappearance of working class opposition to capitalism in the West and the emergence of new social movements around gender, 'racism', ethnicity, sexual orientation, disability, and other issues. In this situation, critique can no longer be based on a single story of the origins of, and prospects for overcoming, oppression; and especially not one organised around the concept of social class. This may be why the poststructuralist emphasis on the constructed character of narratives, and their diversity, has become so appealing. It must be noted, however, that, while many critical social researchers continue to write as if politics involved just two sides (see, for example, van Dijk 1993b), poststructuralism (to the extent that it does not remain wholly negative) opens up the prospect of many different critical research projects committed to diverse, even conflicting, goals, and engaged in advocacy on the part of social groups which are in contention with one another. Moreover, there can be no principled way of choosing among these various political projects, or of integrating them into a single struggle. While there is scope for alliances, the enemy is never entirely the same, and the interests of different groups are likely to diverge. We no longer have a single oppositional movement com-

---

[9] It is worth noting in this context that positivism was an important influence on both Nietzsche and Foucault (Dews 1987: 180–1).

mitted to universal ideals, but rather partisan criticism of particular aspects of current social arrangements on behalf of various groups.

Some advocates of critical social research have recognised this problem and have tried to overcome it, notably by appealing to the principle of participatory democracy, to a *real* democracy in which the voices of those currently on the margins will be heard as loudly, if not more loudly, than those at the centre. Thus, Thomas (1993: 4) sees the critical ethnographer as engaged in political representation, as speaking to an audience on behalf of the people studied. However, others have argued that this is itself a form of domination and that people must be allowed to speak for themselves in research texts, even to collaborate in the research process (Clifford 1986; Gitlin et al. 1989). In Foucault's terms, the task of the researcher becomes: 'to lift the barriers which prevent the masses themselves from speaking' (Dews 1986: 74). However, even apart from the problems which surround the concept of participatory democracy, it is very difficult to see how it could be founded on the work of Foucault and other poststructuralists, given their extreme interpretation of the social constitution of subjectivity (see Walzer 1983: 483). Critical theory, in the form of Habermas's work, provides a more promising basis for such an argument. However, as I noted earlier, his position is not without serious problems, and he appeals to a rather abstract standard of democratic process which seems likely always to be more appropriate in the university than in any wider public sphere, and one which is currently threatened even there. Many critical social researchers express a commitment to democracy along these lines, but without troubling to clarify what they mean by that problematic term, and how arguments for it could be justified. And yet, as Saward (1994: 202) has noted, 'what democracy means, or what it should mean, is arguably more uncertain than ever before.'

In summary, despite the diverse interpretations of, and considerable problems involved in, the rationale for 'critical' inquiry, critical social researchers seem to assume that its justification is obvious, and/or they resort to an implicit relativism. This neglect or cavalier treatment of the issue of philosophical grounding might be excusable in an approach which drew a clear distinction between social research and philosophy. It is indefensible in one which claims superiority over others on the basis of its own reflexivity (see, for example, Simon and Dippo 1986).

## Some reasons for not being 'critical'

In the light of all this, it is not clear what meaning should be given to the term 'critical social research'. Scholem (1982: 210) reports being told by Walter Benjamin that the term 'critical theory' was invented as a euphemism for Marxism by members of the Frankfurt School during their period of exile in the United States, where the word 'Marxism' was taboo. Perhaps it still serves a similar function. The ideas of Marx have been subjected to such diverse interpretation and criticism, and are so contaminated by association with 'actually existed socialism' and its overthrow in Eastern Europe, that they now attract unjustified opprobrium. And, as we have seen, the diversification of Leftist struggles has rendered Marxism an inadequate basis for critique; hence the development of various kinds of post-Marxism (see, for example, Laclau and Mouffe 1985). In this context 'critical' can provide an appealing banner behind which many can gather, despite their differences. Its appeal stems from the fact that, as I noted earlier, within the academic world at least, being critical is almost universally regarded as desirable: no one wants to be seen as *un*critical. In these terms, though, the differences between 'critical' and other forms of social research seem to be reduced or obscured.

This is misleading, however. Critical social researchers are not reticent concerning what they believe is distinctive about their work. Here, for example, is part of Quantz's account of critical ethnography:

> Critical ethnographers impose a value system that requires the researcher to place any culture into a wider discourse of history and power, which serves an emancipatory interest, whereas other ethnographers impose a value system that requires the researcher to treat every culture as if it were independent of or, at most, interactive with history and power. From a critical perspective, these studies ultimately serve the interest of the status quo. While having an ethical orientation does not separate critical ethnography from other . . . ethnography, the pointed effort of critical researchers to reveal their own value perspective to the reader may differentiate critical ethnography from other forms and it may be this openness about their values which prompts criticism more than anything else. (Quantz 1992: 471)

There are three separate arguments involved here, which are widely found in advocacy of critical approaches. The first is that, unlike other kinds of inquiry, critical research locates the phenomena studied in their wider socio-historical context, this being essential for a true understanding of them. The second is that, while all research is actually value committed, only critical research makes its values explicit; by contrast, 'traditional' inquiry involves a spurious claim to value neutrality. The third argument is that while critical researchers direct their efforts towards countering oppression, traditional researchers do not; and, as a result, their work serves to support it.

None of these arguments has much force in my view. At one level, the first is an uncontroversial point. It is a commonplace that in trying to understand something we often need to take account of its context. However, to insist that we must understand *all* social phenomena in one *particular* context is certainly distinctive and requires justification. It demands a social theory of a power and persuasiveness which makes huge methodological demands (see Hammersley 1992a: ch. 6). More than this, though, it is by no means clear that a social phenomenon must *always* be examined in *the same* context; that is, on the basis of *the same* theory. What is an appropriate context is likely to vary not just with the nature of the phenomenon, but also with the problem we are investigating, and with our purposes. Indeed, as a result of the diversification of the political causes to which critical researchers may be committed, this is likely to be increasingly true even for them.

The second argument does not get to grips with the complex relationship between values and inquiry, and thereby misunderstands the principle of value neutrality. Research guided by that principle is based on a commitment to the value of truth: the belief that knowledge is of value in itself and/or has desirable consequences in the world. It may also use values to define the phenomena it investigates, focusing on those which are politically or practically relevant. And it is, needless to say, subject to unwitting bias from the value commitments of researchers. Finally, such research may use values as a basis for proposing conditional evaluations or policy prescriptions. However, all of this can be recognised and accepted without abandoning the principle of value neutrality, as proposed by Weber. What that principle *does* rule out, however, is the commitment of research to advocacy of some particular set of values or in favour of some social group. It assumes, rightly in my view, that the chances of discovering the truth are maximised by not taking for granted any value commitments which are not intrinsic to the task of producing knowledge (see Chapter 7).[10]

Quantz's argument about the role of values in research is also false in what it implies about the practice of critical social researchers. For example, one will look in vain in Harvey's (1990) book, which summarises a large number of critical studies, for any sustained exploration of the values underlying critical social research. Instead, there are simply appeals to 'democracy', 'equal opportunities', 'justice', 'oppression', etc. The value principles and judgments to which these terms relate are treated as if they were well understood rather than highly contested. And this is by no means atypical. The same is true not only of Quantz's own article (Quantz 1992), but also, for example, of Carr and Kemmis's (1986) book on critical action research, and of van Dijk's writings on critical discourse analysis (1993a, b). Yet it is unclear

[10] It is, of course, precisely the argument of critical theorists and of some Marxists that their value commitments *are* intrinsic to that task. But, as I have tried to show in the case of critical theory, this is not an argument which can be sustained. See also McCarney (1990).

what legitimate function such appeals to vague and unexplicated values could perform in the context of research.

The third argument is equally unconvincing. Evidence is rarely offered to show that traditional research has supported oppression, or that critical research has countered it (rather than unwittingly supporting it). The assumption seems to be that the effects of research can be read off from what are taken to be their implications on the page (for example, Gillborn and Drew 1992; see Hammersley and Gomm 1993). This is highly implausible, however, given the scope for multiple readings built into all texts (Newton 1990), the difference between interpreting the meaning and the significance of statements (Hirsch 1967), and the highly mediated character of causal relations in the social world (Hage and Meeker 1988). Furthermore, the case against traditional inquiry requires more than just the establishment of the effects of particular studies. It implies some sort of necessary relationship; and, in proposing this, reliance is typically (if implicitly) placed on functionalist argument. But this sort of argument has been subjected to considerable criticism, both substantive and methodological, and not least by those on the Left.[11] Nor is it clear why we should see research as one-sided, as necessarily serving one side of a struggle or the other; or why political issues should be regarded as involving just two sides.[12] For the most part, all of this is simply assumed, and conventional researchers are sneered at as 'uncritical' (van Dijk 1993a: 131) or as apologists for the status quo (Quantz 1992: 450).

None of these arguments constitutes a sound case for critical social research, then. However, they do point to its distinctive feature: commitment to political goals as part of an attempt to unify theory and practice. In the form of critical theory the validity of these goals is assumed to have been established through a process of rational reflection. The justification for the label 'critical' is clear here, even if it is not cogent. With the adoption of a relativist position, the justification for the term is less obvious. It could refer to a commitment to explicate the values on which critique is based, though as we have seen in practice this is rarely done. Furthermore, the term no longer refers to a single enterprise, nor is there any conceptual limit to the political causes

---

[11] Honneth (1987) points out the reliance of much critical theory on functionalism, and Walzer (1983: 484) argues that Foucault's arguments are often functionalist. Many of the contributions to the debate over functionalism in the 1960s are contained in Demerath and Peterson (1967). For more recent assessments of functionalist arguments in the context of critical theory, Marxism and social theory generally, see Geuss (1981), Cohen (1978) and van Parijs (1981), respectively.

[12] For criticism of the assumption of two sides in the context of research on 'race', see Modood (1992).

which could be embraced. Certainly, there is no reason why the 'critical' banner should be restricted to the Left.

Even more important to recognise, in my view, is the conflict in orientation between the pursuit of political goals and the activity of research. This conflict is denied by critical theory, on the basis of the Enlightenment assumption that the pursuit of knowledge is closely related to, if not identical with, the practical realisation of the good society. But this is an assumption which was rejected by the poststructuralists; and in this respect their judgment is surely sound. The priorities of research and politics are very different. If political goals are pursued consistently, the line of action engaged in is unlikely to be recognisable as a form of research. Virtually all the usual commitments of researchers would tend to be downplayed, if not abandoned. For example, avoiding error and bias in arguments are not the *primary* consideration when one is seeking to advance a political cause. Indeed, this is recognised by some of those advocating politically committed research. Gitlin et al. (1989: 245) comment that in such research: 'The question is not whether the data are biased; the question is whose interests are served by the bias.' This amounts to an abrogation of the framework of assumptions which constitutes the practice of research, in favour of that characteristic of political action.

It might seem here that I am moving towards advocacy of a very different form of critical social research from that which usually goes under the name, one based on critical rationalism. Certainly, I accept that social research is necessarily critical in a methodological sense. Indeed, I believe that considerably more emphasis needs to be given to methodological criticism by researchers (Hammersley 1990). And this implies that they must consciously resist being guided by what Becker (1967) calls the conventional hierarchy of credibility. It is part of the licence granted to them that they can explore ideas which are contrary to common sense, even though it is a licence which is continually in danger of being revoked. This means that the arguments they discuss, and some of the conclusions they reach, may carry critical implications for what is taken to be common-sense knowledge and for the operation of social institutions. This is essential to the value of research. It serves as a counter to the tendency for people to take the presuppositions on which they act almost entirely for granted, and/or to accept whatever it is convenient for them to believe. However, there is an important difference between this and an unswerving commitment to be critical of current social beliefs and institutions, or to question everything. These are orientations which have little general value.

In these terms, one might see the generalised valuing of criticism, in the form of 'critical' social research, as the extension of a principle which is appropriate in the field of intellectual inquiry to other fields, like politics, where it is not. There is probably some truth in this, but it is worth noting that undiscriminating criticism is not a virtue even in intellectual work. In the absence of a foundation of empirical givens whose validity is absolutely certain, it is possible continually to raise doubts about any claim to knowledge: no account can ever establish itself beyond all possible doubt; there is always further scope for criticism. However, it is not desirable to pursue criticism when, on any reasonable judgment, an account is valid. Of course, there is likely to be considerable disagreement about what is and is not reasonable (see Hammersley 1993b; Troyna 1993), and this should normally be resolved in favour of the critic. But there are always points beyond which almost everybody would agree that criticism is of no value. There is no justification for unlimited criticism, then, even in a methodological sense.

In short, there are no grounds for advocating a distinctively 'critical' form of social research, even when this is defined in critical rationalist terms. I see no reason to depart from what I suggested at the beginning of this chapter is the common-sense approach to criticism whereby, in abstract terms, it is neither good nor bad. Criticism can be appropriate or inappropriate depending on the circumstances, but it is not a good in itself.

## Conclusion

In this chapter I have explored the concept of 'critical' social research, arguing that it does not represent a single, coherent approach, and that the philosophical presuppositions on which it is based are open to serious question. Diverse attempts have been made to ground its fusion of epistemological and political critique, but none has been successful. Indeed, poststructuralists and postmodernists, among others, have questioned the very possibility of this. Instead, they have encouraged a celebration of negativity and/or the transformation of critical research into a support service for diverse local political struggles. As a result, the label 'critical' has lost any cognitive value it may have had: it is an empty rhetorical shell. Its use amounts to an attempt to disguise a particular set of substantive political commitments as a universal position that gives epistemological and moral privilege.

Many accounts of critical social research pay little or no attention to the fundamental problems which surround it. They imply a sound and unproblematic philosophical basis, though in practice they oscillate between critical theory, poststructuralist relativism and some sort of scientific realism. Yet these three positions are incompatible, and the first two undermine the very basis for research. If they are taken to their logical conclusions, political goals override commitment to the production of knowledge. Of course, fighting oppression is a good thing: that is almost a logical truth. However, it is not the only good thing, and it is a different activity from doing research. The two should not be confused. Doing so serves neither well.

The very idea that to be critical is a political or even an intellectual virtue needs to be questioned. Like most other actions, criticism may be more or less appropriate and desirable, depending on circumstances. To frame a whole approach to social research as critical is to render what in an appropriate context may be a virtue into an abstract programme that cannot but be a vice.

# 3

# On Feminist Methodology

It is widely accepted among feminists that feminism implies a distinctive approach to inquiry. And for some this is not just a matter of the grounds on which topics are selected for investigation, or even of the theoretical ideas that are treated as relevant. Rather, feminism is taken to carry distinctive methodological and epistemological implications (Cook and Fonow 1986; Harding 1987; Miller and Treitel 1991; Reinharz 1992).

In this chapter I want to assess the arguments for a distinctively feminist methodology. My first task, though, is to provide some detail about what this is taken to entail. There are, of course, important differences among feminists who have written on this topic, and in the course of the discussion I will highlight some of these. I certainly do not want to suggest that what I am assessing is a single position, nor am I claiming to represent the basis on which most feminists actually do research. My concern here is solely with feminist writing about methodology.

## Themes in feminist methodology

There are four themes to be found in many discussions of feminist methodology which are taken to mark its distinctiveness. I will sketch each of these in turn.

### The omni-relevance of gender

Not surprisingly, a key feature of feminist methodology is a central concern with gender and gender asymmetry. It is claimed that human social relations of all kinds are heavily structured by differences in the social position of women and men, and most important of all by differences between them in power. From this point of view, gender is a crucial issue in all areas of social life and must be taken into account in any analysis.[1] And, of course, it is often argued that since gender differences structure personal experience and belief, and given male dominance in society generally, conventional social science is primarily

---

[1] For useful discussions of recent developments in the sociology of gender, see Deem (1990) and Maynard (1990).

an expression of the experience of men presented as if it were human experience (see, for example, Westkott 1979; Smith 1987).[2] From these ideas emerge the methodological injunctions to explore women's experience, to study gender differences and relations, and to subject conventional social science to critical assessment for male bias.

### Personal experience versus scientific method

A second common feature of feminist methodology is an emphasis on the validity of personal experience as against the conventional (and, it is claimed, masculinist) emphasis on scientific method. It is argued that the latter neglects the researcher's embeddness in the socio-political world, and in particular the effects of gender in structuring the knowledge produced. In this way, it promotes masculine forms of knowledge as if they were knowledge *per se* (Code 1991).[3] By contrast, feminist methodologists often affirm the validity of direct experience:

> To address women's lives and experience in their own terms, to create theory grounded in the actual experience and language of women, is the central agenda for feminist social science and scholarship . . . To see what is there, not what we've been taught is there, not even what we might wish to find, but what is. (Du Bois 1983: 108–10)

Thus, one of the major tasks of feminist research is to explore the experience of women, this experience being treated as valid in its own terms: 'Feminism insisted that personal experiences couldn't be invalidated or rejected, because if something was felt then it was, and if it was felt it was absolutely, real for the woman feeling and experiencing it' (Stanley and Wise 1983b: 53).

In addition, the experience of women is often treated as providing access to truths about the social world which are not available to men. Thus, Harding declares that in feminist research women's personal experience comes to be taken as a 'significant indicator of the "reality" against which hypotheses are tested' (Harding 1987: 8). She argues that this is because this experience is 'a more complete and less distorting kind of social experience' (Harding 1987: 184). There are at least two arguments used to support this view. One appeals to the very nature of the relationship between oppressor and oppressed:

> As objects of oppression [women] are forced out of self-preservation to

---

[2] Sometimes this critique verges on a rejection of science and even of rationality itself. For reviews of these arguments, see Radcliffe-Richards (1980), Jansen (1990) and Rooney (1994).

[3] I have been accused of doing this in the present chapter, see Ramazanoglu (1992), and Hammersley (1994a).

know the motives of their oppressors. At the same time they have experienced in their own psyche and bodies how oppression and exploitation feel to the victims, who must constantly respond to demands made on them . . . Men often do not have this experiential knowledge, and therefore lack empathy, the ability for identification, and because of this they also lack social and sociological imagination. (Mies 1983: 121–2)[4]

Alternatively, the argument about the validity of women's experience may be formulated as an appeal to women's double consciousness – to their knowledge of the dominant culture and of their own, necessarily deviant, perceptions and experiences:

> We see and think in terms of our culture; we have been trained in these terms, shaped to them; they have determined not only the ways in which we have been able to perceive and understand large events, but even the ways in which we have been able to perceive, structure and understand our most intimate experiencing. Yet we have always another consciousness, another potential language within us, available to us. We are aware, however inchoately, of the reality of our own perceptions and experience . . . (DuBois 1983: 111–12)[5]

These ideas sometimes result in an insistence that only women can do feminist research and that only women researchers can truly understand women and their situation; indeed, that only women should study women (Stanley and Wise 1983b; see also Hearn and Morgan 1990).

The emphasis on personal experience also often leads to a rejection of structured research methods in favour of unstructured or qualitative methods, on the grounds that these give access to women's experience in a way which other methods do not. Equally, though, structured methods are criticised because they seem to deny the personal and social character of the research process, implying that it involves the following of rules which preserve objectivity on the part of a neutral and uninvolved researcher (Reinharz 1979; Graham 1983; Hollway 1989; but see Strathern 1987; Stacey 1988). Objectivity and neutrality are often dismissed as elements of an erroneous, masculinist perspective on the world that is obsessed with the exercise of control, both over nature and over other humans. For instance, Stanley and Wise (1983b: 169) describe objectivity as 'an excuse for a power relationship every bit as obscene as the power relationship that leads women to be sexually

---

[4] Smith (1987: 78–81) provides an elaborate development of this argument using Hegel's account of the relationship between master and slave. See also Flax (1986).

[5] Hartsock (1983) combines both these ideas, building an account of the feminist standpoint on the basis of an analogy with the work of Marx and rooting the epistemological superiority of feminism in the sexual division of labour.

assaulted, murdered, and otherwise treated as mere objects. The assault on our minds, the removal from existence of our experiences as valid and true, is every bit as objectionable.' Even where an attempt is made to retain the concept of objectivity, this is distinguished from neutrality and is grounded in women's experience (Harding 1992).

*Rejection of hierarchy in the research relationship*
Equally important is the view that the relationship between researcher and researched should be a reciprocal one, that 'hierarchical' distinctions between researcher and researched should be broken down. Thus, Oakley (1981) criticises prescriptions for interviewing that proscribe the researcher sharing personal experiences with interviewees or providing aid to them. Similarly, Reinharz (1983: 186) comments: 'as researchers, we should be interested only in information derived from authentic relations', by which she means relationships where 'genuineness is experienced by both parties'. And this leads some feminists to argue for the equal participation of the people studied in the research process. Thus, Reinharz (1983: 183) also suggests that research subjects should participate in the analysis of data so that it builds on what is meaningful to them as well as on what is significant to the researcher. And Mies advocates a version of the idea of 'conscientisation', the key characteristic of which is:

> that the study of an oppressive reality is not carried out by experts but by the objects of the oppression. People who before were objects of research become subjects of their own research and action. This implies that scientists who participate in this study of the conditions of oppression must give their research tools to the people. (Mies 1983: 126)

Another aspect of the rejection of hierarchy is the idea that the researcher must be included in the research focus: 'The best feminist analysis . . . insists that the inquirer her/himself be placed in the same critical plane as the overt subject matter . . .' (Harding 1987: 9). And Stanley and Wise (1983b: 196) argue that '. . . we must make available to others the reasoning procedures which underlie the knowledge produced out of "research".' Indeed, they imply that research should be (and in one sense cannot but be) focused entirely on the experience of the researcher(s) (see also Stanley 1992).

There seem to be three arguments underlying this rejection of hierarchy, though under certain conditions they coalesce. One is ethical: that only non-hierarchical relationships are legitimate among women, and therefore in research by feminists dealing with women. A second is methodological: that the truth will only be discovered via 'authentic' relations, hierarchy resulting in distortion of data. Finally, there is a practical recognition that if research is to be effective in consciousness-raising (see the discussion of the emancipatory function of research below), then it may be essential to involve the researched in the research process.

### Emancipation as the goal or research

Many feminists define a central goal of their research as the emancipation of women, rather than the production of valid knowledge *per se*. For instance, Mies argues that research must be subordinated to the political aim of the women's movement, which 'is not just the study but the overcoming of women's oppression and exploitation' (Mies 1991: 61).

Often combined with the adoption of this goal is the claim that the truth can only be discovered in and through the struggle against women's oppression: 'It is only through . . . struggles that one can come to understand oneself and the social world' (Harding 1987: 8). Mies makes much the same point, quoting Mao's dictum that 'in order to understand a thing one has to change it' (Mies 1983: 125). And she takes this argument further, suggesting that truth is to be judged in terms of contribution to the goal of emancipation:

> According to [the historical, dialectical and materialist theory of knowledge] the "truth" of a theory is not dependent on the application of certain methodological principles and rules, but on its potential to orient the processes of praxis towards progressive emancipation and humanization. (Mies 1983: 124)

From this point of view, feminist research is necessarily a process of 'conscientisation' for both researcher and researched, and is to be judged in terms of its success in this respect.[6]

The obverse of these arguments about the emancipatory character of feminist research is that 'Description without an eye for transformation is inherently conservative' (Cook and Fonow 1986: 12). And 'those who do not struggle against the exploitation of women in everyday life are unlikely to produce social science research about any subject at all that is undistorted by sexism and androcentrism' (Harding 1987: 12). Indeed, Mies argues that research has, hitherto, been 'largely an instrument of dominance and legitimation of power elites' (Mies 1983: 123).

These, then, seem to be the main themes of feminist methodology. In the next section I want to consider how far they represent a distinctive and defensible conception of social research.

---

[6] See Mies' distinction between the focus of consciousness-raising on group dynamics and relationship problems and the concern of 'conscientisation' with the social relations that govern patriarchal societies (Mies 1983: 126–7). This can be contrasted with Stanley and Wise's rejection of even consciousness-raising as elitist.

**An assessment of feminist methodology**

As we have seen, the argument that there is a specifically feminist methodology implies not just that feminists select research topics on a different basis to non-feminists, or employ distinctive theoretical resources, but that when a feminist investigates a particular topic the whole process of research will reflect her commitment to feminism. What is involved here, then, is a radical methodological proposal.[7]

*The significance of gender*
There is no doubt that the growth in influence of feminism in the social sciences over the past few decades has increased the salience of gender within those fields. This aspect of social relations had not been completely neglected previously, but it had been given relatively little attention in comparison with others like class and ethnicity. This is true in two respects. First, relatively little research had focused on gender differences, and the experiences and perspectives of women and girls had been neglected. Secondly, in research on all topics the significance of gender as an extraneous variable had been underplayed. A result was the tendency to generalise from research on boys and men to human behaviour in a way that neglected potentially significant gender differences. Even more notably, awareness of the effects of gender difference on the research process itself was almost completely absent before the influence of feminism.

In my view, this heightened attention to gender, in all three respects, has been an extremely valuable product of feminism. Looking back, the previous neglect of gender is scandalous. Nevertheless, I want to question the unique importance given to gender by some advocates of feminist methodology. It is not at all clear on what grounds this primacy is based (beyond the idea that female emancipation is the main goal of research, an idea I will examine below).

In many investigations, other variables seem likely to be at least as important as, if not more important than, gender. This is a point which has been made, with some feeling, by black feminists arguing for the significance of racism (La Rue 1970; Carby 1982; Lugones and Spelman 1983; see also Stanley and Wise 1990). And it seems to me that an inevitable effect of privileging gender is to strip away other relevant aspects of the phenomenon studied and its context. Furthermore, there are problems with gender categories themselves. As Flax (1987: 638) has noted: 'feminist discourse is full of contradictory and irreconcilable conceptions of the nature of our social relations, of men and women and the worth and character of stereotypically masculine and

---

[7] See Mies' (1991) criticism of other feminists for diluting its radicalism.

feminine activities.' All this may suggest, as Alcoff has argued, that 'the politics of gender or sexual difference must be replaced with a plurality of differences where gender loses its position of significance' (Alcoff 1988: 407).

Thus, while gender is very important, and must be studied in itself, as well as being taken as a potentially relevant extraneous variable in most social research, in my view it should not be given any general priority over other variables. Moreover, in methodological terms, while we need to subject social research to assessment for male bias, feminist bias is also a danger.

*Experience versus method*

Appeals to direct experience as against reliance on method are not distinctive to feminism. They are quite common in discussions of qualitative methodology generally (see, for example, Blumer 1969). But such arguments founder on the fact that all experience is a human construction. This is not to suggest that it is an entirely conscious construction, or to deny that it refers to phenomena which are independent of it. The point is simply that we have no direct access to the truth, even to the truth about our own perceptions and feelings. The idea that we can 'see what is there' rather than being deluded by cultural assumptions involves a false contrast. What we see is always a product of physiology and culture, as well as of what is there.

It is also true, of course, that, whatever the method used, the data collected and the findings produced will be shaped to some degree not just by the personal biography of the researcher but also by the social and political relations of the context in which he or she works. In other words, research is part of the social world it studies. However, it cannot be concluded from this that one feature of that social background – gender – has so great an effect on the knowledge produced that conventional social research findings can be dismissed as masculinist. Nor do background features, including masculinity, necessarily have negative effects on the validity of knowledge. They may equally lead to insights.

I am not suggesting that there is no point to feminists' and others' emphasis on experience. It may serve a useful purpose in underlining the importance of being open to what there is to be learned from observation, from listening to or reading the accounts of others, and from examining one's own experience. But to be sustainable it needs to be reformulated to refer to the use of an approach which minimises the chances of false cultural assumptions being embedded in the data, rather than avoiding such assumptions completely. And the possibility of error even in data produced by such unstructured methods must be recognised, as must their relative disadvantages in terms of efficient data collection.

In my view we should emphasise neither method nor experience, but rather seek to correct experience by use of method, and method by the use of experience. It is worth stressing that few philosophers of science or social scientists advocate (and none could practice) an exclusive reliance on method or procedure; and probably few feminist or qualitative social scientists would reject method completely. What method amounts to, it seems to me, is making public (and therefore open to collective assessment and improvement) the means of doing research. By making explicit how research is done, reflecting on and discussing the strategies we use, we can come to conclusions (always tentative) about which strategies are more appropriate for particular sorts of purpose in particular types of circumstance. There is always a danger inherent in such a process that the conclusions of these deliberations will be taken as established beyond all doubt and applied in an unreflective way. That must be guarded against. Every piece of research is unique, and for that reason we can never assume that existing methodological wisdom can be applied unproblematically. It must be applied as a trial, in a tentative manner, drawing on judgments about the results being produced and their relationship to the goals of the research. And it may well be necessary to modify, change or reconstruct the methods used in the course of any piece of research.[8]

Feminist arguments about the importance of experience versus method may, then, serve a useful function in countering the rigidity of methodological ideas. However, they carry the danger that they may encourage treatment of some of the researcher's or participants' own experience and assumptions as beyond question when these actually require scrutiny.[9] It is very tempting to treat what one wishes to believe as proven by experience. It seems to me that the essence of science is a communal questioning of assumptions, not of all assumptions but of those judged to be open to reasonable doubt. What it involves, fundamentally, is a commitment to suspend assumptions which are not shared by the whole research community, and a preparedness to try to establish their validity without relying on any other non-shared assumptions.

As I noted, the emphasis on the importance of direct experience rather than method is often associated with the idea that women have uniquely valid insights. This is characteristic of what has come to be called feminist standpoint epistemology (Hartsock 1983; Harding 1987; Stanley and Wise 1990). This parallels similar arguments ascribing privileged insight to other groups; for example, claims that only a

[8] To reject method completely would be to leave us with nothing to appeal to but our own experience; yet this would be an empty appeal since all experience is unique.

[9] See Joan Huber's (1973) critique of the methodological writings of Herbert Blumer on precisely these grounds.

black person can understand other black people (see Merton 1972). An important influence here is the argument of some Marxists that proletarian consciousness represents the truth about capitalism because it derives from the proletariat's oppressed position in that economic system (Korsch 1970; Lukacs 1971). For Marx, the proletariat's special role as the universal class destined to liberate everyone is taken to give it special access to the truth. A similar argument, though of course on a quite different basis, was advanced by Nazi scientists. For example, Johannes Stark, a Nobel prizewinner in physics, claimed that only those of Aryan ancestry had access to authentic scientific knowledge and that the theory of relativity should therefore be dismissed as 'Jewish science' (Merton 1972: 12). In all these cases we have an appeal to a genetic criterion, an appeal to who holds or originated the beliefs in order to validate their truth. In my view such appeals are unsound from whatever political direction they come.

There is no doubt that those in different social locations will be able to draw on different experience and different cultural assumptions, and that this diversity can be extremely fruitful for inquiry: both in producing novel theoretical ideas and in generating criticisms of established ideas. However, we must beware of claims that one group or category of people necessarily has more valid insights than another. Since all experience is a construction, it always carries the capacity for error as well as for truth. There is no such thing as raw experience. In becoming conscious of anything, we process information about it. Even feelings of pain are a product of our sensory apparatus and are affected by variation in the operation of that apparatus as well as by previous experience, cultural conditioning, social context etc.

It is worth looking, briefly, at the two specific arguments offered in support of the claim that women have unique insight. The first, about the insight of oppressed groups into the motives of oppressors, is not very convincing. It is two-edged: presumably the oppressors know their own motives, and for them to be successful they must have at least some understanding of the behaviour of the oppressed. There is no clear basis for a claim to superior insight here.[10] The second argument, that women have access both to the dominant culture and to 'the reality of their own experience', involves the sort of appeal to direct experience I criticised earlier. It could be reformulated to avoid this, in terms of dominant and subordinate cultures. In this form there is some truth in it. However, what is implied is not access to guaranteed truths,

[10] Similarly, Smith's argument (1987: 78–81) drawing on Hegel's parable of the master and the slave, is questionable because it draws too crude and sharp a distinction between rulers and ruled. Also, see the discussion in Descombes (1980) of the debate about the master–slave relationship in recent French philosophy.

but the relative accessibility and inaccessibility of particular sorts of insight to those in different social positions. Moreover, women are not the only category of persons who experience more than one culture. Indeed, it could plausibly be argued that this is the norm in large, complex societies.

As a footnote to this discussion, we should note that arguments by Marxists to the effect that the proletariat has access to uniquely valid insights into the nature of capitalist society have always involved some means of distancing the true proletarian vision from the beliefs of actual members of the proletariat.[11] This is both because the latter are diverse and often inconsistent, and because they frequently fail to match what it is assumed that the proletariat *ought* to believe. Such deviation is usually explained as the product of bourgeois ideology. Feminists face the same problem with the category 'women', and sometimes adopt a similar solution, implicitly or explicitly restricting the claim of insight to feminists involved in the struggle against patriarchy. I shall examine the justification for this argument in the next section, but it should be noted that the problem of diversity and inconsistency of view is to be found even among feminists. Of course, those who fail to evidence the appropriate insights, or who show inappropriate ones, could simply be excluded from the feminist community by definition; but the problem arises of how the correct view is to be selected from among conflicting feminist experiences and interpretations.[12]

Another way of dealing with this problem, that adopted by Stanley and Wise (1983a, b), is to treat all experiences and views as valid in themselves:

> What we're trying to do is to point out that 'scientific knowledge', 'objective knowledge', are all social constructs, and as such are exactly similar to all other forms of knowledge-held-in-common . . . Different states of consciousness aren't just different ways of interpreting the social world. We don't accept that there is something 'really' there for these interpretations to be interpretations of. Our differing states of consciousness lead us into constructing different social worlds. (Stanley and Wise 1983b: 130–1)

However, this suffers from the well-known problem of self-refutation associated with relativism (Scheffler 1967), and provides no basis for the rational resolution of disagreements. Also, it leads these authors to reject the idea that there are real conditions of women's oppression independent of particular women's experience of them (Stanley and Wise 1983b: 81; but see the later discussion in Stanley and Wise 1990).

---

[11] See Kolakowski's (1978) discussion of Lukacs and Korsch.

[12] For an excellent account of this and other related epistemological issues in the context of feminism, see Hawkesworth (1989).

We can recognise the diversity of view across different categories and groups of people, and its advantages in our attempts to minimise the effects of bias. Indeed, that has long been part of the rationale for the capacity of research communities to pursue knowledge. As Merton (1972: 40) comments, we must 'trade on the distinctive strengths and weaknesses of Insider and Outsider perspectives that enlarge the chances for a sound and relevant understanding of social life'. But arguments which privilege the viewpoint of some category of person, or that declare all points of view to be equally valid, are not a sound basis for research methodology; indeed, if they are held consistently, they are incompatible with research, and probably with life itself.

Finally, as I noted, one of the consequences of feminists' emphasis on experience as against method has been their tendency to adopt 'unstructured' methods, notably depth interviewing, rather than more structured approaches. There is no doubt that such methods can be of great value, especially where the aim is to explore people's perspectives. However, it would be a mistake to conclude that such methods are appropriate to all purposes. And, indeed, this is recognised by many feminists, both in practice and in principle (Jayaratne 1983; Reinharz 1992).

*Hierarchy*
There has been much discussion within ethnographic methodology about the variety of roles that a participant observer can play, and about variations in the role of the interviewer.[13] In large part the concern has been how to avoid disturbing what is being investigated, but ethnographers have not been unaware of the ethical issues involved, including their obligations to the people they study (Barnes 1979; Bulmer 1982; Burgess 1984; Punch 1986, 1994; Homan 1991). Few, if any, researchers in the qualitative or ethnographic tradition would argue that the researcher can, or should try to, act as a neutral and uninvolved observer, even though they would not usually advocate commitment to a particular group within the field of investigation and active intervention on the part of that group. Similarly, the idea that the researcher's own values should be made explicit is also to be found in the non-feminist literature (most notably Weber 1949; Myrdal 1970). And, again, the advocacy and practice of collaborative research involving the people studied in the research process has emerged in a number of other fields: in work on education and development in the Third World (Latapi 1988); in educational research (Stenhouse 1975; Carr and Kemmis 1986; but see Weiner 1989; Chisholm 1990); and in some

[13] For a feminist discussion of the role of gender in research relationships which draws on this existing literature, see Warren (1988).

versions of action research in industrial settings (see, for example, Gustavsen 1986). In this respect too, then, the ideas put forward by feminists about social research methodology are not distinctive to them. Furthermore, while there is no doubt of the importance of the ethical and political issues they raise, in my view their arguments are not always convincing.

I identified three feminist arguments against hierarchy in the research relationship, appealing to ethical, methodological and tactical considerations respectively. Let me begin by considering the idea that hierarchy should be eliminated from the research process because there is an ethical requirement that women researchers always treat other women as equals not as subordinates. One obvious problem here is the assumption that feminists only study women. Some feminists have pointed to the importance of 'studying up', of researching the powerful (Harding 1987: 8), and this inevitably means studying men. However, the problem is more general than this: since the lives of women and men are so closely interrelated it would be very difficult to study women alone. The only way to do this would be to restrict one's focus to women's experiences, but this may not tell us much about the world that produced those experiences. And where men are included as sources of data, hierarchy probably cannot or should not be eliminated from the research process. The men may impose a hierarchy and, whether they do or not, presumably feminist researchers must exploit whatever resources they have to exert control over the relationship, on the grounds that in present circumstances the only choice is between being dominant or being dominated. This implies an important qualification to the feminist commitment to non-hierarchical research techniques. And it is worth adding that there are some women in powerful social positions in dealing with whom feminists may also be forced into hierarchical relationships, one way or the other.

Over and above this practical issue, though, I want to question the desirability of the principle of non-hierarchical relationships, if by that is meant equality of control over the research process between researchers and researched (which seems logically to imply the abolition of the distinction between the two). One of the problems with many feminist discussions of this issue is that the concept of hierarchy which is employed is one-dimensional and zero-sum: it implies control that is all-pervasive and that is always exercised by one person or group at the expense of others. On this view, the only alternatives are domination by either one side or the other, or equality/democracy. Yet, power is rarely all-encompassing, it is more usually restricted to particular domains, especially in large societies with complex divisions of labour (Giddens 1973). Thus, conventional researchers do not claim the right to control the lives of the people they study in some all-enveloping sense. The control they seek is restricted to the particular research project. They claim the right to define the research topic, to decide to a large extent how and what data are to be collected, to do the analysis and to write the research report. This does not even represent a claim to total control over the research process itself. Researchers do not, and could not, demand access to all settings, insist on interviewing anyone whom they desire to interview, or require the divulging of all relevant information. More importantly, the research they do is usually a small and marginal part of the lives of the people being studied. The control researchers seek to exercise is more limited than, say, that claimed by employers over employed or professionals over clients. If the researcher–researched relationship is a form of domination then these other relationships are also, and to a much greater degree.

What seems to be implicit in some feminist methodologists' opposition to hierarchical relationships, then, is a rejection of all inequalities in power and authority. But we must ask whether this is a reasonable goal. Could it be achieved? Is even its approximation desirable? Even if we take democracy as an omni-relevant ideal, does it not involve some people making decisions on behalf of others, acting as their democratic representatives? Every decision could not be made by a plebiscite. And is democracy always the best way of making decisions? At the very least these issues need discussion.

Following on from this, we must ask whether researchers' exercise of control over the research process is necessarily, or even typically, against the interests of others, including those of the people studied. This is only obviously so if it is assumed that 'having a say' in decisions, all decisions, is an overriding interest in every circumstance. And it is not clear to me why we should assume that this is the case. As far as research is concerned, advocacy of this view often seems to be based on the assumption that research findings are simply an expression of opinion by the researcher, and that her opinion is no better than that of any other woman. On this assumption the greater likelihood of the researcher's 'opinion' being published as against those of the women studied represents dominance by the one over the other. However, the premiss on which this argument is based is false. Research necessarily and legitimately involves a claim to intellectual authority, albeit of a circumscribed kind. That authority amounts to the idea that the findings of research are, on average, less likely to be in error than information from other sources. And this stems from the operation of the research community in subjecting research findings to scrutiny and thereby detecting and correcting errors (see pp. 76–7 below).

While I accept that everyone has the right to come to their own opinions on any issue, I do not believe that this implies that we must treat everyone's opinions as equally likely to be true, and therefore equally worthy of attention. Nor do I believe that we do this or could do this in everyday life. This is not to say that only research findings are of value as a source of information. For example, we also tend to privilege sources of information based on first-hand experience as against second-hand reports, and justifiably so.[14] Nor is it to say that research findings should be accepted at face value. The point is simply that it is rational to give them more attention than the opinions of people who have no distinctive access to relevant information. In short, research is not the only source of intellectual authority and its authority is limited and does not automatically imply validity, but research does inevitably involve a claim to authority.

Some feminist methodologists reject any claim to intellectual authority on the part of researchers, on the grounds that this conflicts with a commitment to equality, that value being taken to imply the right of all individuals and groups to 'define reality for themselves' (see, for example, Stanley and Wise 1983a, b). But this argument is based on a concept of knowledge production which assumes too direct a relationship between understanding one's situation and changing it; as if one could always change one's situation simply by redefining it and getting others to accept the redefinition. To the extent that successful action depends on accurate information, and it sometimes does, expertise in knowledge production may be of value. This conclusion could only be avoided by adopting an anti-realism which denies the very possibility of such expertise.

The consequences of denying the intellectual authority of research are illustrated by the work of Stanley and Wise (1983b), who take the feminist argument against hierarchy to its logical, and contradictory, conclusion:

> We most certainly don't want to be seen to be telling other feminists how things are and should be, for a start because we don't know anyway, but also because we really don't want there to be a, one, feminist 'line' on research or anything else . . . One of our main arguments has been that the analytic use of feeling and experience in an examination of 'the personal' should be the main principle on which feminist research is based. To this extent, at least, we're willing to provide a recipe and tell other women what they should be doing. This may be a contradiction at the heart of what we believe and what we've written, but neither of us minds being contradictory. (Stanley and Wise 1983b: 177–8)

On the one hand, these authors wish to deny any claim on their part to knowledge which must be treated as valid by others; on the other, they

[14] It is also true that researchers have sometimes claimed and been accorded too much intellectual authority (see Hammersley 1992a: ch. 7).

recognise that in effect their book inevitably makes just such a claim. And their solution to this problem is to tolerate contradiction, abandoning a principle which is essential for the development of knowledge, and indeed for communication itself.

Moreover, the fact that, whether we like it or not, researchers necessarily claim some intellectual authority by publishing their findings also carries an important implication for the organisation of research. The other side of the claim to intellectual authority is an obligation on the part of the researcher to ensure that, as far as possible, the information provided is valid. And this is a responsibility which cannot be shifted on to the people studied, or on to anyone else. For this reason researchers *should* make the decisions which guide the process of inquiry.

The second rationale for the abolition of hierarchy, indeed of any asymmetry in the researcher–researched relationship, is methodological in character: it is suggested that data deriving from hierarchical relationships will be distorted by that context and therefore be invalid. Once again, this seems to me to rest on an assumption which is unsound. If we were to assume that data took the form exclusively of accounts from informants, so that the only barrier to valid research findings was how full and accurate informants were prepared to make their accounts, then this argument would have some plausibility. Presumably, the more informants are treated as part of the research team, the more they are committed to its goals, the better the information they are likely to provide; though even in this case they will have other commitments which may well interfere with the quality of the data, and the danger of reactivity is likely to be increased. However, what we have here is an extremely restricted view of the nature of social science data. It is unreasonable to assume that the only data available consist of the information about the social world provided in the accounts of informants. Indeed, these accounts are not sufficient in themselves because we cannot assume that informants understand the wider social forces which lead them to behave in the ways that they do, that they are always reliable observers, or even that they will always know their own motives.[15] Informants' accounts can and should be examined not just for what they tell us about the phenomena to which they refer but also for what we can infer from them about the informants themselves. Furthermore, many data are observational in character, consisting not of what people tell the researcher but of her/his observations of what they do.

Once we recognise this variation in the character of data, the role of

---

[15] Feminists often accept this in recognising the role of masculinist ideology in obscuring the truth about their situation from some women.

the researcher becomes much more active, involving the piecing together of information from a diversity of sources; and this information is always subject to a variety of forms of potential error. It seems to me that one should use whatever information is available, but in all cases must examine its context with a view to assessing likely sources and directions of error. The idea that there is some single ideal or authentic situation in which data are necessarily error-free and that data from other situations must be rejected is false.

The final argument against hierarchy is the idea that if research has the practical goal of bringing about female emancipation, then the women studied need to be involved in the research if they are to be mobilised effectively. This argument depends on acceptance of that practical goal, and this will be my focus in the next section.

In summary, then, the choice is not between a hierarchical and an egalitarian/democratic form of relationship between researcher and researched. This dichotomy does not capture the relevant complexity of human relationships. Even feminists are not able to implement non-hierarchical relationships in all their research because this is at odds with the nature of the surrounding society. But even more importantly, there are serious questions about the wisdom of attempts to abandon the differentiation of role between researcher and researched. In my judgment, research inevitably involves a claim to intellectual authority (albeit of a severely limited kind) and a corresponding obligation on the part of the researcher to try to ensure the validity of the findings.

Furthermore, from an ethical point of view, the question of how much, and how, one should intervene in the lives of the people one is studying, and whether and in what respects they should be incorporated into the research process, is difficult to decide in general, in ethical or in methodological terms. What is appropriate depends in part on who one is and whom one is studying, in what aspect and for what purpose. This has been recognised by some feminists. Smart (1984), for example, reports that she could not employ a collaborative orientation in studying male solicitors. And Clegg (1975) suggests that collaborative methods are inappropriate for feminists studying men. Even collaborative research by women with other women is not always easy to sustain, as Acker et al. (1982) illustrate. They report a number of problems, including the demand from some of the women for the researchers to provide more of their own sociological analysis (p. 42). And Finch notes the danger that feminist researchers interviewing informants 'woman to woman' could be exploitative because information is elicited which would not otherwise be obtained and that could be used 'against the collective interests of women' (Finch 1984: 83). Finally, Stacey (1988: 22) asks whether the appearance of greater respect for and equality with research subjects in the ethnographic approach 'masks a deeper, more dangerous, form of exploitation'.

In my view, the proper relationship between researcher and researched is not something which can be legislated by methodology, feminist or otherwise. It will depend on the specifics of particular research investigations.[16] Furthermore, we should avoid naive contrasts between the dilemmas and inequalities involved in the research process and some idealised conception of 'authentic, related [personhood]' (Stacey 1988: 23). The rest of life is full of dilemmas and inequalities, even more than research, and while ideals are important they should not be applied irrespective of circumstance. In short, advocacy of a non-hierarchical relationship between researcher and researched rests on some doubtful ideas about the social world and the relationship of research to it.

*Emancipation as goal and criterion*
The idea that scientific inquiry should be concerned with changing the world, not just describing it, goes back to Marx and beyond (Lobkowicz 1967). There have also been those who have argued that truth should be defined and/or judged in terms of practical efficacy of one kind or another. For instance, William James reformulated Peirce's pragmatic maxim in this direction (see Bird 1986); and some Marxists and critical theorists have adopted a similar instrumentalism, framed in terms of a contribution to emancipation (see, for example, Habermas 1968b). Once again, then, we should recognise that what feminists are proposing is to be found in the non-feminist literature; and some of the problems with these ideas are well known.

I want to argue against both aspects of the emancipatory model of inquiry: the idea that changing the world should be the immediate goal of research, and that its success in this respect is the most important criterion by which it should be judged. It seems to me that the concept of emancipatory inquiry is based on a simplistic notion of practice (political and social). This is conceived as struggle for emancipation from oppression in a world that is neatly divided into oppressors and oppressed. As slogans, the terms 'oppression' and 'emancipation' may be appealing, but as analytic concepts they are problematic. For one thing, there is no single type or source of oppression. It is now widely recognised that 'racial', ethnic and sexual oppression cannot be reduced to class oppression. Nor can other types of oppression be reduced, directly or indirectly, to sexual oppression. Given this, we find that many people will be classed as both oppressors and oppressed

---

[16] Exactly the same point applies to the argument for a conflict methodology in dealing with powerful groups, see Lehman and Young (1974), Douglas (1976) and Lundman and McFarlane (1976).

from different points of view. At the very least, this introduces a considerable degree of complexity into the application of the oppressor–oppressed model. This problem has been highlighted by black feminists who have challenged the neglect of racism by white feminists (Davis 1981; Carby 1982). And, of course, even black women living in Western societies may be regarded as part of the oppressor group when the focus includes international exploitation.

There are also problems involved in the very concept of oppression, as Geuss has pointed out in a discussion of critical theory:

> It seems unrealistic under present conditions of human life to assume that any and every preference human agents might have can be satisfied, or to assume that all conflict between the preferences of different agents will be peacefully and rationally resolved. Some frustration – even some imposed frustration – of some human preferences must be legitimate and unexceptionable. (Geuss 1981: 16)

In addition, the concept of oppression involves the assumption that we can identify what are real or genuine needs relatively easily. Yet, as Alcoff has noted, this is not the case:

> most if not all theories of need rely on some naturalist conception of the human agent, an agent who either can consciously identify and state all of her or his needs or whose 'real' needs can be ascertained by some external process of analysis. Either method produces problems: it seems unrealistic to say that only if the agent can identify and articulate specific needs do the needs exist, and yet there are obvious dangers to relying on 'experts' or others to identify the needs of an individual. Further, it is problematic to conceptualize the human agent as having needs in the same way that a table has properties, since the human agent is an entity in flux in a way that the table is not and is subject to forces of social construction that affect her subjectivity and thus her needs. (Alcoff 1988: 426–7)

Thus, the identification of needs is not a matter of simple description. Rather, it is a reconstruction on the basis of what we feel and know, and what others say and do, and may well involve dealing with inconsistencies and disagreements. As a result, the needs ascribed to a group may not match the beliefs of many of its members (Geuss 1981: 45). How do we smooth out the contradictions in what people say and do about their needs? How do we deal with inconsistencies and disagreements in our own orientations? How do we decide what are genuine desires, and what desires are against a person's own interests (or against those of others)? Geuss comments that 'To speak of an agent's "interests" is to speak of the way that agent's particular desires could be rationally integrated into a coherent "good life"' (Geuss 1981: 47–8). This highlights the danger of defining the 'real needs' of an oppressed group falsely. Worse still, the question arises: are there not likely to be several alternative rational reconstructions, especially since such judgments depend on value and factual assumptions? If so, there is room for genuine disagreement about needs and interests (Moon 1983; Fay 1987).

These problems with 'oppression', and with the associated concepts of 'needs' and 'interests', also create difficulties for the notion of 'emancipation'. If oppression is not an all or nothing matter, is not restricted to a single dimension, and is a matter of judgment which is open to reasonable dissensus, it is not clear that it can be overcome in the form of the total, once and for all release from constraint which the term 'emancipation' implies. In Marxism these problems are obscured by a view of practice that portrays it as a historical process which brings reality into line with theory, that theory itself being a product of, and legitimated in terms of, its position and role in history. According to this view, desire and social obligation are miraculously harmonised as contradictions between subjectivity and objectivity, fact and value are resolved by the historical dialectic (Lobkowicz 1967; Prokopczyk 1980). As I noted earlier, Marx argued that the triumph of the proletariat would abolish all oppression because the proletariat is the universal class. Most feminists would probably doubt whether a successful proletarian revolution would lead to women's emancipation; and not without reason. But the argument works the other way too: as some feminists recognise, there is no good reason for assuming that women's emancipation (if such a concept is viable, given the problems outlined above) would abolish 'racial', ethnic, class and other forms of oppression. Indeed, it is possible that it could worsen them. Historicism, whether in Marxist or feminist form, is not convincing in my judgment (Hammersley 1992a: ch. 6). However, without it the concept of emancipation becomes highly problematic. In its absence, negative critique can be little more than negativism for the sake of it.[17]

I am not denying the existence or illegitimacy of inequalities between the sexes, including power differences. Nor am I suggesting that feminist politics must stop until the analytical problems outlined here have been resolved. I am simply pointing to important problems whose resolution may require considerable rethinking; and this is (at least in part) the responsibility of researchers. And one result of such rethinking should be a less instrumentalist view of the relationship between 'theory' and 'practice'. Once we recognise the complexities of practice, it should become clear that research cannot play the commanding role it is given by some interpretations of the idea of research as directed towards bringing about female emancipation (see Chapter 7).

The other issue I want to raise about the emancipatory conception of

[17] See Kristeva (1980: 137) for an example of such negativism; and Descombes (1980) for something of the philosophical context in which this view arose.

inquiry concerns the idea that truth is to be judged in terms of a pragmatic criterion: in terms of its contribution to emancipation. It is fairly obvious, I think, that in practice it is not uncommon for successful action to be based on some false assumptions (this is fortunate, since otherwise humanity would not have survived). Equally, it is quite possible for action based on sound assumptions to fail; for example, because of contingencies which could not have been anticipated. Truth and effectiveness are in my view different values that, while not completely unrelated, have no *necessary* connection. And this has important implications for the nature of research and for its relationship to practice. Since its value cannot be judged entirely in terms of practical success, the research process must be given some autonomy from practical concerns if researchers are to be able to assess the validity of their products effectively. And this argument runs counter to the claim, to be found in some versions of feminist methodology, that any inquiry which is not directed in some relatively immediate way to bringing about emancipation is illegitimate.

Clearly, political movements like feminism must involve reflection on their goals and strategies, as well as some information-gathering, as part of their practice. However, that process of inquiry will be shaped by the constraints and requirements of the practice. This will carry both benefits and costs. On the one hand, it should encourage an efficient balance between inquiry and the other necessary elements of practice, and appropriate judgment about what it is and is not relevant to inquire into. On the other hand, the pressures of practice and commitments of the audience to which inquiry is directed may restrict topics of inquiry, and limit the degree to which assumptions are tested to what is relevant to relatively narrow and short run concerns. It may be difficult, or perhaps even counter-productive from the point of view of practice, to raise questions outside these limits. And yet those issues may be important when the political practice is viewed in a longer term and/or in a wider perspective. Given this, it seems to me that there is a case for institutionalised inquiry that is not geared to the immediate requirements of any single political or social practice. Such inquiry would produce knowledge that is potentially of relevance to a wide range of practices. Of course, by its very nature inquiry of this kind could not be specifically directed to pragmatic goals and could not be judged primarily in pragmatic terms, though it *would* need to be judged in terms of public relevance (Hammersley 1992a). It is on some such view of inquiry that scholarship, science and universities have long relied. In my judgment that view needs to be defended against those who, for whatever reason and whatever their values, wish to tie inquiry to their own practical goals, and this includes some feminists.

# Conclusion

In this chapter I have outlined and assessed the arguments for a distinctively feminist methodology. There is no doubt that feminism has made, and continues to make, a major contribution to the social sciences. However, in my opinion the arguments in support of a feminist methodology do not establish it as a coherent and cogent alternative to non-feminist research. Many of the ideas on which feminist methodologists draw are also to be found in the non-feminist literature. Furthermore, many of these are defective. Over and above this, though, I want to argue against the very idea of a specifically feminist methodology. It is yet another instance of an attempt to set up a separate methodological paradigm based on distinctive political and philosophical assumptions which are held to motivate a unique form of research practice. Ramazanoglu (1992) provides an extreme example, dismissing the assumptions on which Western scholarship and science are based as 'blatantly sexist and racist', and seeing feminists as operating from a quite different standpoint.

Like all attempts to set up a new paradigm, the effect of this is to homogenise other research and other views: to neglect what is held in common; and to assume a stronger inferential link between political and philosophical assumptions, on the one hand, and research decisions, on the other, than is to be found in reality and than can be justified. Research is a more pragmatic enterprise than this implies, and rightly so. Worse than this, though, the setting up of distinct methodological paradigms may create an obstacle to open debate, encouraging dogmatism on both sides. As Merton (1972: 13) points out, it can lead to a 'balkanisation' of social science; and we all now know where that leads. It is also counter-productive as a way of re-orientating social research. After all, if the arguments outlined in the first section of this chapter were to constitute a specifically feminist methodology, then there would be no obligation on the part of non-feminists to take any account of them. If, on the other hand, they are arguments about social research methodology put forward by feminists for general consideration, there is an obligation on the part of others to address them and to engage in discussion about them. This chapter is offered in the spirit of such a discussion.

# 4

# Research and 'Anti-racism': a Critical Case

> The distinctive character of social science discourse is to be sought in the fact that every assertion, no matter how objective it may be, has ramifications extending beyond the limits of science itself. Since every assertion of a 'fact' about the social world touches the interests of some individual or group, one cannot even call attention to the existence of certain 'facts' without courting the objections of those whose very *raison d'être* in society rests upon a divergent interpretation of the 'factual situation'.
>
> (Louis Wirth, Preface to Mannheim's *Ideology and Utopia*, 1936)

In this chapter I want to look at the critical response that has arisen to some recent sociological work on the issue of racism among teachers in British schools. This response raises some fundamental problems about social research, including the question of how we should decide what is sufficient evidence to accept or reject the findings of a study, and of how researchers ought to deal with views with which they disagree. It also allows us to explore contrasting views about how social research should be pursued, and to what end.

In an empirical study of a multi-ethnic, inner-city school which was formally committed to multi-cultural/anti-racist education, Peter Foster argued that there was little evidence of racism among teachers, or of school practices that indirectly disadvantaged black students. He claimed that this was true whether one looked at the allocation of students to ability groups or at their treatment in lessons (Foster 1989, 1990a). His conclusions conflicted with general claims made on the basis of studies in other schools; and, in order to understand this discrepancy, he examined a number of widely cited studies that claimed to document racism on the part of teachers. He argued that these studies suffered from serious methodological flaws: that they involved vague and doubtful conceptions of racism, as well as questionable assumptions about the motivations of the teachers involved in the incidents described, and about the effects of those incidents. Furthermore, he suggested that the small number of examples provided did not give a sound basis for the generalisations frequently made on the basis of these studies (Foster 1990b, 1993a–c).[1]

---

[1] I should declare at the start that I am in substantial agreement with Foster's arguments, and regard most of the criticisms of his work as unconvincing. I am grateful to

The response to Foster's work was predominantly negative. In outlining the criticism of Foster and the presuppositions on which it seems to be based, I will not try to reconstruct the actual views of Foster's critics in detail – this is neither possible nor necessary; but I have drawn on what they have written wherever possible. Most of the criticism of his work seems to come from those committed to some version of 'anti-racism', and my interest is in what critics of this kind could say, in what their most distinctive and forceful arguments would be.[2]

The criticism of Foster's work can be classified under two broad categories. First, there are factual criticisms: to the effect that various elements of Foster's arguments are false, including his theoretical and methodological assumptions. Secondly, there are what I will call practical value criticisms: criticisms of Foster's motives, of his behaviour as a researcher, and of the consequences of making public the arguments he presents. I will look at these two sorts of criticism separately.

## Arguments about validity

Various sorts of criticism have been directed at the validity of Foster's work. Some is substantive in character; in other words, it consists of a questioning of his claims on the basis of appeals to what is taken to be well known from other sources. For example, Connolly (1992: 134) argues that the fact that Foster's findings 'challenge the growing "perceived wisdom" of a number of research and theoretical perspectives developed since the mid1980s . . . raises numerous important issues concerning the study's political, ethical and theoretical orientation and, consequently, the research methods used'.

Accompanying such substantive criticisms, very often, are methodological criticisms: these question the inferences Foster draws on the basis of his own or others' data. For instance, both Connolly (1992)

---

Peter Foster for providing me with copies of some unpublished responses to his work. Published discussions include: Wright (1991); Connolly (1992); Gillborn and Drew (1992); Blair (1993). See also Foster's replies (1991, 1992). My thanks go to Maud Blair, Peter Foster, Roger Gomm, Donald Mackinnon and Peter Woods for comments on earlier drafts of this chapter.

[2] There is a problem with the term 'anti-racism' which motivates my use of quotation marks around it. While as a matter of semantics the meaning of the term is purely negative, in common usage it is associated with specific ideas about the nature, distribution and origins of racism, and about how it must be dealt with. The result of this ambiguity is that the term carries the implication (given the assumed dichotomy) that those who do not accept these ideas are not against racism – in fact, are racist themselves. It is important not to be misled by this ambiguity or by rhetorical exploitation of it. It is also true, of course, that 'anti-racists' differ about many issues, but for the purposes of my task in this chapter these differences are probably not significant.

and Gillborn and Drew (1992) challenge Foster's claim that there was little evidence of racism on the part of the teachers in the school he studied, on the grounds that he took insufficient account of black students' views. They argue that he explains away the unsolicited complaints of racism on the part of teachers voiced by three of the students he interviewed through treating these as products of a general anti-school attitude. The critics also argue that the fact that so few of the students reported the existence of racism among teachers resulted from the influence on them of Foster's own status as a white, middle-class male whom they identified with the teachers. Another methodological criticism that has been made of Foster's study is that the school he investigated was atypical and therefore does not constitute a sound basis for generalisation to other schools (Gillborn and Drew 1992: 558–9).[3]

Interestingly, these methodological criticisms parallel in character, if not in force, those that Foster himself makes of other studies, including those on which his critics rely in their substantive criticisms. And he, and others, have responded to the attacks of the critics with further methodological arguments (Foster 1991, 1992; Hammersley and Gomm 1993).

What we have here, then, is a body of substantive and methodological issues which are interpreted in conflicting ways by Foster and his critics. One response to this situation might be to call for further research designed to resolve the disagreement. I would not want to discourage this, but I doubt whether it would succeed. It seems to me that the roots of the disagreement lie more deeply than these substantive and methodological criticisms themselves. We get an inkling of this from the fact that Foster's critics sometimes combine such criticisms with what I will call 'meta-methodological' arguments. These concern defects in what they take to be the presuppositions on the basis of which Foster approached his own data and that of others. The clearest published example of such criticism is provided by Connolly (1992). He argues that, as a result of his adoption of a Weberian orientation, Foster was unable to recognise the racism that was taking place 'under his nose' (p. 142). Connolly sees Foster's work as controlled by a deterministic model of research in which the findings are constrained by his starting assumptions, in such a way as to rule out the detection of many forms of racism. Gillborn and Drew (1992: 558–9) hint at the same point, criticising Foster's definition of racism as too narrow.

---

[3] A related methodological criticism is that Foster draws the false conclusion from his work that there is no need for further investigation of intra-school processes to detect possible racism (Troyna 1991: 365; 1992: 46). However, this accusation is based on a mis-quotation of Foster and therefore does not require attention.

In part, what seems to be implied in these arguments is that the evidence which Foster offers in his study, and his questioning of the findings of other studies, must be rejected because they are incompatible with the widely accepted theoretical assumption that racism is institutionalised in British society, that it is part of the fundamental structure of that society. On this basis his critics argue that while discrimination may not seem to be occurring in some particular setting, once we view this setting in the context of British (or English) society as a whole it will be seen to form part of a larger pattern of racism.

Here Foster's claims are being questioned on the grounds of his presumed commitment to an inadequate methodological framework, one which gives a misleading priority to micro-empirical evidence at the expense of macro-theoretical perspective. This can be summarised as the charge that Foster's work is empiricist (Gillborn and Drew 1993). And, of course, this argument connects with much discussion of the methodology of qualitative research today, in which the empiricism of quantitative research, and of some qualitative work as well, is challenged on the basis of alternative epistemological assumptions.[4]

What is being rejected here is a foundationalist epistemology: the notion that research conclusions are founded, in some rigorously determinate fashion, on a body of evidence whose own validity is beyond question (for example, because it consists of reports of intersubjectively observable behaviour). Thus, Troyna criticises Foster for 'methodological purism', which he interprets as requiring evidence that rules out all possible alternative interpretations (Troyna 1993; see Hammersley 1993b). Foundationalism has, of course, been subjected to very damaging criticism in philosophy, as well as in the social sciences, over the past 30 or 40 years, and I think it is clear that it is not defensible.

There is little agreement about what is the alternative to foundationalism, but we can identify three radical positions which have become increasingly influential in social research methodology in recent years; and whose influence is detectable in the writings of some of Foster's critics. These positions are: relativism, standpoint theory and instrumentalism. They are not always clearly distinguished, and are sometimes used in combination. However, I will try to show that none of them is acceptable.

Applying relativism to the case under discussion, it would be argued that the validity of Foster's appeal to the canons of good research is

---

[4] See, for example, Smith (1989), Eisner and Peshkin (1990), Guba (1990) and Lather (1991). I am not concerned at this point with whether Foster's work does rely on empiricist presuppositions. An implication of arguments presented later in this chapter is that it does not.

relative to a particular methodological framework, namely positivism or post-positivism; and that other frameworks would produce different conclusions.[5] We may, for instance, decide to treat the claims of some black pupils that they and others have been subjected to racist treatment by teachers as true in their own terms, as reflecting their experience and the framework of assumptions which constitute it, that framework being incommensurable with the one adopted by Foster. Something like this may underly Connolly's question: 'how can Foster as a White middle class male construct his own definition of racism to then use to judge the accuracy of Black working class students' definitions?' (Connolly 1992: 144). If treated as valid, this argument has the effect of apparently undercutting Foster's empirical research in the sense that it need no longer be treated by others as representing reality. Yet, at the same time, from this point of view Foster's arguments remain valid in their own terms; in fact, they remain as valid as those of his critics. This seems to lead to a sort of stalemate. And, of course, there is the problem that relativism is self-undermining: if it is true, then in its own terms it can only be true relative to a relativist framework; so that from other points of view it remains false.[6] As a non-relativist, this leaves Foster free to claim, quite legitimately (even from the point of view of relativism), that his views represent reality; whereas a relativist critic could not make the same claim for his or her views but must treat them simply as representing a particular framework of beliefs to which he or she happens to be committed.

The second view I want to consider is sometimes associated with versions of the first, but must be kept separate because it involves a quite distinctive and incompatible element. I will refer to this as standpoint theory. Here people's experience and knowledge is treated as valid or invalid by dint of their membership of some social category.[7] Here again Foster's arguments may be dismissed because they reflect his background and experience as a white, middle-class, male teacher. However, this time the implication is that reality is obscured from those with this background because of the effects of ideology. By contrast, it is suggested, the oppressed (black, female and/or working-class people) have privileged insight into the nature of society. This argument produces a victory for one side, not the stalemate that seems to result from relativism; the validity of Foster's views can therefore be dismissed. However, in other respects, this position is no more satisfactory than

---

[5] Some of Gillborn and Drew's (1993) discussion seems close to this position.

[6] For a useful discussion of this and other aspects of relativism, see Scheffler (1967).

[7] This view derives from the Hegelian and Marxist traditions, but the label comes, of course, from feminist standpoint epistemology. On these sources, see Hammersley (1992a: ch. 6), and Chapters 2 and 3.

relativism. We must ask on what grounds we can decide that one group has superior insight into reality. This cannot be simply because they declare that they have this insight; otherwise everyone could make the same claim with the same legitimacy (we would be back to relativism). This means that some other form of ultimate justification is involved, but what could this be? In the Marxist version of this argument the working class (or, in practice, the Communist Party) is the group with privileged insight into the nature of social reality, but it is Marx and Marxist theorists who confer this privilege on them by means of a dubious philosophy of history.[8] Something similar occurs in the case of feminist standpoint epistemology, where the feminist theorist ascribes privileged insight to women, or to feminists engaged in the struggle for women's emancipation (Harding 1986). However, while we must recognise that people in different social locations may have divergent perspectives, giving them distinctive insights, it is not clear why we should believe the implausible claim that some category of people has privileged access to knowledge while others are blinded by ideology.[9]

Finally, there is instrumentalism. Here, the validity of knowledge is defined solely according to whether action on the basis of it has desirable effects. We can find this idea among pragmatist philosophers like James and Dewey, as well as in Marxism, 'critical theory' and some forms of feminism.[10] The implication of this position is that research must be pursued in close association with practical activities and judged in terms of its contribution to those activities. If it facilitates their success it is true, if it does not it is false. Thus, the validity of Foster's work could be assessed in terms of whether or not it serves the fight against racism. And, indeed, some of the criticism of his work does focus on its assumed consequences in this respect.[11]

I will consider such arguments as they apply to the issue of the relevance or value of his work later; here I am concerned simply with the epistemological interpretation of instrumentalism. And this seems to

---

[8] For a discussion of the ethical implications of this in the case of Marxism, see Lukes (1985).

[9] For a sustained assessment of this claim, see Merton (1972). Connolly's (1992) critique of Foster hovers uneasily between relativism and standpoint theory, beginning from the implied relativism of the claim that the findings of research are determined by political assumptions, but later appealing to the authority of 'the black perspective'.

[10] See Bird (1986) for a sympathetic discussion of James's pragmatic definition of truth. For a similar treatment of Dewey, see Tiles (1989). On this aspect of Marxism, see Prokopczyk (1980). One of the clearest examples of instrumentalism in discussions of feminist methodology is Mies (1983).

[11] Gillborn and Drew (1992) seem to use this form of argument indirectly against Foster and directly against the work of Smith and Tomlinson (1989). See Hammersley and Gomm (1993).

me to be decidedly weak. While we may recognise that the value of academic work should be judged partly in terms of its political and social relevance, the claim that its validity should be judged in this way is much more questionable. In so far as the production of desirable consequences is taken as defining validity, this position proposes a replacement for the correspondence theory of truth, yet implicitly relies on that theory. This is because claims about the effects of acting on the beliefs being assessed cannot themselves be judged instrumentally (otherwise we are in an infinite regress). Even where instrumentalism implies treating desirable consequences only as an indicator of validity, this assumes a much stronger relationship between the truth of a belief and the practical consequences of acting on it than is justifiable: it is clear, I think, that validity of assumptions is neither a necessary nor a sufficient condition of practical success.

So, to summarise, there is apparently intractable disagreement at the level of substantive and methodological arguments between Foster and his critics. And it seems that this probably results, in part at least, from some more profound differences of view, differences which are indicated by what I have called meta-methodological criticisms, criticisms that challenge the methodological framework on which Foster is assumed to be operating. Effectively, he is accused of empiricist foundationalism, a position that does not seem to be defensible.

I have examined three currently fashionable alternative positions to this view, traces of which can be found in the writings of Foster's critics. But I have argued that none of these alternatives is sound. This clearly leaves us with a problem, and it is my task in the next section of this chapter to try to show how it might be resolved, and what conclusions follow from this.

### Exploring the implications of non-foundationalism

In the discussions of non-foundationalist philosophers of science and others we can identify an empirical model of how scientists actually judge claims in the absence of a foundation.[12] This involves a process in which consistency with existing beliefs plays a key role. While this model does not rule out the acceptance of new ideas that are incompatible with existing beliefs, it makes this less likely than on the foundationalist model, where these would simply be accepted if supported by decisive evidence. Ideas that are in conflict with existing beliefs will be initially resisted and subjected to severe scrutiny, however

---

[12] I have drawn rather selectively on a variety of work in philosophy and the philosophy of science here, including that of Quine (1953, 1960; Quine and Ullian 1970), Polanyi (1958), Wittgenstein (1969), Kuhn (1970) and Lakatos (1970, 1975).

apparently strong the evidence available in support of them. Obversely, the non-foundationalist model makes the acceptance of new ideas that are consistent with existing beliefs easier than it would be on the basis of foundationalism: in this case little evidence may be needed. This model can be elaborated by the addition of a distinction (or, better, a dimension) between core and peripheral beliefs. Where new ideas threaten relatively peripheral existing beliefs, change may occur without much resistance. However, where new ideas challenge core beliefs change is much less likely. What distinguishes core and peripheral beliefs is the extent to which other beliefs depend on them, so that if they are modified much of the rest of the belief system will need to change. Ease of acceptance is an inverse product of how much reassessment and reorganisation of what is currently taken to be established knowledge would be required to accept the new claim and retain overall consistency. Furthermore, defensive cognitive strategies may be developed specifically to protect the core from criticism (Lakatos 1970).

An obvious implication of this model is that evidence running counter to accepted core beliefs may not be taken seriously. Kuhn, for instance, argues that over a period when scientific work in a particular field is dominated by a single paradigm, anomalous evidence (that is, evidence which cannot be accounted for within that paradigm) accumulates but is ignored. It only becomes significant if and when an alternative paradigm is identified which looks as though it may be able to account for all the evidence covered by the old one and the anomalies as well; at which point there may be a scientific revolution leading to paradigm change, though even then this usually depends on generational replacement of the 'old guard' by the new (Kuhn 1970). If we apply this argument to the multi-paradigmatic case of the social sciences, where there are debates among parties adopting sharply discrepant assumptions, we can see why discussions among them may well be inconclusive, or at least will take a very long time to resolve.[13] Thus, the goal of the early advocates of the foundationalist model – to find a method that would produce consensus by convincing everyone relying solely on reason – seems to be beyond reach.

If we look at the case of Foster and his critics from this point of view, I think we get the following result. On the foundationalist model, whether others would accept Foster's arguments depends entirely on whether he shows that the findings of the studies he criticises do not derive logically from brute data and that those of his own study do. But, given the absence of any foundation of absolutely certain knowl-

[13] Of course, Kuhn did not apply his paradigm model to the social sciences; indeed, he explicitly rejected this possibility. However this does not affect the force of my argument here.

edge, Foster can only do the former, not the latter. And once we switch to a non-foundationalist position, we no longer have an absolute standard by which to decide even whether Foster's criticisms of others' work are sufficiently convincing to be accepted. Whether or not they are accepted will depend in part on judgments about the relative benefits and costs of accepting them, in terms of the reorganisation of existing beliefs, and this will vary among audiences. (Of course, exactly the same point applies to his critics' substantive and methodological questioning of Foster's own empirical research.)

I think this enables us to see why the responses of 'anti-racists' to Foster's work have been so negative. As noted earlier, 'anti-racism' generally involves the core theoretical assumption that racism is institutionalised in British society, and that it must be directly confronted in all its forms. On this basis, it follows necessarily that there are substantial inequalities in outcomes for members of ethnic minority groups – in terms of school achievement, jobs, freedom from harassment etc. – and that these derive not from features of ethnic minorities themselves, nor from idiosyncratic personal characteristics of individual members of the majority community, nor even just from the organisational structures and cultures of particular agencies like schools, firms, police forces etc. Rather, they result from the most fundamental structures of society, whether these are conceived in terms of capitalist social relations and/or of national cultural features (state racism, imperialist past etc.). What we have here is an application to the social level of the distinction between core and periphery that I outlined earlier in relation to cognition. It is being argued that racism is not a peripheral feature of British society but is built into its very core, so that its elimination requires fundamental social change.

The problem with Foster's argument for 'anti-racists', then, is that it seems to challenge a core assumption of their position: it suggests that some of the evidence on which this position is based, establishing the ubiquity of racism, may be unsound. And, complementarily, Foster's own research implies that he has discovered at least one place where racism is not endemic. Both these claims, negative and positive, may be seen as posing a fundamental threat to 'anti-racism'. As a result, even if 'anti-racists' were to find Foster's evidence credible at face value, on the Kuhnian model it would probably be treated by them as anomalous, at least until a satisfactory alternative position is found. This provides a partial explanation for the nature of their response to his work.

Up to now I have presented the non-foundationalist model as explanatory, as accounting for why the response to Foster's work has taken the form that it has. However, like foundationalism, the non-foundationalist model is also often presented as prescriptive, as indicating how researchers ought to respond to claims. And, while I do not want to conflate factual and value issues, I think that non-foundationalism is not only more accurate factually but is also a more reasonable basis on which social researchers ought to assess claims. However, its adoption clearly complicates any judgment we might make about the soundness of Foster's arguments and the appropriateness of the responses to them. One obvious implication is that judgments of what is sound may differ between people, depending on their current beliefs and on their judgments about the likelihood of finding a suitable reconstruction which would incorporate what they believe to be true in those beliefs and what is sound in Foster's case. The same argument applies to Foster himself. Despite the judgments of his critics, from the point of view of the non-foundationalist model his scepticism about the claim that there is widespread racism among teachers in British schools may also be legitimate, given his own presuppositions. And we cannot avoid presuppositions, nor can we ever be sure that our own are correct.

In this way, exploring the implications of non-foundationalism may appear to lead us to something like the stalemate which resulted from the relativist position. However, I do not believe that this is the case. While relativist conclusions have sometimes been drawn from the non-foundationalist model, they do not follow automatically (Phillips 1987, 1990a, b). And, as we saw earlier, there are good reasons to avoid such conclusions if we can. Let me outline a way round this problem.

In my view, it is precisely the model of scientific research, suitably formulated, which offers a solution. I suggest that the assessment of substantive claims within a research community should be based on judgments about the plausibility and credibility of evidence. By 'plausibility' here I mean what I referred to earlier as consistency with existing knowledge whose validity is taken to be beyond reasonable doubt. By 'credibility' I mean the likelihood that the process which produced the claim is free of serious error. Here I am assuming that factual claims vary in their credibility, both according to their own content and according to the circumstances in which they were produced. Where a claim is neither sufficiently plausible nor credible to be accepted at face value, the evidence for it must be examined in terms of *its* plausibility and credibility, and so on until a judgment can be made or until judgment must be suspended for want of the necessary evidence.[14] Where disagreements arise, such as that between Foster and his critics, attempts to resolve them should be pursued through a search for common ground, in terms of plausible and credible evidence, and an attempt to argue back from this to some conclusion that all will accept.

[14] For a more detailed account of this position, see Hammersley (1992a: ch. 4).

Ideally, this process will result in the acceptance of one or other of the two original positions, or (more likely) the construction of a third position (for example, through clarification of the concept of racism); though by contrast with foundationalism there is no guarantee that disagreement can be resolved.

In order to maximise the chances that agreement will be reached in this way, and that the resulting consensus will capture the truth, a research community needs to operate on the basis of the following norms:

1   The overriding concern of researchers is the truth of claims, not their political implications or practical consequences.
2   Arguments are not judged on the basis of the personal and/or social characteristics of the person advancing them, but solely in terms of their plausibility and credibility.
3   Researchers are willing to change their views if arguments from common ground suggest that those views are false; and, equally important, they assume (and behave as if) fellow researchers have the same attitude – at least until there is very strong evidence otherwise.
4   Where agreement does not result, all parties must recognise that there remains some reasonable doubt about the validity of their own positions, so that whenever the latter are presented they require supporting argument, or reference to where such argument can be found.
5   The research community is open to participation by anyone able and willing to operate on the basis of the first four rules; though their contributions will be judged wanting if they lack sufficient knowledge of the field and/or of relevant methodology. In particular, there must be no restriction of participation on the grounds of religious or political attitudes.[15]

In my view, a research community committed to the above norms maximises the chances of discovering error in empirical and theoretical

---

[15] It should not escape attention that these norms rule out meta-methodological arguments about the validity of empirical claims based on relativism, standpoint theory and instrumentalism. What this suggests is that those epistemological ideas conflict with the constitutive principles of rational discourse. In Peirce's words, they block the road of inquiry (see Skagestad 1981). Of course, these norms also proscribe racism, in the sense of the exclusion of participants from the research community on the basis of, or judgment of their contributions in terms of, 'race'. The conception of rational discourse employed here is similar in many respects to Habermas's concept of the ideal speech situation, on which see McCarthy (1978). There is also a parallel with Merton's specification of the ethic of science (see Merton 1973: ch. 13).

claims, and of discovering the truth about particular matters. It encourages the cumulative development of a body of knowledge whose validity is more reliable on average than that of lay views about the same issues. This is not to say that in any particular instance current research-based knowledge will be correct and common sense wrong; simply that it will usually be closer to the truth. Furthermore, it should be noted that this advantage is bought at considerable cost in terms of the time taken to complete inquiries in this way, and (correspondingly) the limited size of the body of research-based knowledge that can be produced.[16]

Even natural science does not conform perfectly to this ideal of communal organisation, but it approximates it more closely than social science. In the natural sciences obstacles to the operation of the five rules are likely to come mainly from internal factors such as individuals' commitments to particular theories and facts on the basis of their career interests.[17] While other concerns, such as religious and political commitments, play a role in some areas of natural science (for instance, as regards evolution), in general they have little influence. In the social sciences, on the other hand, such commitments have a much more wide-ranging effect because the topics investigated usually have much more direct social significance. These commitments have the consequence of reducing the likelihood that views will be changed on the basis of counter-argument, and that others will be seen as prepared to change their views. This may even lead to a rejection of the priority which the scientific model gives to the concern with the truth of claims.

Nevertheless, it seems to me that to the extent that social scientists are committed to the provision of accurate knowledge of the world, and therefore have an obligation to maximise the chances that their findings are valid, then the aim should be to approximate the process of assessment of arguments that this model implies. What this means is that in judging claims we must rely not just on our own assumptions about their plausibility and credibility, but also on the judgments of other members of the relevant research community. Anything that we do not find plausible or credible, or that we believe or know a substantial number of other researchers in the field will not find plausible or credible, requires support by evidence that *is* so regarded; and there

---

[16] It is worth emphasising that this view sees the findings of research as correcting rather than replacing common-sense assumptions, and that in my judgment the value of research for practice is more limited than commonly recognised (Hammersley 1992a: ch. 7) (see Chapter 7).

[17] Of course, in the case of research carried out in commercial or governmental organisations, commitment to these norms may be undercut by organisational interests and pressures.

must be a commitment to resolve disagreements by searching for and working back from such common ground. Within the framework of this model it is in the interests of both sides of a disagreement to resolve it, since they share the same goal; it is certainly not in their interests to prolong disagreement by spurious scepticism.[18] Furthermore, just as researchers must write with the anticipated assumptions of their audience in mind, providing evidence sufficient to convince that audience, as readers of research reports we must judge claims not only in relation to our own assumptions but also in relation to those which we expect to be accepted as beyond reasonable doubt by other members of the research community.

This proposed resolution of the problem of the failings of foundationalism is, of course, much less radical than the three alternatives which I discussed earlier. It retains much more of the conventional view of research than they do. Notably, it assumes something like the correspondence theory of truth, the idea that research is designed to, and can, represent social phenomena which are independent of it, though it does not need to assume a naive realism (Hammersley 1992a: ch. 4). It provides a meta-methodological rationale for empirical research of the kinds carried out by both Foster and many of his critics, and for the substantive and methodological criticisms which they make of one another's work; though I do not suggest that it is the only possible rationale for these, and of course it does not in itself give them validity. Most important of all, it indicates a way in which their disagreement could be resolved in principle, even though it does not guarantee a resolution.

However, it seems likely that this basis for resolving the dispute would not be accepted by many of Foster's critics; and not just because they have discrepant epistemological commitments. This becomes clear when we look at the ethical and political criticisms which they have directed at his work; and it is to these that I now turn.

### Practical value criticisms

The practical value criticisms made by Foster's critics are concerned with his intentions, with some features of his research practice, and with what they see as the consequences of the publication of his work. He has been accused, for instance, of lacking proper commitment to racial equality, indeed of producing work that is racist (Connolly 1992: 145). It has also been claimed that one of the interview questions he used with teachers invited them 'to articulate racist stereotypes', and

---

[18] This seems to be what Troyna has in mind by 'methodological purism' (see Troyna 1993; Hammersley 1993b).

thereby gave these respectability (Connolly 1992: 143). Finally, it is suggested that he can and will be read as 'blaming the victim' (Wright 1991: 354; Connolly 1992: 143; but see Foster 1991, 1992); and that the publication of his work plays into the hands of those who seek to deny the existence of racism for political reasons, thereby undermining the efforts of 'anti-racist' activists: it is 'disabling rather than enabling' (Blair 1993: 64).

In terms of the model of the research community I outlined in the previous section, these practical value criticisms are only directly relevant if they indicate deviation on Foster's part from the proper orientation of the researcher specified in that model. This orientation involves researchers being primarily committed to the discovery of the truth by means of rational discussion, being prepared to offer evidence for their claims where there is disagreement, being willing to change their views on the basis of compelling evidence, and assuming that all this is true of other researchers unless strong evidence to the contrary emerges. Some of the practical value criticisms of Foster imply such deviation, suggesting for instance that he 'has not stopped to critically examine the ideology which informs his own practice' and that in his empirical research he was 'keen to demonstrate that [the] teachers were not racist' (Blair 1993: 64). The implication here seems to be that he had a hidden political agenda. Convincing evidence is required to establish this claim, of course, and dismissal of Foster's work on these grounds without strong evidence is itself a breach of the norms.[19]

Most of the value criticisms of Foster's work, however, fall outside what is directly relevant according to the model outlined in the previous section. Examples are the charges that he 'lacks commitment to racial equality' and that his research 'disables' those fighting racism (Blair 1993: 64). This does not mean that these criticisms should automatically be ruled out of account by those operating on the basis of the model, however. There are two indirect ways in which ethical issues can still be relevant. First, there are forms of action on the part of researchers which are allowed by the model but which may need to be proscribed, temporarily or permanently, because they threaten the continued practice of research. We find this sort of argument quite commonly in debates about the legitimacy of covert methods of research, where it is sometimes argued that such research worsens future researchers' chances of gaining access (see, for example, Erickson 1967). However, this does not seem to be a major component in the arguments of Foster's critics.

The other way in which ethical arguments, apart from those which

---

[19] Foster's critics do not provide much evidence for this claim, and what they do provide is not convincing in my judgment.

are directly implicated in the model, can be relevant relies on the fact that the identity of 'researcher' is never the only one that a person has. And even when someone is acting as a researcher her or his other identities, and the ethical prescriptions and proscriptions associated with them, retain some relevance. Especially significant here is the identity of 'person' itself, and the ideas associated with it about what one person should do for, and should not do to, others. Many of the ethical and political arguments that Foster's critics advance could be understood in these terms, though establishing their force would require careful, casuistical argument that they do not supply.

Still, it seems unlikely that this is what the critics have in mind. Much recent writing on social research methodology has rejected the idea that the role of researcher can be separated from that of the person or the citizen. This is one reason why research is often seen as an intrinsically political enterprise. We find such views among feminists, critical ethnographers and many advocates of action research. Here the idea of research as an activity which is even semi-autonomous from practical and political activities is rejected. This perspective suggests that rather than being primarily concerned with producing knowledge, research should be directed towards maximising the success of particular practical or political projects. It seems that many 'anti-racists' adopt this view.[20] After all, 'anti-racism' is not simply a scientific theory (though it seems likely that it is intended as that in part); it is a practical enterprise directed towards changing British society. On this basis, research is required to serve the goal of bringing about social change of appropriate kinds, and may even be judged primarily in terms of its success in this respect.

I think we can see how criticisms of the intentions behind and consequences of Foster's research would arise in this context. From this perspective, those intentions and consequences, especially the latter, could be of more importance than the validity or otherwise of his empirical and methodological claims. While he declares his commitment to racial equality, and hopes that his work will contribute to the achievement of this, it is clear that he does not regard it as desirable for research to be geared directly towards the achievement of practical goals, not even this one. We are faced here, then, with a rather deep-seated disagreement between Foster and his critics about the character and purposes of social research.

Nevertheless, I think questions can be raised about the practical value criticisms made of Foster's work even from the point of view of this activist conception of social research. Central is a distinction

[20] That some 'anti-racists' are committed to a view like this is indicated by Troyna and Carrington (1989).

between two ways in which research may serve practical purposes. First, it may provide information about the world in which a practical activity is carried out and on the basis of which its goals and means should be developed, reviewed and perhaps changed. Secondly, it may serve a propaganda role, it may be used to legitimate the goals and means adopted or to criticise those of opponents. Much political activity involves debate between opponents, and while no one would suggest that conflicts are usually resolved in a purely discursive way, propaganda is a factor that has some weight (especially in liberal democratic societies), not least in mobilising the support of others.

Now, of course, the same research findings may serve both of these functions, but how findings are assessed by political activists will need to vary depending on which function is treated as primary. If the first is dominant, there will be particular concern with the accuracy and relevance of the information provided. While I do not assume that for action to be successful it must be based on true assumptions, nor that true assumptions will automatically lead to success, I do believe that there is a positive relationship between the two in general. By contrast, from a propaganda point of view the truth of the findings is less significant than whether relevant others regard them as true and what they take their implications to be. What is important here is what role the findings can play in the propaganda war.

Recognising the propaganda role of information involves a view of political debate and conflict which places it at a considerable distance from the sort of rational discourse that is central to the model of the research community which I outlined in the previous section. In such debate, dissembling, the suppression of evidence, the dismissal of opponents' views on the basis of their motives, accusations of ideology and racism etc. may be rational techniques, at least from a short-term and partisan perspective. This is not a novel view of politics, of course. And it matters not at all for my argument here whether this is taken to be the universal character of politics or whether it is specific to a particular historical period.[21] Let us simply accept, for the sake of argument, that this is how politics is today.

Looking at the critical response to Foster's work in the light of this, I think we need to recognise that the judgments that 'anti-racist' activists will and should make about the validity, or at least the implications, of Foster's work may be different from those that researchers (on my model) should make. Not only may the belief in widespread racism among teachers be more deeply entrenched for them than it is for some researchers, on the basis of practical experience and commitment, but also they are not under the same obligation as researchers to

---

[21] As in the view of Marx, see Lukes (1985).

treat as in need of supporting argument all that the research community does not currently accept as beyond reasonable doubt. Of course, in discourse with fellow practitioners, and with those with whom they must deal in the course of their practice, they will need to take account of what is and is not shared knowledge. However, this may be different from what is accepted by researchers, especially where the boundaries of the practitioner community are politically defined, as they are in the case of 'anti-racism'. Furthermore, in such contacts practical considerations will be most salient, including for instance the costs of different sorts of error. Finally, disagreements may be resolved (legitimately or illegitimately) by other means than rational discussion, including coercion, manipulation, negotiation, delegation, democracy etc. (Lindblom and Cohen 1979).

This is not to say that practitioners, such as 'anti-racist' educators, should simply ignore the findings of research. The point is rather that they should judge those findings in relation to their own practical knowledge and according to what is required to pursue their work well. On this basis, it might be quite reasonable for 'anti-racists' to continue with their campaign against racism among teachers despite the doubts that Foster has raised; but they would be foolish to ignore those doubts completely.

All this said, the criticisms of Foster's work do not seem to derive primarily from such practical judgments about his findings. Many of them seem more motivated by a concern with its possible propaganda consequences: not only can Foster's work not be used to support the 'anti-racist' campaign against racism among teachers, it could be used by the other side. Indeed, it seems to be suspected by some of the critics that Foster is working for the opposition. The key question, for some at least, is 'whose side are we on?'[22]

I do not doubt that propaganda considerations are necessary ones for practitioners engaged in political activity to take into account. While in an ideal world, perhaps, disputes would be resolved on the basis of discussion in pursuit of the truth, it is clear I think that the world we live in is very far from that ideal. However, great danger arises if propaganda concerns come to outweigh other practical concerns. In these circumstances, practical activity is likely to fail because erroneous assumptions accumulate; and its failure may do widespread damage.

It would be a mistake, then, it seems to me, for 'anti-racists' to dismiss Foster's work. To the extent that it throws doubt on the accuracy of some of the assumptions on which they operate, they ought to con-

---

[22] Troyna and Carrington (1989). The use of military metaphors is striking in this context; see especially Gillborn and Drew (1993).

sider its validity seriously and not simply ignore, reject or even try to suppress it.[23] It may point to a necessary reconstruction of 'anti-racism'. This might be required if it were true that racism on the part of British teachers was not widespread or that it did not play a significant role in the generation of 'racial' inequality. Accepting this would not involve a denial that there may be features of the British education system and society that generate the underachievement of black pupils. Indeed, Foster himself suggests one mechanism for this: the disproportionate allocation of black pupils to schools that are less effective educationally.[24] Of course, there still remains the question of what level or sort of evidence should persuade 'anti-racists' that Foster is right. I do not want to speculate about this here, merely to point out that there should be some level of confirming evidence at which 'anti-racists' would accept his arguments. And even if Foster does not provide that level of evidence, his work could be accepted by them as making a potential contribution to increasing the effectiveness of their activities.[25] In my view these considerations should outweigh any negative propaganda effects that Foster's work is likely to have. After all, racists have seldom found it difficult to invent arguments and evidence to support their position, and have generally shown scant regard for the difference between such inventions and more soundly based scientific conclusions.

I want to conclude by going even further than this and suggesting that 'anti-racists' are unwise to reject the conventional model of research in favour of an activist conception. One reason for this is that the propaganda capacity of research is to a large extent parasitic upon the conventional model. Once research becomes seen as geared to the pursuit of particular political goals, with research results being selected (even in part) according to their usefulness in political campaigns, its propaganda value is gone.

There are also dangers in integrating research with other sorts of practical activity. It is likely to be difficult for practitioners of

[23] Suppression was certainly regarded as desirable by some of Foster's critics. One comment from a journal referee was: 'we do not believe that we should be giving wider circulation to Foster's dubious arguments' (Foster, personal communication).

[24] For some evidence regarding this, see Smith and Tomlinson (1989); but see also Gillborn and Drew (1992, 1993) and Hammersley and Gomm (1993).

[25] We must remember in all this that Foster does not offer, and does not claim to offer, evidence that racism among teachers is not widespread in British schools. He simply raises doubts about the evidence taken to establish that it is. His case, therefore, illustrates a corollary of what Wirth (1936) says in the quotation given at the beginning of this article: that even to question whether some claim has been well established may attract objections from those who believe that their *raison d'être* relies upon the truth of this claim.

'anti-racist' education, as for practitioners of other kinds engaged in pressure group politics, to give separate consideration to the informational and the propaganda implications of arguments and evidence. The virtue of the research community is that it is, or ought to be, concerned exclusively with the validity of those findings, not with their propaganda significance. And while the judgments of the research community in this respect are no substitute for practitioners making their own assessments, they can make an important contribution to those assessments.

So, there is a danger that if research is fully integrated into the practitioner context it will fail to exercise its role properly. All activities have their own peculiar vices. Academic researchers are often criticised for investigating trivial issues and neglecting important ones, and for being excessively sceptical about 'what we all know'. Conversely, professional practitioners are sometimes criticised for being unreflective, for being blinded by prejudices deriving from their experience. It should not escape us that these criticisms are mirror images of one another. Vice is sometimes simply virtue taken to excess, and different circumstances facilitate different virtues and vices. In my view, without autonomy research will lack the capacity for its virtues not just for its vices. And I remain convinced that, in exercising autonomy, research can be of some benefit to practice, even to the practice of 'anti-racists'. While it may make their lives more difficult in some ways, Foster's work is an excellent illustration of the potential value of that autonomy.

# 5

# Writing Wrong: an Assessment of Textual Radicalism

There was a time when very little explicit attention was given by social researchers to issues surrounding the writing of research reports. Even texts on qualitative methodology typically devoted little space to this aspect of the research process.[1] There was a tendency for research reports to be seen as transparent representations of the findings of research, as though once data production and analysis had been done the process of writing was straightforward, in principle if not always in practice. In other words, writing was conceived as a matter of coding pre-existent messages, with reading as the decoding of those messages.[2] Today the situation among qualitative researchers is quite different. As van Maanen (1988: 138) comments: 'fieldworkers' silence about and sleepy indifference to the writing conventions of their craft has been shattered in recent years, and there is now no going back to more complacent or blissful days.' Thus the literature on ethnographic writing is currently growing very rapidly, in both anthropology and sociology. Some of this is primarily concerned with offering practical guidance (Woods 1985; Becker 1986; Richardson 1990; Wolcott 1990), but there has also appeared a considerable body of work of a more theoretical kind, concerned with the presuppositions and effects of different rhetorical strategies.[3]

A major stimulus to the upsurge of interest in the character of research texts has been the influence of structuralism and poststructuralism. The rejuvenation of the field of literary studies that these have brought about, and the publicity they have attracted, has led to their influence spilling over into many areas of the social sciences. Of course, the terms 'structuralism' and 'poststructuralism' represent heterogeneous trends; and their influence has been accompanied by that of

---

[1] An early exception was Schatzman and Strauss (1973).

[2] See Sperber and Wilson (1986) for criticism of this model of communication.

[3] While most of this work has been concerned with qualitative research in anthropology and sociology, some of it ranges more widely; see, for example, McCloskey (1985), Nelson et al. (1987) and Simons (1988). For an overview of this literature, see Hammersley (1994b).

others, including postmodernism, ethnomethodology, and the revival of interest in classical rhetoric.[4] As a result, the literature on social research writing is quite diverse in character, and in this chapter I want to consider just one of its central themes: what I will call 'textual radicalism'. This has emerged primarily in the context of discussions of ethnographic writing, but it has much more general relevance.

## Criticism of ethnographic realism

One immediate concern of work on ethnographic rhetoric, particularly in sociology, has been to document the literary devices by which researchers have constructed their accounts (van Maanen 1988; Atkinson 1990). For example, van Maanen identifies three sorts of 'tales of the field': realist tales, confessional tales, and impressionist tales.[5] He shows how each of these has a structure which relies on characteristic conventions. For example, realist tales, by far the most common kind, have the following features:

- They involve an appeal to the experiential authority of the ethnographer. Indeed, van Maanen suggests that they presuppose a doctrine of 'immaculate perception', and present the ethnographer as an impersonal conduit through which what he or she saw and heard is carried to the reader. This is reflected in a studied neutrality of tone, and the relative absence of the author from the account. In terms of another metaphor, the ethnographer generally remains invisible, like someone behind a camera.
- There is presentation of precise mundane details about the phenomena described and explained, with what is typical being demonstrated through close description of the singular, often employing the 'ethnographic present tense'.
- 'Native points of view' are presented through brief quotes at strategic points in the ethnographer's account, in such a way as to highlight the actuality of that account.
- The ethnographer exercises 'interpretive omnipotence': he or she has the last word, and thereby closes the text rather than leaving it open to multiple interpretations.

---

[4] On structuralism and poststructuralism, see Sturrock (1979) and Dews (1987); and on postmodernism, see Best and Kellner (1991) and Docherty (1992). The influence of ethnomethodology can be detected in Woolgar (1988) and Ashmore (1989). For a useful introduction to the revival of rhetoric, see Vickers (1990); and for the application of rhetorical analysis to research reports, see Edmondson (1984).

[5] He stresses the looseness of his categories, and notes the existence of other kinds of ethnographic story, see van Maanen (1988: 9, 127–38).

Van Maanen (1988) does not reject ethnographic realism as a literary mode, though his preferences clearly lie elsewhere. Others have been more critical, often rejecting ethnographic realism on both epistemological and political grounds. Anthropologists, in particular, have been increasingly concerned with the nature of representation in their texts, and with the political implications and consequences of different sorts of representation. Central have been questions like: how far is it possible to represent other cultures accurately? Is cognitive representation always political representation, or perhaps even political repression? To what extent does ethnographic research constitute a form of domination, the researcher imposing his or her definitions on others, furthering the hegemony of white, Western elite culture? In this context, realism stands accused of claiming a transparency of representation it cannot deliver, of presenting as neutral and comprehensive what are very particular and politically loaded points of view, and of seeking to control the interpretations of readers.

These criticisms of ethnographic realism can also be found in sociology. A recent example emerges in a dispute about Whyte's classic study *Street Corner Society* (Whyte 1955). The debate was stimulated by an article challenging Whyte's conclusions, on the basis of more recent fieldwork (Boelen 1992). Some of the responses to this critique, including that by Whyte himself (Whyte 1992), confront the criticism in a straightforward way, challenging the evidence offered in support of it, and thereby relying on realist assumptions. But not all of the contributors do this. For instance, Denzin argues that:

> there is, in a sense, no final truth or final telling. There are only different tellings of different stories organized under the heading of the same tale: in this case, Bill Whyte's story of Cornerville. Now we have two different versions of the same story, and it becomes a different story in the new telling. (Denzin 1992: 124)

We could interpret Denzin as saying no more than that we shall never know with absolute certainty who is right about the nature of Cornerville. But his point seems to go beyond this to imply that since we can never know with absolute confidence which one of these accounts is true, we must simply accept the validity of the different accounts in their own terms. More than this, Denzin takes the opportunity to criticise the realist assumptions of both Whyte and Boelen, claiming that realism 'functions to perpetuate the status quo' (1992: 130) and must be overthrown:

> poststructuralism undermines the realist agenda, contending that things do not exist independently of their representations in social texts. Accordingly, if we want to change how things are, we must change how they are seen.

How they are seen is itself determined by the older, realist and modernist agendas that presumed worlds out there that could be mapped by a realist, scientific method. It is this hegemonic vision that must be challenged . . . (Denzin 1992:126)

So, the objection to realism is not just that it is epistemologically unsound but also that it is morally and politically unacceptable:

Whyte and Boelen entered this urban space and, like voyeurs, attempted to lay bare its underlying structures. Each found different structures because their angles of vision were different. But each of their texts endorses the validity of the cultural voyeur's project. They refused to challenge and doubt their own right to look, write, and ask questions about the private and public lives that go on in Cornerville. Consequently, they keep in place the disciplinary eye of a positivistic social science. This science justifies its existence in terms of its 'positive' contributions to a surveillance society that requires greater and greater information about the private lives of its citizens. As the twentieth century is now in its last decade, it is appropriate to ask if we any longer want this kind of social science. (Denzin 1992: 131)

Here, then, first of all, we have the claim that the phenomena described in Whyte's and Boelen's texts are constructed in and through the rhetorical strategies they employ: a rejection of the realist idea that texts represent phenomena which exist independently of them. Secondly, there is the argument that the hegemony of realism must be challenged because of its political implications or consequences. On this view, literary realism involves deception of readers and perhaps also self-deception on the part of the writer. Furthermore, it is seen as suppressing the voices of the people studied and closing down interpretation on the part of readers, rather than encouraging an active and critical participation by all.

### Textual radicalism

This work on ethnographic writing in anthropology and sociology does not consist solely of criticism of conventional forms of ethnographic rhetoric, it also involves advocacy of the exploration of alternative kinds of writing. These include dialogical and other sorts of multivocal text, including, for example, the sustained use of indirect speech (Krieger 1983), and also such techniques as textual collage (Clifford 1981).[6] The rationale for these alternative forms of writing is that they avoid the epistemological deceits and unacceptable political implications and consequences of ethnographic realism. Regarding epistemology, Atkinson remarks in connection with the influence of postmodernist theory on sociological writing:

[6] For useful discussions of these alternatives, see Marcus and Fischer (1986) and Atkinson (1992). For examples of textual collage, see Dorst (1989) and Pfohl (1993).

If culture itself is seen as fragmentary and incoherent, then the texts of its representation may appropriately be likewise. The ethnographer can no longer subordinate all of his or her 'data' to unifying themes and models. The work of the text is more overtly recognised as an act of 'bricolage': the fragments of 'data' (which are themselves crafted rather than found) are thus juxtaposed. The textual arrangement becomes a kind of collage . . . The effects of the text are derived from the contrasts and juxtapositions rather than from a sense of cumulative evidence, unfolding narrative, or logical progression. (Atkinson 1992: 41–2)

Such texts do not claim to describe the world, in any simple sense, and they do not seek to control the interpretations of readers. They are 'writerly' in Barthes's (1975) terms, leaving great scope for readers' interpretations. Similarly, multi-vocal texts are often viewed as giving voice to the people studied in a more unrestrained way than the controlled quotation used in conventional ethnographic writing. And the people studied by ethnographers are, of course, often those at the margins of Western society who have little or no voice within it.

At one level, then, what I mean by 'textual radicalism' is the use of these 'experimental' modes of writing. However, often lying behind this is the idea that by writing differently the wrongs of the world can be righted. In this way 'textual radicalism' acquires political as well as aesthetic meanings. To a considerable extent, it is epistemological constructivism which allows the fusion of these two realms: the idea that social phenomena are constituted in and through the texts in which they are described. And it is sometimes concluded from this, as seems to be true in the case of Denzin, that the writers of texts can change the world by changing what they write. Here we have not just a blurring of non-fictional and fictional genres but actual erasure of the distinction between fiction and reality. According to this view, ethnographic fictions must be recognised for what they are, and put to politically desirable uses. The obverse of this, of course, is that conventional ethnographers, by relying on realist rhetoric, are responsible for preserving the socio-political status quo through the very manner in which they write. This is an extension of the common Marxist argument that particular sorts of account serve ideological functions because of their substance, for example their theoretical orientation (see, for example, Asad 1975). Thus, Brodkey reports that new theories 'variously known as social construction, negative critique, poststructuralism, and deconstruction' have heightened interest in the extent to which scholarly writing practices 'have contributed to the marginalization of such politically and often economically disenfranchised groups as minorities and women, not to mention the vast and undifferentiated group commonly referred to as the working class' (Brodkey 1987: viii).

We can identify different strands of argument underpinning textual radicalism. Some commentators recommend the adoption of modernist techniques of textual experimentation. Thus, we have Clifford (1981) drawing explicitly on surrealism. He charts the close relationship between the surrealist movement and the development of French anthropology in the 1920s and 1930s, and portrays the spirit of that movement as follows:

> The world of the city for Aragon's *Paysan de Paris*, or for Breton in *Nadja*, was a source of the unexpected and the significant – significant in ways that suggested beneath the dull veneer of the real the possibility of another, more miraculous world based on radically different principles of classification and order. (Clifford 1981: 542)

But Clifford's interest in surrealism is not merely historical. He seeks a revival of a surrealist ethnography dedicated to displaying ironic incongruities and juxtapositions of the phenomena of the everyday world. This is an ethnography which seeks not simply to comprehend 'the diversity of cultural orders, but which openly expects, allows, indeed desires, its own disorientation' (1981: 558–9). Thus:

> To write ethnographies on the model of collage would be to avoid the portrayal of cultures as organic wholes, or as unified, realistic worlds subject to a continuous explanatory discourse . . . The ethnography as collage would leave manifest the constructivist procedures of ethnographic knowledge; it would be an assemblage containing voices other than the ethnographer's, as well as examples of 'found' evidence, data not fully integrated within the work's governing interpretation. Finally, it would not explain away those elements in the foreign culture which render the investigator's own culture newly incomprehensible. (Clifford 1981: 563–4)

In much the same spirit, though drawing on feminism and later French sources, Lather (1991: 8) writes of her 'desire . . . to "interrupt" academic norms by writing inside of another logic, a logic that displaces expectations of linearity, clear authorial voice, and closure'.

Arguments about the ethical and political significance of aesthetic form are not new, of course, as Clifford's appeal to surrealism indicates. But probably the most fully developed rationale for textual radicalism as simultaneously aesthetic and political is to be found in the work of the Frankfurt Marxist, Theodor Adorno.

The guiding idea of Adorno's work was discovering and redeeming unintended truths, disclosures of utopia, within bourgeois thought.[7] These truths lie in the contradictions of the bourgeois social world and

---

[7] Adorno was strongly influenced by Walter Benjamin, who drew on the ideas of both the expressionists and the surrealists. In turn, his work and Adorno's influenced French poststructuralism: see Jay (1984).

the possibility of it being transcended. Adorno believed that because those contradictions could not be overcome by thought alone, they must be represented explicitly in genuine thought. He took as his guide art, which he saw as the pursuit of objective truth; this being facilitated, paradoxically, by the fact that unlike science its task is not simply to represent 'things as they are'. His model was Schoenberg's view of the role of the composer as a craft worker, acting on the material historically provided according to its inner logic, and following that logic wherever it led. In this way avant-garde art could be progressive even when it had no consciously political intent; indeed, for Adorno it should not be directly geared to political praxis, in the way that Brecht's was, since in doing so it would be diverted from its pursuit of the truth towards propaganda.

The task of philosophy for Adorno, then, was the demystification of contemporary reality, and what this required was the creation of constellations of dialectically opposed concepts which would allow the significance of particular objects to be released, and opened up to critical understanding:

> Adorno considered that his task as a philosopher was to undermine the already tottering frame of bourgeois idealism by exposing the contradictions which riddled its categories and, following their inherent logic, push them to the point where the categories were made to self-destruct. (Buck-Morss 1977: 64)

This was not just a matter of revealing similarities in opposites but also of showing the immanent logical relations between apparently unrelated phenomena. This line of thinking led to a characteristically dense style:

> Adorno didn't write essays, he composed them, and he was a virtuoso in the dialectical medium. His verbal compositions express an 'idea' through a sequence of dialectical reversals and inversions. The sentences develop like musical themes: they break apart and turn in on themselves in a continuing spiral of variations. The phenomena are viewed as Freud viewed dream symbols: They are 'overdetermined', so that their contradictory complexity needs to be disentangled through interpretation. But there is no affirmation, no 'closing cadence'. The contradictions are unraveled; they are not resolved. (Buck-Morss 1977: 101; see also Rose 1978)

For Adorno, the distinction between social structure and cultural superstructure, like all distinctions, was open to question. He saw the cultural realm as no less embodying the social relations of capitalism than economic institutions. By aesthetically radical treatment of their material, cultural workers could contribute to revolutionary change more generally, though Adorno was always ambivalent about the possibility of realising any utopia.

Adorno's work seems to have had little or no influence as yet on textual radicalism in the field of ethnographic rhetoric, but it offers much the most substantial rationale for it based on artistic modernism. Other forms of textual radicalism show less influence by the modernist avant-garde in art and music, and represent a more direct attempt to construct texts which exemplify a political ideal. This is especially true of dialogical and multi-vocal formats, the idea often being that such texts embody participatory democracy. There is a desire on the part of many advocates of these forms of writing to redress the imbalance in the influence of voices at the centre and at the margins of society, through creating a poly-vocal polity (Krupat 1992: 4) or discursive democracy (Dryzek 1990). This parallels arguments in favour of democratising the research relationship through collaboration between researcher and researched, and the development of practitioner or indigenous research (Carr and Kemmis 1986; Clifford 1988; Gitlin et al. 1989). Intrinsic to this commitment to participatory democracy is the idea that everyone should speak and write on their own behalf (in fact that no one can do anything else), and that everyone has a right to equal expression. At the same time, it is not unusual to find the notion that some voices are more authentic or truth-revealing than others. In particular, those 'on the margin' are held to be less subject to the sway of ideology and therefore more likely to see through misleading appearances (Harding 1992).

In short, then, textual radicals criticise conventional forms of ethnographic writing as philosophically and politically unsound: as based on epistemological misconceptions and as reinforcing the socio-political status quo. And they recommend the adoption of alternative forms of writing that avoid these alleged failings in the belief that by doing so they can right wrong.

### Can writing right wrong?

Social researchers' newly acquired interest in the character of academic writing is surely to be welcomed, despite a danger that this aspect of the research process will be given more attention than it deserves compared to others. However, in my view the textual radicalism which informs much of the work in this field is fundamentally misconceived. It is mistaken in both its epistemological and its political presuppositions.

As I noted earlier, textual radicalism is frequently based on the idea that the phenomena described in texts are constituted in and through the strategies by which they are represented, such that they have no existence beyond that representation. We can see this as an application to research writing of philosophical ideas which have been influential throughout the nineteenth and twentieth centuries. Initially the argument was framed in terms of the role of *a priori* categories in the constitution of experience and empirical knowledge. Later, it came to be formulated in cultural and linguistic terms, so that human experience was recognised to be culturally diverse and socio-historically constituted. Finally, whereas in some earlier versions analysts had escaped the implications of their own analyses, usually through an appeal to a distinctive method, transcendental or scientific, now the argument came to be applied even to them. Thus, social scientific accounts themselves began to be seen as constituting the social world through the presuppositions on which they are based.

These constructivist arguments can very easily degenerate into an extreme form of epistemological scepticism or relativism that is literally indefensible. It is indefensible because it rests on precisely the sort of claim it rules out as illegitimate: it denies the existence of objects which are independent of our accounts of them, but that denial necessarily involves a claim to knowledge about those objects (that they do not exist!). So, on its own account, this view can only be a construction, with no more claim to truth than its contrary. In this way, the position is self-contradictory: showing it to be true would demonstrate that it is false in one case at least (itself), and it can provide no justification for its own exceptional status.[8] This is not to deny that there are genuine and serious epistemological problems involved here. It is important, however, not to see scepticism as following immediately from those problems, as if it carried no theoretical baggage, thereby representing the only alternative to a naive realism which treats our knowledge, or some of it, as the product of direct acquaintance with the world. As Williams (1991) has shown, scepticism shares the same presuppositions as the naive realism it criticises. Once we question those presuppositions, we find that more sustainable forms of realism are possible (Phillips 1990a, b; Hammersley 1992a).

As regards the political grounds on which textual radicalism rests, these too are open to serious doubt. In order to be convinced by Adorno's case for the radical political potential of modernist art forms, a case not accepted by many modernist artists (including Schoenberg himself), one has to accept a philosophy of history which at the same time claims to reject the philosophy of history. It escapes the problems associated with the teleological accounts of Hegel and Marx only at the expense of a commitment to a wholly negative critique. And this is something it shares with much poststructuralism and postmodernism (see Chapter 2).

---

[8] The Pyrrhonian sceptics recognised this problem and sought to avoid it by making no claims at all, simply accepting appearances; but it is difficult to see how this avoids treating appearances as appearances *of* something.

The argument that research writing should exemplify participatory democracy may have more initial appeal, but it is no more cogent. We must ask why single research texts should embody democracy, rather than the larger discussions to which they contribute. Over and above this, though, we need to consider whether democracy is our only or even our pre-eminent value, and whether it is the most appropriate form of social organisation in the context of research. What is wrong with demands that research be democratic, in my view, is that they confuse democracy, as a political procedure for resolving policy disagreements, with rational discussion, which is a means of producing knowledge. Of course, given extreme forms of constructivism, the latter enterprise may no longer seem viable, but these also threaten the commitment to democracy. Insistence on the social constitution of subjectivity undermines the treatment of voices as autonomous and authentic sources of self-expression. Similarly, poststructuralism negates any omni-relevant distinction between centre and periphery, undercutting the idea of privileging those at the margin.

What often seems to be of primary concern to textual radicals is not so much the actual empirical intentions behind or effects of the publication of research reports as the political implications which can be read off from what has been written. So the focus is on the discursive positioning of the author and of various categories of other in relation to the author and to one another, along with the attributes that seem to be assigned to these. Of course, if one refuses to treat the existence of phenomena as independent of the texts in which they are portrayed, these textual implications might reasonably be regarded as equivalent to empirical consequences. But once one abandons such extreme constructivism the distinction between textual implications and actual consequences must be recognised. And then the question of the effects of research texts becomes an empirical matter that requires investigation (see Weiss 1980). Moreover, there are reasons to believe that these effects will be highly contingent and by no means under the control of the writer. One of the central themes of recent thinking about texts has been the indeterminacy of interpretation (Newton 1990). If we add this to more conventional ideas about the complexities of social causation (Hage and Meeker 1988), it becomes clear that any idea that research reports have a direct and powerful impact on social events becomes highly implausible (see Chapter 7).

Without commitment to an extreme form of constructivism, then, it is very difficult to see writing research reports as a form of political activism. The idea that writing is a means of changing the world directly is a fantasy, one which reflects intellectuals' characteristic overestimation of their own socio-historical significance.[9] This is not to deny that social research may have political consequences, and that researchers should be aware of these and may be obliged to try to counter them. It is to insist, however, that bringing about such consequences should not be the prime goal of research. That goal, mundane as it may seem, is the production of knowledge (see Chapter 6).

## Really writing right

Rhetoric has always been an evaluative and prescriptive, not just a descriptive, discipline. Traditionally, it provided advice for orators about effective and ethical modes of speech, though it was later extended to written language. What it points to above all is that language is used for multiple purposes, and in a variety of contexts; and that both purpose and context carry implications for what is and is not appropriate.[10] What is legitimate language in addressing a political assembly or meeting or in a law court is different from what is appropriate in philosophical discussion or in writing a scientific paper. So the task of rhetorical analysis in relation to social inquiry, in my view, is to identify specific principles about how one ought to write research reports.

Of course, researchers address a variety of audiences, and what is necessary in order to make their accounts comprehensible and persuasive will vary accordingly. However, an over-arching and pre-eminent requirement is that the account lays itself open to rational assessment of its validity. This is essential, whatever the audience, given the primary commitment of researchers to the production of knowledge. And yet many of the rhetorical forms employed by textual radicals, like some of the strategies used by ethnographic realists, actually work in the opposite direction, being likely to mislead or confuse audiences. In particular, they tend to obscure the line of argument being presented, and therefore may deter readers from thinking carefully about what the researcher is claiming and the adequacy of the evidence offered in support of this.

This line of thinking leads me in a very different direction from textual radicalism, of course: towards an insistence on the importance of a clear voice on the part of the author, albeit one which does not

---

[9] This fantasy is also represented in the culturalist bias of Western Marxism, with its stress on the role of ideology in social reproduction and its faith in ideology critique as a means of producing social change. See Anderson (1976) and Abercrombie et al. (1980).

[10] This was recognised in classical rhetoric in the distinctions between forensic, deliberative and demonstrative rhetoric, see Dixon (1971). In this respect classical rhetoric works against deconstruction's tendency to blur genres.

pretend to infallibility or to cultural superiority. It also distances me from normal practice in ethnography, towards arguing for greater standardisation of the structure of research reports, rather than acceptance of their diversification. Indeed, most ethnographers would baulk at the rhetorical structure I want to recommend because it is not far from the conventional format regarded as normative in some parts of natural science and quantitative social research. More than this, though, the very idea of having a standard format is itself anathema to many ethnographers, perhaps because it is seen as stifling creativity, or imposing literary form on reality in an arbitrary way. But of course such arguments can be directed against reliance on any literary form, and we cannot escape such reliance. Moreover, what I am recommending is a relatively loose, not a tightly constraining, structure.

In my view, all research texts must be seen as presenting an argument, and in doing so must make explicit certain essential components. These consist of five sorts of information that readers need access to: about the focus of the study, about the case(s) investigated, about the methods employed, about the main claims made and the evidence offered in support of them, and about the conclusions drawn. The more clearly this information is distinguished and labelled, and the more effort is put into ensuring that what is provided under each heading is adequate, the more effective a text will be in giving readers the information necessary for them to assess the arguments presented. Furthermore, these categories of information represent a logical sequence, and it seems sensible that normally they should be given in the order listed.[11]

Of course, merely to list these types of information leaves open the question of how much detail is necessary under each heading. And no general answer can be given to this. What information is required will depend on the nature of the claims made and what the audience can reasonably be expected to know and take for granted as beyond reasonable doubt. Sufficient evidence must be provided in research reports to establish the claims made from the point of view both of the researcher and of the relevant audience, whichever is the more demanding in any particular case. Of course, the researcher's judgments about the validity of the arguments, and about the audience's likely reactions, may be wrong, in which case they will need to be corrected later. But writing research reports necessarily involves making such judgments.

---

[11] A common argument against such formats is that they do not represent accurately the messiness or disorder of the research process, or indeed that they misrepresent it. But we must remember that research reports do not need to reflect the messiness of the research process in order to convey it; and that most ethnographic accounts, however literary in style, do not attempt to represent the research process itself, nor can that ever be done in an unmediated fashion.

Another question which arises here is how much information is required about the researcher her or himself. Some writers have argued that the researcher must be included in the focus of the research (see, for example, Stanley and Wise 1983b). This reflects the influence of anti-realist arguments to the effect that all understanding is a socio-historical product, that research findings reflect the biographical and situational circumstances of the researcher. There is no doubt some truth in this, but we should not assume that the validity of each piece of research is relative to its author's social position, personality etc. The whole point of research is to produce findings which are of general validity. In doing research and writing up the results, a researcher is expected, as far as possible, to operate as a representative of the research community. This implies treating as reliable only what researchers generally would regard as reliable; trying to eliminate the effects of one's own personal and social characteristics and circumstances where these may lead to bias.

A different way of putting this is to say that researchers must appeal without further justification only to what their colleagues would accept as plausible and credible on the basis of well-established procedures and accepted knowledge. Given this, the only information about the researcher required is that which is directly relevant to an assessment of the validity of the research findings, and this will often be minimal. Some indication of values and expectations, and other personal characteristics which may have affected the data collected or interpretations produced might be relevant, but personal autobiography beyond this is not necessary or desirable.[12]

Another important rhetorical requirement of research reports is that they indicate clearly the different forms of argument which they contain. There is room for disagreement about what the possible forms of argument are, of course, but I would distinguish: descriptions, explanations, predictions, evaluations, prescriptions and theoretical statements. It is important to differentiate these types of argument because each requires different sorts of evidence. Yet, there is often a lack of clarity in research reports about the nature of the argument being presented: for example, about whether it is a description, an evaluation, an explanation or a theory. In my view this does not facilitate the reading and assessment of research reports.[13]

---

[12] Of course, this may be of interest and use for other reasons, for example to give some sense of the experience of engaging in research.

[13] For an extended discussion of what is proposed here, see Hammersley (1990). It is perhaps worth emphasising that the other side of what I am recommending is greater recognition of the diversity of products which research can generate, and the different sorts of argument to be found within any particular piece of research.

This approach to research rhetoric implies a propositional structure for research reports, including clear specification of major claims, evidence and general conclusions. However, it rules out none of the textual strategies commonly used by qualitative researchers, whether of a conventional or an 'experimental' kind. For instance, there is nothing wrong with evocative narratives, extensive quotations from the words of the people studied (whether in direct or reported speech), fictional constructions of average or exemplary types etc. Indeed, these will often be of considerable value as evidence or as illustration. The only requirement is that the use of such techniques is subordinated to the goal of clearly presenting the claims made and conclusions drawn, and providing supporting evidence and information about the research process necessary and sufficient to allow their assessment. Above all, these techniques must not be used to suppress critical reflection on the part of readers, or to invite aesthetic appreciation.

**Conclusion**

It is surely to be welcomed that researchers are more aware than previously of the rhetorical strategies they employ. However, the study of research rhetoric must not be concerned merely with providing a catalogue of textual strategies but also with indicating the grounds on which those strategies should be selected for particular purposes and in particular contexts. The discipline of rhetoric was criticised in the past for being preoccupied with techniques of persuasion and for neglecting logic: for being primarily concerned with how to sway audiences rather than with how to pursue and express the truth. This is what gave 'rhetoric' the bad name it has in common usage. Current discussions of the rhetoric of research reports are in danger of confirming this reputation, by their reliance on a textual radicalism which dismisses logical considerations (in the broadest sense of that term) in favour of a concern with political and/or aesthetic effect.

Textual radicals see much previous research as having been written wrong, not just in a grammarian's sense but in the sense of having played a reprehensible role in bolstering political oppression. What is at issue here is not just the surface matter of the topics studied or conclusions drawn but the very mode of writing deployed. The obverse of this is the belief that by adopting a different mode of writing researchers can right wrong. This is given what plausibility it has by an epistemological constructivism which suggests that reality is only reality-as-it-is-inscribed: there is no really real, no nature, lying behind the artifice of our texts. By employing modernist textual strategies that draw attention to their artifactual character and do not seek to control the reader's understanding, and/or by producing multi-vocal texts, giving those 'on the margins' a voice, it is supposed that we can counter an oppressive socio-political status quo.

In this writing about writing, 'postmodernist' commentators seem to be constructing themselves as gods who create worlds: not surprisingly, perhaps, there is a whiff of a Nietzchean will to power here. But neither the epistemological nor the political arguments associated with textual radicalism can support it. The former suffer the same fate as all arguments for relativism and scepticism: self-refutation. The political arguments rely on a faith in the links between the influence of the cultural avant-garde and political change that are unconvincing, or on arguments about democracy which are little more than slogans.

# 6

## Is Social Research Political?

There was a time when most social researchers would have denied that research is political. Today, the situation is different. There are, no doubt, still some who reject the idea that their work is political, but it is much more common to find declarations, or at least admissions, that it is. At the same time, claims that research is or should be objective, value neutral and non-partisan are under attack. In a recent issue of *Social Research* Margaret Jacob, a historian of science, described this shift in attitude as a cognitive revolution (Jacob 1992). There has certainly been a change, and one that in many respects is to be welcomed; not least because it highlights aspects of the research process which had previously been given too little attention. At the same time, it is difficult to be clear about the nature of the shift that has taken place and its implications. All questions and answers involve presuppositions, and sometimes those presuppositions need to be scrutinised. This is especially true of questions and answers which are ambiguous, in the sense that they can be premissed on more than one set of presuppositions. The question posed in the title of this chapter is a case in point. It could be answered in different ways depending on how one interprets it.

In part, at least, the uncertainty of interpretation which surrounds this question stems from the way in which the statement 'research is political' is frequently used. In some contexts it has come to represent little more than a declaration of allegiance, a statement of which side one is on. In the past, the denial that research is political was part of the assertion by social researchers of the scientific nature of their work, of its distinctiveness and authority, of its superiority to common-sense and practical experience. To a large extent claims to scientific rigour, objectivity and political neutrality were part of the process by which social science disciplines established themselves in institutional terms. We might reasonably suspect that today's declarations of the political nature of research are involved in similar processes, but this time perhaps of institutional differentiation and re-grouping. Where once the interests of social researchers seemed to lie in an alliance with science, some now see those interests as requiring a distancing from it and the forging of closer links with practical life, the humanities and politics.

While such institutional manoeuvrings cannot be entirely ignored, they are not what I wish to focus on here. Instead, I want to discuss the senses in which it is reasonable to describe social research as political, and to consider whether there are any respects in which it is not necessarily, or should not be, political. This requires careful attention to the terms of the question. Most attention must centre on the two key terms: 'social research' and 'politics'. But even the little word 'is' at the start of the question is not without ambiguity. Depending on how we interpret that word, the question may be asking: whether research *could be* non-political; whether, in fact, research as practised *tends to be* political; or whether research *should* be political. In other words, it could be a theoretical, an empirical, or a normative question; and there is an order of priority amongst these possibilities (see Figure 6.1).

The distinction between these three sorts of question tends to get overlooked by those who believe that research cannot be other than political. But the tendency to use 'is' to cover not just factual but also theoretical and normative questions arises from other sources as well: notably from positions which deny the distinction between them, such as some sorts of Marxism and the views of natural law theorists like Strauss and MacIntyre.[1]

This would become a very lengthy discussion if I were to try to address this issue of the relationship between normative, theoretical and empirical issues. But it is important to bear it in mind because what

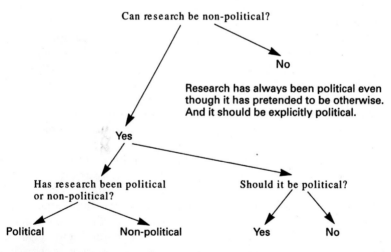

Figure 6.1  *A clarification of the question: is research political?*

---

[1] On Marx, see Lukes (1985). For versions of natural law theory see, for example, Strauss (1953) and MacIntyre (1990).

position we take may affect how we answer the question posed in the chapter's title. My view is that the three sorts of issue are distinct and that as commonly used the statement 'social research is political' denies that such research *can* be other than political and insists that it *should* be explicitly and directly political. I will be primarily concerned, then, with whether social research is necessarily political, and with whether it ought to be governed by political criteria.

Let me turn now to the two main terms in the question: 'research' and 'politics'. The first can be dealt with briefly; the second will be the focus of most of the rest of this chapter.

### Defining 'research'

The meaning of the term 'research' has probably always been open to diverse interpretations, but in recent years it has become particularly unclear, partly through the promotion of various sorts of policy, action and practitioner research. We can distinguish what we might call narrow and wide definitions of the term. A narrow definition would be one which portrayed it as an activity directed towards the accumulation of knowledge within a discipline, carried out by specialists, where the immediate audience is other researchers working in the same discipline or subdiscipline. A wide definition of 'research', by contrast, interprets it as that process of search for (and processing of) information which occurs in a great range of circumstances, not just in universities, publicly funded institutes and commercial research organisations, but also in government bureaucracies, news media agencies, political parties and pressure groups. Indeed, on the broadest of definitions, research is an activity carried out by all of us when we are faced with a problem whose solution seems to depend on obtaining relevant information.

How one defines 'research' may affect the way one answers the question raised in the chapter title. However, the argument that research is political often involves the claim that *all* research is of necessity political. Given this, the prime target is those forms of research which claim in some sense to be non-political or to be politically neutral. The area where this claim has been promoted in the most sustained manner is in relation to disciplinary research in universities. In many respects this represents a test case for the argument, and much of my discussion will tend to focus on it, though it will have clear implications for other sorts of research as well.

### Defining 'political'

The term 'political' is subject to even more diverse usage than 'research'. Again, there are narrow and broad interpretations. At one extreme, its use may be restricted to issues subject to dispute between contending national political parties or pressure groups; or, alternatively, to the interests of nation states (Schmitt 1932). At the other extreme, we have the argument that micro-political processes are to be found in all realms; or, indeed, that all human relations and contacts are political, as implied by the slogan 'the personal is political'. For the purposes of this chapter, I will begin with a wide interpretation of what counts as political, otherwise the answer proposed runs the risk of succeeding (if at all) solely by definitional fiat.

There are at least two, distinct but closely related, ways in which research may be seen as political. From the first point of view politics is to do with the exercise of power. From the second, it concerns the making of value judgments and action on the basis of them.

### Research as power

The claim that research is political, in the sense of being implicated in power relations, represents a counter to the idea that research institutions, especially universities, are autonomous from the state or from powerful interests in society. From the latter point of view, researchers are at most involved in, as the phrase has it, 'talking truth to power'. Closely associated with this, often, is the idea that power is a source of corruption which research must be insulated against if it is to be pursued effectively.

One line of criticism here is to question the view of power which is presupposed, denying that it is corrupting, and thereby rejecting the need for or possibility of autonomy. This may be done by re-evaluating politics; for example, by moving away from a perspective which sees it as a necessary evil (and perhaps only temporarily necessary) towards one which treats engagement in democratic politics as the essential human activity. Much the same effect can be achieved by the reverse process: by an interpretational devaluation of everything, including research, to the level of sectional interests, a form of cynicism whose traces can be found in some forms of poststructuralism and postmodernism. However, most critics of the view that research can be autonomous seem to retain the idea that state power and other forms of power in modern societies are oppressive. So, most criticism of claims about the autonomy of research takes two other forms: either questioning the latter's independence from external power or pointing to the power exercised by research institutions and researchers themselves.

*Autonomy from external power*  This first criticism involves a denial of the autonomy of the institutions in which research takes place, and thus of the work that researchers do, from the state and from other powerful interests in society. A famous example of this is Martin Nicolaus's attack on sociology in the 1960s. Addressing a plenary session of the American Sociological Association, he declared that:

> This assembly of sociologists here tonight is a conclave of high and low priests, scribes, intellectual valets and their innocent victims, engaged in the mutual affirmation of a falsehood . . . The profession is an outgrowth of nineteenth century European traditionalism and conservatism, wedded to twentieth century American corporation liberalism . . . The professional eyes of the sociologist are on the down people, and the professional palm of the sociologist is stretched out to the up people ... he is an Uncle Tom not only for this government and ruling class but for any. (quoted in Gouldner 1970: 10; see also Nicolaus 1972)

The idea that social research forms part of the ideological state apparatus of modern capitalism is still influential in some quarters. And, in recent years, a more ambivalent and elusive version of the argument has become popular, as represented by the work of Michel Foucault. He has traced the correspondence between the emergence of the human sciences and new less overtly coercive, less centralised, but more powerful modes of social control. He does not claim any direct causal relationship between these intellectual and general social trends, one way or the other. But he emphasises the close articulation between the two.[2]

There is certainly some truth in arguments about the involvement of universities and other research institutions with state power, and with power of other kinds. They have never been completely autonomous and in the late twentieth century there has been a trend towards the increasing dependence of universities upon the state in Western societies. Furthermore, this intensified in the 1980s at the same time that the state's relationship to capitalism was being restructured, resulting in increased representation of business interests and the growing institutionalisation of corporate management practices within universities. However, arguments like those of Nicolaus and Foucault do not depend much on claims about such specific historical trends or about particular relationships between research institutions and powerful social interests: they portray the involvement of universities with external sources of power as a longstanding if not essential feature of late capitalism or of modernity. And, in doing so, they exaggerate the functionality of research institutions for the state and other powerful interests, as well as the influence of the latter on research.

There is no doubt that some earlier conceptions of the autonomy of universities were overdrawn. And, as I have indicated, it is true that the dependence of universities on state power and other interests has

---

[2] See, for example, the accounts in Sheridan (1980) and Dews (1987).

increased, and that this has opened them up to increasing influence from outside. But it seems clear that some relative autonomy, indeed a considerable looseness of coupling, remains. This, in fact, is what current government-sponsored reforms of British universities are designed to reduce, in order to make the latter serve national economic goals more effectively. More than this, though, it is quite false to suggest that research is in some sense *necessarily* a tool of the state or of the ruling class, or of some ill-specified force such as that christened knowledge/power by Foucault. Certainly, the critics provide no convincing evidence of this; and, given the functionalist character of the argument, it is difficult to see how they could do so.[3]

*Research as the exercise of power*  The second way in which the claimed independence of research from power relations may be denied involves pointing out that research institutions exercise power on their own behalf and in their own interests. It is suggested that they are an influential force within modern societies, and that their interests shape the character of social research. Two forms of power exercised by researchers have been identified.

First, and most important in general terms, researchers claim expertise, and thereby authority, over some areas of knowledge. They claim a right to be heard and taken notice of in those areas. Furthermore, this is an asymmetrical right: their words demand more attention than those of lay people. Criticism of this authority claimed by researchers is an extension of the Leftist critique of the professions which developed in the 1960s and 1970s; a critique continued by the New Right in the 1980s and 1990s, with devastating effect. Here professional claims to authority are challenged, being portrayed as self-serving devices designed (or at least functioning) to protect and increase professional power. A crucial element of the argument of some critics was that, irrespective of any specific benefits of professional work, it has the general negative effect of rendering lay people dependent on professionals. It is claimed that professional power denies people the competence and confidence necessary to judge the services provided, and dissuades them from searching for alternative services or from dealing with their problems themselves.[4]

Criticism of research as a profession has also appealed to radical

---

[3] The argument is dependent on many of those functionalist sleights of hand exposed by critics of sociological functionalism in the 1960s. See, for example, the articles collected in Demerath and Peterson (1967, esp. chs 6 and 7) and also van Parijs (1981).

[4] The most controversial area where these arguments have been developed is in relation to the treatment of mental illness. For a spirited Leftist counter-critique that takes in the work of Foucault, see Sedgwick (1982).

epistemological arguments and to the ideal of participatory democracy. Critics deny the justification for researchers' claims to authority, portraying these as simply the exercise of power – as, in effect, researchers seeking to impose *their* meanings on others. What is being rejected here, in part, is the realist epistemology that underpins most research, and the conventional role of the research community which derives from that.

This challenge is frequently based on sceptical or relativistic arguments to the effect that all accounts of the world are constructions, including those of social researchers, and that these constructions rely on presuppositions whose validity cannot be established beyond all doubt. From this it is sometimes taken to follow that all accounts must be treated as valid in their own terms: everyone not only has a right to express their opinion but also a right to that opinion being heard and given equal weight.[5] In other words, the only sort of representation that is possible is political representation; and marginal individuals and groups must be represented; indeed, strictly speaking, each person must represent her or himself.

Alternatively, critics may appeal to standpoint theory, to the idea that some people have privileged access to truths about the social world by virtue of their social position. This idea has its origins in Marxism, where it is the working class who, as a result of their oppressed position in capitalist society, are judged to be best placed to see through bourgeois ideology. More recently, this view has been adopted and developed by some feminists (see, for example, Harding 1986, 1992). On this basis, too, the authority claims of researchers have been challenged.

Whichever of these epistemological positions is adopted, the conclusion reached is that research excludes, and may serve to silence, the voices of those on the margins of the current organisation of society. What is required instead, it is suggested, is the promotion of forms of social organisation in which all voices are heard and given equal weight; or, on the basis of standpoint theory, a society in which voices on the margins are amplified. Such an argument is exemplified in Lather's (1991: 47) interpretation of the 'subtext' of Foucault and Lyotard as saying that '*who speaks* is more important than *what is said*.'[6] Along the same lines, Apple (1991: ix) argues that 'We must shift the role of critical intellectuals from being universalizing

---

[5] In practice, those who put forward this view do not always extend this relativistic tolerance to everyone; they engage in what Woolgar and Pawluch (1985) call ontological gerrymandering: they move the boundaries between what is taken to be real and what is treated as interpretative construction to suit their political purposes.

[6] Lather is quoting Said at this point. See Sheridan (1980 Pt 2, ch. 1) for the background in the case of Foucault.

spokespersons to acting as cultural workers whose task is to take away the barriers that prevent people from speaking for themselves.' In other words, researchers should renounce their power, and/or put it at the disposal of the marginalised or dispossessed.

Again, there is some truth in these arguments. It is the case that the publication of research findings, like all writing and indeed like all speech, involves a claim to authority. At the same time, it is important to recognise the distinction between claiming authority and exercising power. One aspect of this is that authority, unlike power, requires a rationale. And I believe that researchers can legitimately claim a limited and fallible authority in relation to the production of knowledge.[7] Rejection of the realist epistemology, on which the challenge to the authority of research is based, involves a confusion of naive realism with all forms of realism (Hammersley 1992a: chs 3 and 4). And it is based on alternative epistemologies – relativism and standpoint theory – which suffer from major defects.

The problem of the self-refuting character of relativism is well known: in claiming that all truth is relative to a framework, it makes its own truth relative, and thus false in terms of other frameworks even from the point of view of relativism itself. Relativism also implicitly relies on a discredited foundationalism.[8] The problem with standpoint theory is equally serious. The claim that some group has privileged knowledge cannot itself be validated in terms of that privileged knowledge, otherwise the argument is circular. But this indicates that there must be a higher epistemological authority even than the voices of the oppressed, one which can in principle overrule these. In the case of Marx, and it seems that of Harding too (Harding 1992), this higher authority is science; and, indeed, it is difficult to see what reasonable alternative is available.[9] But here we have come full circle back to the authority of research.

Another difference between authority and power is that some types of authority do not rely on, indeed do not have access to, power resources for enforcing due respect.[10] To a large extent this is true of the author-

---

[7] In my view, researchers have often exceeded the boundaries of their authority. For discussion of an example of the misuse of educational research in this way, see Hammersley and Scarth (1993).

[8] While highly critical of the authority claims of conventional social research, Harding (1992) rejects epistemological relativism on this latter ground. For a sustained exploration of this argument in relation to scepticism, see Williams (1991).

[9] In the history of Marxist politics, of course, the Party has often usurped this role; and something similar seems likely in some forms of feminist research; see, for instance, Mies (1991).

[10] See Flathman's (1989) discussion of the distinction between being 'an authority' and being 'in authority'.

ity granted to researchers. In their claims about the power exercised by researchers, the critics tend to over-estimate the influence of research. They neglect the highly mediated, selective and distorting fashion in which the findings of research reach audiences; and the equally selective and instrumental fashion in which these findings get used. There is a tendency to exaggerate both the impact of research on culture and the significance of cultural reproduction for social reproduction. Research on the impact of social research on public policy underlines that its effects are diffuse and weak, rather than direct and powerful in the manner portrayed by the engineering model, where research findings are seen as being directly implemented in policy decisions (Weiss 1980; Bulmer 1982; Finch 1986). What is important for my argument here is that recognising the highly mediated character of the effects of research forces a weakening of any claim that researchers exercise substantial power through the publication of their findings. No doubt researchers do have an effect in this way, to varying degrees, but their impact is easily exaggerated; and often the effect is not even in a direction they desire. Furthermore, I suspect that this is not simply an empirical fact but indicates a theoretical point about the limited power that research *can* have over practice (Lindblom and Cohen 1979). (See Chapter 7.)

The other respect in which researchers are said to exert power on their own behalf is in their relations with the people they study. Here it is emphasised that it is generally the researcher who decides what topic is to be researched, how it is to be investigated, how the data are to be analysed, and how the findings are to be written up and for what audience. In these ways, it is suggested, the people studied are unempowered if not disempowered – to a large extent they are treated merely as objects of the research process.

This sort of argument is also largely unconvincing, in my judgment.[11] For one thing, it assumes that research has, or ought to have, a central role in the lives of the people being studied; when in most cases it manifestly does not, and there is no reason for it to do so. We are all on the margins of *some* of the activities in which we participate. We cannot be, nor in my view should we try to be, central to all of them. To argue otherwise is to believe in a form of society in which the high level of structural differentiation, the division of labour characteristic of large-scale modern societies, is abandoned or overcome. I see no prospect for this, aside from the effects on social life of widespread ecological disaster, nor am I convinced that it would be desirable.

It is also worth drawing attention to what is meant by the phrase 'exercise of power' in the context of arguments about the relationship

---

[11] For a useful discussion of the various meanings of 'empowerment', and the problems associated with some of these, see Gomm (1993).

between researchers and the people they study. Here it seems to mean little more than the taking of decisions in relation to the research process. Yet making these decisions is not in itself the exercise of power. Or at least if one defines 'power' in this way one has obscured some very important distinctions that the term is conventionally used to mark. Thus, researchers do not normally form part of the permanent power structures in the settings in which they do research.[12] They typically have to negotiate access to the settings, groups or people they study; and there have always been settings to which, and informants to whom, access is barred. Even where access is gained, once in the field researchers have to ask people to meet their requirements, to agree to be interviewed or observed for example: participation is almost always voluntary; sanctions against those who refuse to comply are not usually available, and even if they are will not usually be used. In these terms, the relationship between researcher and researched involves little exercise of power by the researcher. Indeed, very often it is the people studied who have most of the power, including the power to exclude the researcher from the research site, a power that is occasionally deployed. The bald declaration that research involves the exercise of power over the people studied runs the risk of obscuring such complexities.

In summary, there are respects in which research is subject to, and is involved in, the exercise of power. However, researchers are not *locked into* social relations that serve dominant groups within society; and, while historical trends have left them more dependent on the state than hitherto, they still retain some autonomy. Nor is the authority that researchers claim on their own behalf simply a matter of the imposition of one person's views on another. This authority, while fallible and limited, can be justified. Certainly, the radical epistemological arguments used to challenge it are not convincing. Moreover, what power researchers do exercise, both in relation to the people they study and through the publication of their findings, is for the most part slight. Research is political in all these senses, then; but no more so than many other human activities, and not in a way that necessarily prejudices the pursuit of knowledge as traditionally conceived.

*Research and values*
The other main basis for the argument that research is political involves pointing to the various ways in which value judgments are implicated in the research process. Here the political character of research is contrasted with claims regarding its value neutrality or value freedom. From this point of view, there are several respects in which research may legitimately be described as political.

[12] The situation can be different with action research, of course.

First, and most basically, it rests on a commitment to the goal of producing knowledge. In other words, it assumes that knowledge is in general preferable to ignorance. This may be regarded as a somewhat old-fashioned interpretation of the goal of research. As I noted earlier, there are those who deny that knowledge, in the conventional sense of accurate representation of reality, is possible. There are also those who deny that the production of such knowledge should be the sole or even the main goal of research. At this point in my argument, though, all that is important is that research must presuppose *some* valued goal: it cannot be value free or politically neutral in this fundamental sense.

A second way in which values are implicated in research is that there are certain social, political and economic conditions which have to be met for research to be possible on any scale, and decisions must be made to establish and maintain these, decisions which rely on value judgments. Again, what these conditions are is a matter of dispute. But, at the very least, in external terms research requires resources, and in modern times these are likely to come from the state. Given that these resources could be used for other purposes, to allocate them to research expresses a value choice. And here the judgment being made is not just that knowledge is preferable to ignorance, in a general sense, but that at some particular margin it is worth allocating resources to research as against the other directions in which modern states expend, or could expend, resources. Also, as we have seen, another external condition required for research to be possible, many believe, is a relatively high level of institutional autonomy from the suppliers of those resources. Here again, a value judgment is involved, about the desirability of such autonomy: a value judgment which has always been contested, and is increasingly questioned in influential circles today.

These external conditions apply to all forms of research, including work in natural science and the humanities. But in the case of social research there is also the need for *access* to settings, informants, documents etc. I noted earlier that this is by no means automatic. Decisions have to be made by gatekeepers and others about whether research of the kind proposed is desirable in the circumstances and at the time intended, given the costs. More generally, there are arguments, growing in influence, that men should not study women, that whites should not study blacks, that the able-bodied should not study the disabled and so on. Also, increasingly, certain research strategies, notably those involving high levels of deception, are being ruled out on ethical grounds. These developments and the disputes surrounding them point to further respects in which value judgments are associated with the research process.

There are also some internal conditions that probably have to be met for research to be possible, concerning relationships among researchers;

but what these are depends, of course, on what is taken to be the goal of research. Still, even the traditional definition of that goal, in terms of the production of knowledge, requires some internal conditions to be satisfied. These have often been interpreted in terms of an ideal political model believed to be approximated by the community of natural scientists (see, for example, Polanyi 1968). Equally, relationships among researchers, and between researchers and researched, have been criticised on political grounds; for example, because they are held to be undemocratic. Without wishing to enter into the debate that surrounds these matters, I want simply to make the point that value judgments must be made about how research communities should be organised, given both the goal of research and relevant ethical considerations.

A third sense in which research is subject to the influence of values arises from the fact that it is founded on intellectual presuppositions. At one time, the distinctively scientific, rather than political, character of research was held to derive from the fact that it involved drawing conclusions on the basis of incontestable evidence by means of ineluctable logic. If that view was ever believed by a majority of philosophers of science, it is accepted by hardly any today. Instead, there is a recognition that presuppositions are always involved in inquiry. In other words, once we abandon foundationalism – the idea that our knowledge can be validated by appeal to a foundation of givens such as sense data – we must recognise that our claims to knowledge always rest on presuppositions that have not been subjected to empirical test and none of which can be proved beyond all doubt. Furthermore, these presuppositions reflect, in part at least, the cultural values arising from the socio-historical locations of individual researchers and groups of researchers, including their gender and ethnicity. This, too, is sometimes what is meant when research is described as political.

What is at issue here, again, is the authority of research. The claim that research is political, in this form, may amount to a denial that its findings can be of universal validity: that they can represent phenomena in a way which captures the intrinsic nature or universally relevant character of those phenomena. We find something like the idea that science *can* produce knowledge of universal and certain validity from at least Descartes onwards, and in the twentieth century it is represented in the writings of the logical positivists. It is a view which has had a considerable influence on social research. There are several points at which it may be challenged. It can be argued that certainty is never available and that no claim to knowledge *must* be accepted by all: there is always scope for doubt. Another set of criticisms centres on the assumption that phenomena have intrinsic natures. It is argued by some that all accounts reflect the character of those who produce them rather than that of the phenomena studied. And, often, this argument is pursued by highlighting the demonstrably particular character of all researchers, whose socio-historically produced 'prejudices' are not optional extras but are constitutive of the process of inquiry in which they engage. Such arguments are to be found, for example, in the writings of both constructivists and poststructuralists (see, for example, Guba 1990; Lather 1991).

Once again, what the implications of this are for the cognitive status of research is a matter of dispute, but the fact that we are always dependent on unproved presuppositions, and that these are in some degree socio-historical products, seems to me to be beyond reasonable doubt. So in this sense, too, research may be seen as political, in that what counts as knowledge within any research community will have been shaped by the values of that community and by those of the other communities to which researchers belong.

The fourth sense in which values are involved in social research arises from the fact that research has material effects.[13] These occur both through the actions of researchers in the course of doing research, and through the publication of results. People's lives may be affected by being researched, and by being in a context that is affected by research findings. And these effects may be for good or for ill, and can run through the whole gamut of more complex combinations and possibilities that lies between those two extremes. So, in negotiating access and collecting data, researchers have to make decisions that involve ethical considerations about such principles as respect for privacy, and about the likelihood of damaging consequences of the use of particular research strategies. Similar considerations surround the publication of research findings (Becker 1964). There are, of course, different views about how much account researchers should take of the likely effects of their research in these respects. But even if one believes, along with Becker, that within broad limits such considerations should be subordinated to the goal of producing knowledge, the relevance of at least some ethical concern with consequences on the part of the researcher is another respect in which values do and must influence research.

I suspect that it would be generally agreed that values are relevant to social research in these four ways: that all research has a valued goal, requires external and internal conditions to be met for its pursuit, is founded on presuppositions which have not been established beyond all possible doubt, and has material effects. In all these respects, value judgments have an impact on, or enter into, research. However, it is also important to note that these features are characteristic of many

---

[13] This is distinct from the exercise of power, since (as I noted earlier) the effects of research may not be those intended.

other, if not of all, human activities. They are not, therefore, respects in which research is *distinctively* political.

Now, it is not clear whether those who argue that research is political are claiming that it is *more* political than other nominally non-political activities, or whether the argument is that *all* human activities are political by nature. In large part, though, as I noted earlier, the argument that research is political, in the sense that values are implicated in it, gains its sense from contrast with a view of research which presents it as value neutral or value free.[14] Yet, there is a great deal of misinterpretation and misconception surrounding this view. Very often the principle of value neutrality is portrayed by its critics, and sometimes even by its supporters, as implying the complete exclusion of values from research. But this is not the sense given to the term by Max Weber, who coined it (see Bruun 1972). Weber was well aware that truth is itself a value; and that, given its commitment to truth, scientific research is necessarily value committed in that sense – it could not be otherwise.

Weber also recognised that social research is almost inevitably influenced by the various other value commitments that researchers have as individuals and as members of the social categories and groups to which they belong. Indeed, his promotion of the principle of value neutrality as an ideal to be striven for was precisely motivated by recognition of the influence on social research of values other than truth, and of the threat that this posed to the validity of its findings. In this sense, too, he recognised that research is not free of the influence of values. But while he believed that this sort of influence was almost inevitable, he regarded it as one which could be and should be minimised.

There were also two other respects in which Weber believed that values not only could but should play a role in research, signalled by his concepts of value relevance and value clarification. First, he argued that we do, and should, rely on values in selecting problems for investigation; and, more than this, that the phenomena investigated by social researchers are *constituted* on the basis of values. This arises from Weber's neo-Kantian conception of the nature of the socio-historical sciences. From this point of view, whereas natural science is concerned with identifying what is common to whole categories of phenomena with a view to developing scientific laws, the idiographic approach characteristic of the human sciences focuses on unique phenomena which are constituted on the basis of values. He uses the French Revolution as an example, arguing that this is constructed by modern historians as an event by means of their own orientation to the values of liberty and equality, as well as the orientation to these values of

---

[14] For a useful discussion of the historical background, see Proctor (1991).

people at the time. The French Revolution does not exist as a distinct historical event independently of that value orientation. Without the latter, the various individuals and groups and their actions which we commonly refer to as the French Revolution would not be gathered together, or distinguished from other events that occurred at the same time and in the same places, in the way that they are. In this sense too, then, Weber did not believe that social research could be free from the influence of values.

Equally important for Weber was value clarification. He believed that social research could make a useful contribution by evaluating policies in terms of their consistency with the ultimate values espoused by those promoting them. And researchers could also formulate policies, conditionally, as the most effective and efficient means of achieving particular goals.[15]

Given all these various ways in which social research involves values, necessarily or legitimately, what meaning can be given to the concept of value neutrality? In what sense, for Weber, should values *not* be involved in research? The answer is that research should not be directed towards the realisation of any ultimate value other than truth, and should not make evaluations of such ultimate values. Weber based this conclusion on two crucial assumptions. The first is that there is no possibility of rational choice among ultimate values. In his own words, one must simply choose one's 'demon'. The other assumption is that in the modern world ultimate values are in conflict: they imply different ways of life. Given this, the resolution of political problems always involves choices between ultimate values, and social conflict is almost inevitable. The principle of value neutrality was designed, in part, to protect science from the effects of such value conflict (Weber 1974). But at least as important, if not more important, for Weber was to protect politics from false appeals to the authority of science. He believed that it is a feature of the modern world that science is used illegitimately to try to 'resolve' political problems on the basis of purportedly technical considerations.[16]

---

[15] I think Weber exaggerated the contribution that research can make to policy in this notion of value clarification. His belief that there can be scientific assessment of the derivation of policies from ultimate values, or scientific recommendation of policies given commitment to particular ultimate values, seems to rest on the idea that one could develop something like a mathematical proof, in which the premises are ultimate values and factual propositions and the conclusions are prescriptions for action that should be implemented by policy-makers. In my view, the relationships among values are much more complex than this allows, involving different preferences depending on who is making the judgment and in what capacity, and shifting preference structures depending on context.

[16] This aspect of Weber's work prefigures the views of Frankfurt Marxists like Horkheimer, Adorno and Habermas.

Weber's assumptions are, of course, open to question, especially the first: that value issues are not amenable to rational resolution.[17] We can recognise that disagreements over value issues involve a considerable degree of intractability without declaring them to reflect ultimately conflicting irrational commitments. But, in my view, Weber is correct to insist that the primary goal of research should be the production of knowledge, and that it should not involve the attempt to realise other values than truth. He was also correct that research can produce evaluations and prescriptions, though it seems to me that such arguments have different implications in academic compared to other contexts: they constitute cases to be assessed rather than calls for action.

The need for detachment from political commitments, for objectivity in other words, is recognised even by some of those who explicitly reject value neutrality and argue for politically committed research. However, in my view they underestimate the institutional requirements for this detachment. Haskell, for example, reviewing a study of the 'noble dream' of objectivity in historical scholarship, sees detachment largely in terms of the psychological attitude of the researcher. He emphasises the need for:

> an ascetic self-discipline that enables a person to do such things as abandon wishful thinking, assimilate bad news, discard pleasing interpretations that cannot pass elementary tests of evidence and logic, and, most important of all, suspend or bracket one's own perceptions long enough to enter sympathetically into the alien and possibly repugnant perspectives of rival thinkers.
> (Haskell 1990: 132)

Important as such asceticism undoubtedly is, one should not underestimate the role of the research community in socialising researchers into it and maintaining their commitment to it, as well as in correcting at least some of the biases which it does not prevent (Popper 1972).[18]

By contrast, Harding (1992), who also explicitly rejects value neutrality while retaining a commitment to objectivity, is much more aware of the power of sources of bias and their ability to affect research despite the psychological detachment of researchers. However, she seems to see bias as coming from only one direction: from the ideology of dominant groups within society. And it is questionable whether her

---

[17] This is the fundamental basis on which Habermas and Strauss criticise him, from the Left and the Right respectively (see Strauss 1953; Habermas 1971).

[18] Haskell does note that 'the kind of thinking I would call objective leads only a fugitive existence outside of communities that enjoy a high degree of independence from the state and other external powers, and which are dedicated internally not only to detachment, but also to intense mutual criticism and to the protection of dissenting positions against the perpetual threat of majority tyranny' (Haskell 1990: 135).

solution – starting from the perceptions and concerns of the oppressed – can even solve the problem as she conceptualises it. One could argue with some plausibility that since the oppressed are the major target of the purveyors of the dominant ideology, and given that any ruling group needs some sound knowledge if it is to remain in power, the powerful are at least as likely to escape the effects of the dominant ideology as the less powerful.[19] But, however this may be, we must surely recognise that there is no single source of ideology. Marxists, feminists and 'anti-racists' identify different oppressor groups, for example; and, on the evidence of the Soviet and Chinese experience, one could make a case for those people and organisations which claim to represent the oppressed also sometimes being a source of ideology. In my view, the most effective, though never fully successful, means of achieving objectivity in the process of inquiry is through the institutionalisation of research communities specialising in the production of knowledge (which is not to say that this is either a necessary or a sufficient condition).

Arguing that the goal of researchers should be the production of knowledge does not mean that they must abandon all other value commitments. It is important to draw a distinction between direct and indirect goals. Researchers may have all manner of motives for doing research or for selecting particular problems for investigation. A researcher may quite legitimately do research in the hope that it will promote some political ideal or other to which he or she is committed. In other words, no restriction should be placed on the indirect goals that researchers may seek to pursue through research. All that is required is that the goal to which their work as researchers is *immediately* directed, and which primarily controls how they do it, should be the production of valid and relevant knowledge.[20]

Given this, there must be resistance to attempts to make research serve other goals, such as maximising national wealth (Department of Science 1993), or attempts to restrict the pursuit and publication of information to suit the political preferences of sponsors or others, as in the increasingly tight restrictions placed by British government departments on the research they fund (Pettigrew 1993). But it is not just governments which represent a threat to research in this respect. Some of those who insist on the political character of research also want it to be directed towards practical goals of one kind or another. For

---

[19] For the argument that ideology is less significant in the process of social reproduction than many Western Marxists and cultural theorists have claimed, and that dominant classes are *more* likely to be misled by their own ideology than subordinate classes, see Abercrombie et al. (1980).

[20] On validity and relevance and their assessment, see Hammersley (1992a: ch. 4).

instance, some critical theorists and feminists argue that social research should be directly, and exclusively, concerned with an egalitarian and democratic transformation of society. Thus, in an article advocating collaborative work between Leftist educational researchers and teachers, Gitlin et al. (1989: 215) require that research methods explicitly embody 'the purpose of emancipation'. Despite sympathy with these political ideals, I do not believe that they should be the goals of research. This is because, as Weber recognised, research cannot play the commanding role that is required of it in such struggles, and the attempt to make it do so will undermine its capacity to fulfil the task of producing knowledge.

In this context, the broad definition of 'political' that I have used up to now obscures a more specific distinction that the word is sometimes used to make, and which is important. As already noted, on the broad definition all human activities are political, to one degree or another. But I have also argued that there is a sense in which research should *not* be political, and a similar argument could be made for other activities, for example in relation to work in the fields of medicine and the law. The narrower definition of 'political' presupposed here might usefully be formulated as referring to any activity that is directly concerned with preserving or changing a particular policy on the part of some public agency, whether this be the state or a state-sponsored organisation. It is in terms of this narrower definition that some social activities are political and others are not. While the latter, including research, will sometimes require political activity to sustain them, their central purpose or point is not political in the narrow sense.

It is also worth emphasising that research is by no means the only or even often the most effective means of pursuing political goals. When we are concerned with persuading someone to do things, we would be sensible to use whatever means we judge to be effective and ethical to do this. While giving them information is one strategy, there are others that in many circumstances will be more effective. And, even where we seek to influence people by providing information, our aim is usually to persuade them to accept what we believe to be the case and its implications. In doing this, we are likely to play down doubts that in other circumstances we might take more seriously. Indeed, in the course of political struggle it is often not sensible to mention evidence which could weaken one's case; and, on occasion, we may even feel that deception and manipulation are justified.

By contrast, such tactics are not reasonable in a research context, since the aim there is to discover, through empirical investigation and rational discussion, which conclusions are sound and which are not, and why. Indeed, to pursue political goals directly through research would not simply increase the likelihood of bias, it could render the concern with bias irrelevant (see Gitlin et al. 1989: 245). And such an orientation would turn social research into a political activity, in the narrow sense, and in so doing it would undermine both the pursuit of knowledge and the authority based in that.[21]

In summary, then, there are various ways in which social research involves values; and, in these terms, it may be regarded as political. But there is also one crucial respect, I believe, in which research should not be value-committed or political: it should be directed to no other immediate goal than the production of knowledge. As Haskell (1990: 151) remarks: 'When the members of the scholarly community become unwilling to put intellectual values ahead of political ones, they erase the only possible boundary between politically committed scholarship and propaganda, and thereby rob the community of its principal justification for existence.'

## Conclusion

I have argued that the question of whether social research is political is not one that can be answered in a straightforward manner. Research is political or is non-political, is political in some respects and not in others, only relative to how one defines the terms involved, and especially the word 'political' itself. Taking two key senses of that term, as concerning the exercise of power and the making of value judgments, I have identified a whole variety of respects in which research may be described as political. And these are important aspects of the research process which have tended to be neglected by those insisting on the non-political character of research. At the same time, I have argued that there is a sense in which research need not be and should not be political: it should not be *directly* concerned with any other goal than the production of knowledge. I have sought to justify this both in terms of the limited capacity of research to contribute to the pursuit of political goals, and the danger that pursuing these in the course of research will undermine the limited value that research has. One final clarification is perhaps necessary. To say that research should not be directed towards political goals is not to say that we should be unconcerned with the political relevance of our research. My view is very much that of Weber in this respect: that research should be value relevant without being designed to serve particular political causes.

---

[21] This would not be the case if pursuit of the truth and pursuit of the good were related in such a way that the two goals could be achieved by the same means. But this idea, characteristic of the Enlightenment and central to the philosophies of Hegel and Marx, is not sustainable (see Chapters 2 and 7).

# 7

# Social Research, Policy-making and Practice: Reflections on the Enlightenment Paradigm

In 1972 Morris Janowitz published an influential paper about the relationship between research and policy-making, in which he distinguished between two conceptions of that relationship: the engineering and enlightenment models. According to Janowitz, the engineering model draws a sharp line between basic research, concerned with producing theory, and applied research, devoted to the application of this theoretical knowledge in order to solve practical problems. On the engineering view, the impact of research, or at least of applied research, is direct and specific. By contrast, the enlightenment model does not involve a sharp division between basic and applied research, nor does it present research as providing solutions to practical problems. Instead, research is seen as supplying resources that policy-makers and practitioners can use: descriptive information about the situations they face, and theoretical concepts which provide an understanding of those situations and the roles of practitioners within them. On this view, the impact of research is less direct but potentially pervasive.

The distinction between engineering and enlightenment models has come to be widely used in discussions of how social research is intended to, and may actually, contribute to policymaking, and to social and political practice generally.[1] However, there are some respects in which Janowitz's distinction is not entirely satisfactory. For one thing, it does not capture the full range of views about the relationship between research and practice. Thus, there are those who believe that practical applications spring directly from the pursuit of basic science, so that there may be little need for applied research.[2] Others see a distinction between basic and applied work, but regard the latter as involving much more than the application of existing theory; indeed, they question whether there is much theory in the social sciences which

---

[1] See, for example, Bulmer (1982), Abrams (1984), Finch (1985, 1986), Hammersley (1992a), and Rist (1994). From this point onwards I will employ the term 'practice' to refer to all forms of social and political practice, including policy-making and implementation.

[2] Polanyi comes close to this position (see Polanyi 1961, 1962, 1964).

could be applied in this sense.[3] Yet others see applied or action research as itself producing both solutions to practical problems and contributions to scientific theory, so that, on an extreme interpretation, there is no need for basic research.[4] There have also been various attempts to distinguish *kinds* of applied research, as with Gouldner's differentiation between engineering and clinical approaches to applied sociology, the key difference being that the latter involves an independent diagnosis of the client's problems (Gouldner 1965: 11ff). There have also been distinctions drawn between different kinds of enlightenment research, notably between interpretive and critical approaches (Fay 1975).

A more important problem with Janowitz's distinction between engineering and enlightenment models, however, is that it draws attention away from what those two models have in common. *Both* of them rest on what we can usefully refer to as Enlightenment ideas. And these have become the target of considerable criticism in recent times. In this chapter I will begin by spelling out some of the history and presuppositions of Enlightenment thinking about the relationship between theory and research, on the one hand, and social and political practice, on the other. Following this, I will look in detail at several models of that relationship deriving from such thinking, diversifying Janowitz's typology a little in the process. In the second half of the chapter I examine some recent challenges to the Enlightenment paradigm, and consider what conclusions we should draw from them.[5]

### The Enlightenment paradigm

Ever since the institutionalisation of the social sciences and of applied social research, there have been recurrent criticisms of them on the grounds that their payoff for practice is poor. Sometimes these criticisms have come from outside, but often they have been promoted by social scientists themselves and have led to various proposals as to how social inquiry could be made more relevant to practice. These have included increased emphasis on applied research (or, contrastingly, on the systematic development of theory), greater concern with the dissemination of findings, and the promotion of various kinds of action and collaborative research. However, both the complaints and the research complained about typically rely on much the same set of assumptions about the proper relationship between research and

---

[3] See Gouldner (1965). For a directly opposed view, see Zetterberg (1962).

[4] See, for example, Kemmis (1988).

[5] I am using the term 'paradigm' here to refer merely to a pattern of thought, rather than employing it in the full-blown sense which has come to be associated with the work of Kuhn, see Chapter 1.

practice, assumptions which can be traced back to the Enlightenment. Central to much Enlightenment thinking was the belief that, through the exercise of the human capacity for reason, it was possible to produce knowledge whose validity is absolutely certain; knowledge not just about the physical world but also about human social life and the ideals that should guide it. Such knowledge was also seen as of universal validity: as valid for all human beings in all places at all times. Differences in beliefs and behaviour within and between societies were often regarded as the product of failure to use reason properly, resulting from its distortion by religion, superstition and tradition. The knowledge produced by reason was believed to provide the foundation for a reorganisation of society which would abolish the sources of unreason and create universal material comfort and spiritual happiness. Some saw this as possible almost immediately, others came to see history as a progressive process, though not necessarily a linear one, in which rationality in thought and social life would eventually prevail.[6]

It is quite common in the current literature of social science to find references to Enlightenment thinking and criticisms of it. These are particularly significant in discussions of poststructuralism and postmodernism, trends of thought which are often represented as anti-Enlightenment. They have this character in the sense that to a large extent they break with meta-narratives like those embodied in the concept of human progress, whether liberal or Marxist. However, the question of what is and is not characteristic of the Enlightenment, and of modernity generally, is not a matter of consensus. The Enlightenment was internally diverse, and those who oppose it nevertheless often inherit much from it. Thus, it is not difficult to show that poststructuralism and postmodernism have something in common with what they criticise. One shared element is a large dose of scepticism; though it is now directed not just against tradition and religion but also against science and even rationality itself. Also, what could be more reminiscent of the Enlightenment than the centrality which Foucault gives to the notion of knowledge/power. While the moral evaluation implied is predominantly negative rather than positive, he still treats knowledge as powerful, in a manner reminiscent of Francis Bacon (see Rouse 1987).

For the purposes of this chapter, I will define the Enlightenment view of the relationship between theory and practice as having three component assumptions:[7]

---

[6] This is necessarily a highly schematic account of Enlightenment thought; but it does capture its most influential themes. For a particularly useful account, centred on the concept of progress, see Bury (1932). See also Brinton (1967a).

[7] This definition of the Enlightenment paradigm gives much more emphasis to French than to British views. The latter will be given attention later.

1   That social life can be improved, in the interests of all, through
    deliberate intervention, piecemeal or radical.
2   That the most effective basis for such intervention is scientific – in
    other words, rational, theoretical – knowledge.
3   That such knowledge is achievable through social research.

As I noted earlier, these presuppositions underly both of Janowitz's
models and, to one degree or another, much other discussion of the
relationship between social research and various kinds of practice.
However, they have been subject to varying interpretations and
emphases.

In its eighteenth-century French version, Enlightenment thinking
saw rational inquiry and the knowledge it produced as a rational whole,
capable of being encapsulated in an Encyclopaedia.[8] One of the
changes since that time, of course, has been the massive expansion in
the volume of knowledge produced, and a concomitant proliferation of
disciplines and subdisciplines, not just within natural science, but also
in the humanities and social research. The idea of scientific knowledge
as a rational whole has persisted, but in practice an alternative model
has emerged of particular disciplines making specific contributions to
particular areas of practice. Indeed, within the social sciences there
has been a tendency for the specialisation of disciplines and subdisciplines to parallel emerging divisions among different sorts of practice.
Thus, the establishment of economics and sociology reflected in part
the institutionalised separation of economic and social policy. And
within sociology we find some specialisation that relates to different
areas of social policy, in terms of various sorts of social issue or problem: crime, education, health, etc.[9]

At the same time, of course, there have been bids by particular social
sciences, notably sociology, to adopt the overarching position previously claimed by philosophy. As Janowitz (1972: 1) notes, 'Sociology
was developed by men of the "great enlightenment", who believed that
with the accumulation of sociological knowledge, gradually and without self-conscious effort, a new basis for social relations would emerge.'
Indeed, Auguste Comte specifically invented the term 'sociology' to
refer to the discipline which would be the crowning glory of the hierarchy of scientific disciplines, and would provide the foundation for a
new type of society. A significant feature of this line of thinking, even

[8] For a critical assessment of the concept of reason underlying this, see MacIntyre
(1990).
[9] Of course, there has also been an increasing differentiation between sociology, on the
one hand, and social administration and policy, on the other; however, there remains
much overlap (see Bulmer 1982).

in its less grandiose forms, is that sociological inquiry is regarded as serving simultaneously both theoretical and practical goals. Thus, referring to Karl Mannheim as an example, Janowitz notes that he 'saw no tension between the development of sociology as a discipline and the knowledge needed for social planning. If anything, the theoretical development of sociology would be enhanced if it analyzed the fundamental issues of social change and social control in contemporary society' (1972: 2).

This sort of Enlightenment optimism about the compatibility of theoretical and practical goals was characteristic of much British sociology even as late as the 1950s and early 1960s. It is exemplified, for example, in the political arithmetic tradition which dominated research in the sociology of education in that period.[10] A.H. Halsey, a central figure, belonged to what he himself has called 'the first group of career sociologists in Britain' (Halsey 1982: 150). And the work of the political arithmeticians was explicitly tied to general theoretical developments in that field and to research in other substantive areas besides education. They saw themselves as contributing to a discipline which was still struggling to establish a secure place for itself within universities.[11] At the same time, equal emphasis was given to influencing policy-makers, both at national and at local government levels. The political arithmeticians were not simply concerned to understand modern society, they wanted to shape it; and they were relatively successful in this respect. Furthermore, this concern with influencing policy was coloured by a particular political commitment. They were working to bring about a democratic socialist society.[12] In their review of the history and character of the political arithmetic tradition, Halsey et al. emphasise this practical political commitment:

These writers were concerned to describe accurately and in detail the social conditions of their society, particularly of the more disadvantaged sections, but their interest in these matters was never a disinterested academic one. Description of social conditions was a preliminary to political reform. They exposed the inequalities of society in order to change them. The tradition thus has a double intent: on the one hand it engages in the primary sociological task of describing and documenting the 'state of society'; on the other hand it addresses itself to central social and political issues. It has

[10] For a brief account of this approach, whose influence was not limited to educational research and whose history can be traced back into the nineteenth-century, see Halsey et al. (1980: ch. 1). See also Glass (1950) and Westergaard (1979).

[11] Sociology was not defined narrowly but in large part by contrast with biological, psychological and economic approaches.

[12] Dennis and Halsey (1988) refer to the political ideals that motivated their research as ethical socialism, which they see as exemplified in the writings of Hobhouse, Orwell, Marshall and Tawney.

never, therefore, been a 'value free' academic discipline, if such were in any event possible. Instead, it has been an attempt to marry a value-laden choice of issue with objective methods of data collection. (Halsey et al. 1980:1)

For the political arithmeticians, then, theoretical and practical political goals operated side by side. Though distinct, they were not felt to be in conflict. Quite the reverse, each was seen as conducive to the pursuit of the other. In particular, scientific sociological investigations were regarded as furthering progressive political goals. This view was possible because these researchers saw modern societies as evolving towards social democracy under the driving force of technological development.[13] Moreover, sociology was to play a key role in facilitating this process of evolution. It provided a map of the path ahead based on theoretical understanding of the past and of developments in other societies. In addition, empirical sociological research showed where the priorities for further progress lay; for example, pointing out that the selective secondary school system was not providing equality of opportunity and not maximising economic exploitation of the available pool of talent, this indicating the need for a shift to a comprehensive system. And, given that progress towards democratic socialism was not only possible but was in the interests of all, it could reasonably be assumed that at least some politicians and policy-makers were predisposed to take account of the knowledge produced by sociologists, and that their actions on the basis of this knowledge would facilitate social progress.[14]

As is clear from this example, Enlightenment thinking assumes that cognitive and political progress are built into the process of historical change, albeit perhaps as potentialities rather than inevitabilities, and that they are closely related to one another. Above all, it involves a substantial optimism about the ability of researchers to produce the knowledge that is required by policy-makers and practitioners, and about the capacity of that knowledge to generate reform.

Such optimism has not entirely disappeared since the 1960s. One can still find examples of it. For instance, Pollard (1984: 192) has argued

---

[13] The introduction to Halsey et al. (1961) gives a clear sense of this technological functionalism. For a critique of American versions of technological functionalism, see Goldthorpe (1967). It is worth pointing out that Halsey and his colleagues did not see the relationship beween technology and social development, or that between education and economy, as simple and unmediated. And their functionalism seems to have been inherited as much from Marx as from structural functionalism. On Marx's functionalism, see Cohen (1978).

[14] I am not suggesting that the political arithmeticians believed that progress was inevitable or assumed that their advice would necessarily be heeded, simply that they took it as given that conditions were open to benign influence.

that researchers must contribute to what is 'socially progressive', and has suggested that 'the developments which are necessary to reinvigorate the contribution of [research] to our social scientific understanding are very close to those which are necessary to make it a more effective source of informed policy' (1984: 179). And he goes on to claim that for both purposes 'it is the quality of the work which is of paramount importance' (1984: 182–3). Despite the fact that Pollard is writing about a different approach to research from the political arithmeticians (ethnography), and one which is seeking to influence a different sort of 'policy-maker' (schoolteachers), he shares their optimism about the prospect of producing sound sociological knowledge and the capacity of that knowledge to shape practice in desirable directions. Similarly, while in her book *Research and Policy* Finch (1986) shows more awareness of the problematic nature of the relationship between research and policy-making, she too retains faith in the capacity of research, especially qualitative work, simultaneously to pursue its own goals and to enlighten policy-makers and produce progressive outcomes (Finch 1985, 1986).

### Diverse Enlightenment models

While strong versions of Enlightenment rhetoric persist, it is increasingly common to find research guided by conceptions of the relationship between research and practice that seem to display a more uneven commitment to the three elements of the Enlightenment paradigm. One, which operates across much academic social research, is what we might call the *disciplinary model*. Here the goal of research is to contribute to knowledge in a particular discipline, with abstract theoretical knowledge being given priority. While research is seen as ultimately making a contribution to practice, that contribution is not intended to be very immediate or specific. What is involved is the production of general-purpose knowledge, which is valued as much for its own sake as for any instrumental value it has. Findings are simply put into the academic public domain for others to use: as, when and if they wish. What is retained here from the Enlightenment paradigm is a belief in the possibility of producing rational knowledge about the social world that is of universal validity and relevance; but there is only a residual commitment to the value of this knowledge for practice, and utilisation is not seen as the responsibility of the researcher.

The sharpest contrast to this disciplinary model is, of course, the *engineering* or *policy research model* (Gouldner 1965; Coleman 1972; Janowitz 1972). On this view, applied social research is a central component of a modern society, which by its very nature is continually attempting innovations as solutions to problems. The role of research is both to provide information that can lead to appropriate innovations, and to evaluate past innovations, thereby preparing the way for future policy. As Coleman (1972: 2) comments: 'the conception is of a society that has an explicit evolutionary mechanism built in, an evolutionary mechanism that employs scientific methods.' So, for policy research, 'the ultimate product is not a "contribution to existing knowledge" in the literature, but a social policy modified by the research results' (1972: 6).

Coleman refers to the policy researcher's role as being to 'carry out a sensitive and accurate translation of societal interests – potential or expressed – so that the very framing of the research problem will not myopically or intentionally favor interests of certain segments of society or further his own ideology' (1972: 8–9). The concept of 'societal interests' is not without its problems, of course, and it is more usual today for the engineering model to take a client-based form: a practitioner or group of practitioners has a problem, the solution to which requires information or understanding which they do not have. The researcher is called in to provide this knowledge or understanding. The parameters of the inquiry process are set narrowly: the aim is to solve the problem, and both the problem and what constitutes a solution are defined by practitioners. This is the Rothschild conception of applied research in natural science (Rothschild 1971), and increasingly this idea seems to underly Western governments' funding of social research. However, its influence extends more widely than this. For example, some versions of collaborative research with professionals are quite similar in being directed at generating technical solutions to practitioner-defined problems.[15]

The engineering model is in many ways a strong version of the Enlightenment paradigm. It retains the commitment to progressive social change and a belief in the essential role of scientific knowledge in facilitating this. However, it deviates from the paradigm somewhat in that the inquiry and knowledge sponsored by this model tend to be specific and concrete rather than general and theoretical in character: the spirit is local rather than cosmopolitan, tied to particular (at the very least national) rather than universal interests.

There is a third, distinctive view of the relationship between research and practice derived from Enlightenment thinking, the *critical research model*. Here research is conceived as properly directed towards the achievement of progressive social change, this often being conceptu-

---

[15] See, for example, Carr and Kemmis's (1986: 202) discussion of technical and practical action research. There is an interesting parallel between Coleman's view that the product of research should be an effective social policy and Stenhouse's argument that teacher research should be designed to develop and test curricular proposals (see Stenhouse 1975; Hammersley 1993a).

alised in emancipatory terms. The main source, directly or indirectly, is usually Marxism; notably its conception of history as having a *telos* which implies future human self-emancipation, and its assumption that theory plays a crucial role in guiding the process of change. In many ways this model is the closest of the three to the Enlightenment paradigm. However, it has been subject to a process of internal decomposition. Thus, in recent forms of critical research, the emancipation aimed at has not been conceptualised in universalistic terms. For instance, in the case of feminist research the goal is, first and foremost, the emancipation of women. Similarly, critical theorists influenced by poststructuralism focus on local struggles of diverse kinds, rejecting overarching theories or general conceptions of emancipation. There is also disagreement within the critical research tradition about *how* research is to bring about change. At one extreme, as in some forms of Western Marxism, research must produce a theory which encapsulates not just how the world is but how it should be and how it can be changed for the better (see, for example, Fay 1975, 1987). At the other end of the spectrum, the capacity of research of conventional kinds to produce anything of value is downplayed, in favour of seeing the knowledge required as being generated through the process of struggle, in which researchers collaborate with oppressed or marginalised groups to transform their situations (see Hall et al. 1982; Latapi 1988). An extreme example is the Maoist *Gauche Prolétarienne* in France, for whom the role of the intellectual was 'not to produce theory, but to erase her/himself as intellectual in the service of the people' (Dews 1986: 65).

These three models, though by no means exhaustive, give us a sense of the range of ways in which the Enlightenment paradigm has been interpreted, all involving some deviation from that paradigm. Moreover, the history of their implementation raises further questions about the extent to which they can realise Enlightenment ideals. Little more needs to be said in these terms about the disciplinary model: it represents a diluted form of Enlightenment thinking, in which the relationship between research and practice is downplayed. Work inspired by this model produces knowledge whose indirect and generally low practical payoff has been much criticised.

Problems have also arisen, however, with the implementation of the engineering or policy research model. Ray Rist (1994) has reviewed the situation from his position in the US Accounting Office, which has funded large amounts of both quantitative and qualitative research of a policy-related kind. He comments that 'what policy researchers tend to consider as improvements in their craft have not significantly enhanced the role of research in policy making'. And he identifies what he calls a centrifugal tendency in such research: 'spinning off more methodologies and variations on methodologies, more conceptual frameworks, and more disarray among those who call themselves policy analysts' (Rist 1994: 545). Furthermore, what investigation there has been of the impact of applied social research, for example that of Carol Weiss, suggests that any expectation of substantial direct impact is misplaced (Weiss 1980). These problems challenge what is generally seen as the strongest feature of the engineering model: its capacity to shape policy and practice. But, of course, it has also been criticised for a tendency to produce research which furthers the interests of those who finance it (usually the powerful) at the expense of others.

The critical research model displays persistent problems of implementation as well. Once the attempt is made to complexify it, to take account of multiple sources of oppression, of conflicts between equality and freedom, its capacity to produce a coherent movement for progressive change is greatly weakened, if not completely lost. And there are unresolved tensions between the priorities of research and those of action (Papadakis 1989). Indeed, much critical research is carried out at some distance from political struggles, and in practice often comes close to the disciplinary model.[16]

### Challenges to Enlightenment thinking

This account of the influence of the Enlightenment paradigm on social research suggests that it has some inherent problems. Thus, the political arithmetic tradition of the 1950s and 1960s was undermined by criticisms of the technological functionalism on which it was based, and by a growing disillusionment in the 1970s with the effectiveness of social science as a basis for policy (Marquand 1983). Similarly, the influence of Marxism was weakened by the theoretical criticisms of the structuralists and by the political criticisms of feminists and anti-racists. And in recent years even more fundamental theoretical challenges to Enlightenment thinking have developed, from diverse sources, which imply severe limits on the contribution that social research can make to practice. These are not new (see Shklar 1957), but they have been given renewed emphasis in recent years.

The most general of these challenges relates to the idea of progress, and to the assumption that there is a coherent set of universal values in terms of which any set of social arrangements or actions can be judged. The Enlightenment idea of progress, particularly as developed by Saint-Simon, Comte, Hegel and Marx, has been subjected to a great deal of

---

[16] For a critique of radical sociology along these lines, see Shaw (1975). See also Mies's (1991) criticism of feminists for failing to engage research directly in the service of the women's movement.

criticism. Certainly, any notion of some automatic process of improvement, some *telos* built into history, has been largely abandoned on the grounds that it is a metaphysical if not theological concept (Löwith 1949; but see Blumenberg 1983). And, of course, the associated idea that Western culture represents the highest form of human social life has been largely rejected as a result of the influence of twentieth-century anthropologists, and of external and internal critics who have drawn attention to its ethnocentrism. This has led to considerable disillusionment about the civilising mission of the West, even in establishment circles. Symbolic here is the amount of attention given recently, particularly in the United States, to Fukuyama's view that while Western liberalism is the almost inevitable outcome of progress, it is by no means obviously the most desirable form of life (Fukuyama 1989, 1992).

As part of these critiques, the concept of universal human values proclaimed by the Enlightenment has also been questioned. In fact, of course, it had been rejected almost immediately by the romantics and historicists of the late eighteenth and early nineteenth centuries, who emphasised the integrity and distinctiveness of diverse national and local cultures (see Iggers 1968). Equally important, the Enlightenment assumption that Western values form a coherent and interdependent whole, whose pursuit is a single project, was challenged in the nineteenth century by Nietzsche, Kierkegaard and others. The influence of these anti-Enlightenment ideas has grown in the latter half of the twentieth century, currently being celebrated under the heading of postmodernism.

In more specific terms, each of the three elements of the Enlightenment paradigm which I identified – social intervention as capable of bringing about desirable change, the role of scientific knowledge in facilitating this, and the capacity of social research to produce such knowledge – have been put in doubt.

*The scope for desirable change*
The idea that social life can be improved through deliberate intervention, notably on the part of the state, was never an undisputed element of Enlightenment thinking, and it was always more influential in France than in Britain and America. Indeed, it was strongly rejected in the nineteenth century by the *laissez-faire* tradition in British social and economic thought. As late as 1892, we find Herbert Spencer writing: 'Acts of Parliament do not simply fail; they frequently make things worse . . . Moreover, when these topical remedies do not exacerbate the evils they were meant to cure, they constantly induce collateral evils; often graver than the original ones' (Spencer 1946: 131, 133; quoted in Sieber 1981). By that time, though, even in Britain, public opinion had

swung towards a more favourable view of state intervention, leading to the liberal welfare reforms of the first half of the twentieth century.[17]

In recent decades, of course, opinion has been moving in the other direction, especially in the Anglo-American context. In the 1960s and 1970s, on the Left, the role of the state was a major focus for criticism; there were claims, for example, that state-sponsored social policy and schooling functioned to serve and preserve capitalism.[18] From a Marxist point of view, the criticism was not of state intervention as such but rather of its role under advanced capitalism. However, there was within the New Left a more general opposition to the state, fuelled by libertarian ideas. The 'administered society', East and West, came to be the target for attack, and for many such a society was seen as the natural product not so much of capitalism *per se* as of the 'dialectic of enlightenment'.[19] Indeed, for some the problem was not just that the instrumental side of reason had come to dominate, but that the very notion of a rationally ordered society was oppressive: representing a Western and/or masculinist illusion.

More recently, of course, criticism of state intervention has come from the Right, where there has been a resurgence in the influence of *laissez-faire* ideas, again drawing on a form of libertarianism. From this point of view, state intervention is oppressive because it interferes with the freedom and responsibility of individuals. These ideas have been developed into comprehensive political philosophies by writers like Hayek and Nozick (Hayek 1967b; Nozick 1974).

Perhaps even more significant than criticism from established Left- and Right-wing positions is the fact that some of those previously committed to, and involved in, social intervention have become pessimistic about its effectiveness, on much the same grounds as Spencer (1946). An example is Nathan Glazer:

> I participated as a writer, and occasionally as an official or consultant, in the remarkable burst of social reform that accompanied the Kennedy and Johnson administrations and that was to continue, scarcely abated, through the Nixon administration. We believed in those years . . . that our rich country had both the material resources and the intelligence to eliminate poverty, eradicate slums, overcome the differences between the educational achievement and health of the rich and the poor. Social scientists . . . were pulled into the design and administration of new government programs aiming at

---

[17] For a discussion of the complex question of whether there was a *laissez-faire* age in nineteenth-century Britain, see Taylor (1972). And on the origins of the liberal welfare reforms, see Hay (1975).

[18] For an account of how the US state was construed as a social problem by both New Left and Radical Right in the 1960s, see Warren (1993).

[19] On Horkheimer and Adorno's (1973) development of this view, see Jay (1973: ch. 8)

these results. A new discipline of policy sciences or policy studies expanded, and new schools were founded to teach it. [The journal] *The Public Interest* . . . was founded in 1964 . . . it heralded a new age in which we would rationally and pragmatically attack our domestic social problems . . . By the end of the 1960s I was not alone in thinking that something had gone wrong, that we had been somewhat too optimistic . . . We seemed to be creating as many problems as we were solving and . . . the reasons were inherent in the way we . . . thought about social problems and social policy . . . Whatever our actual success by some measure in dealing with a social problem, it seemed that discontent steadily increased among the beneficiaries of these programs, those who carried them out, and those who paid for them . . . We were enmeshed in a revolution of rising expectations, a revolution itself fed by the proposals for new social policies. Their promise, inadequately realized, left behind a higher level of expectation, which a new round of social policy had to attempt to meet, and with the same consequences . . . Rising expectations continually enlarge the sea of felt and perceived misery, whatever happens to it in actuality. Alongside rising expectations, and adding similarly to the increasing difficulties of social policy, was the revolution of equality. This is the most powerful social force in the modern world . . . And just as there is no point at which the sea of misery is finally drained, so, too, there is no point at which the equality revolution comes to an end, if only because as it proceeds we become ever more sensitive to smaller and smaller degrees of inequality. More important, different types and forms of equality inevitably emerge to contradict each other as we move away from a society of fixed social orders. (Glazer 1988: 3–4)

At one level this sort of argument may be taken to suggest that in the past social interventions have been based upon inadequate social science knowledge, so that no criticism of the Enlightenment paradigm is implied. However, in many ways, it goes deeper than this. Thus, Glazer argues that the regressive effects of social policy interventions arise from the fact that they weaken those institutions which have traditionally dealt with the social problems they are directed towards remedying, notably the family. Here the commitment to the rational planning of society, characteristic of much Enlightenment thinking, is at the very least qualified by a belief in the essential role of tradition and/or of 'spontaneous' forms of social organisation, echoing the views of the counter-Enlightenment and of the *laissez-faire* tradition respectively.

*The nature of policy-making and practice*
I noted earlier that investigations of the impact of applied social research on policy-making suggest that high expectations about its influence are ill founded. It has long been recognised that there are resistances to the adoption of research findings on the part of policy-makers, practitioners and others. However, these have generally been treated simply as irrational barriers to change which need to be overcome (Glass 1950; Gouldner 1965; Finch 1986). Indeed, those working

within the critical tradition have sometimes appealed to the Freudian concept of resistance to explain why the oppressed do not always embrace emancipatory theory (Habermas 1968b; Fay 1975: 89; Keat 1981). More significant, and more of a challenge to the Enlightenment paradigm, however, are arguments to the effect that research *should not have* a direct relationship to practice; in other words that policy-makers should not base their decisions primarily on research findings. In their book *Usable Knowledge*, Lindblom and Cohen (1979:10) point out that, whereas researchers tend to assume that problems can be solved by policy-makers gathering and analysing information, with research findings being the major input, in fact much problem-solving 'is and ought to be accomplished through various forms of social interaction that substitute action for thought, understanding and analysis'. As examples, they cite delegation, negotiation, voting and the market mechanism. From this point of view, public policy-making is a political process, not a matter of intellectual problem-solving (see Gregory 1989); and even where a knowledge-based solution is sought, research information is usually only a small part of the knowledge that needs to be used – practical experience and skilled judgment are generally much more important.[20]

These doubts about the role of research in relation to policy-making reflect, in part, revisions of older, rationalistic versions of decision-making and organisation theory, which were modelled on the concept of the business firm as a machine for making and implementing decisions, in which information about alternative courses of action is collected and assessed and those calculated to maximise profits are adopted. Much recent work in this field has been critical of the idea that organisations actually operate this way, or that we should try to make them run like this. It has been suggested, for example, that profit maximisation is not the goal even of business organisations; and that many organisations are 'organised anarchies', in which goals and preferences are unclear and contradictory, and the means by which these can be pursued ill understood or not under effective control. Furthermore, decision-making is now seen as a process occurring over time in which various individuals and groups participate in contingent, and often unknowing, ways, with unpredictable effects. In these circumstances, decisions are not, and cannot be, made by the application of some technical procedure. Nor are they or should they be based solely on technical considerations: politics in the broadest sense – internal and external, micro and macro – always enters.[21]

[20] One can trace a sort of parallel, very different in spirit, within the critical tradition in the work of Sorel, who stresses the necessary role of myth and violence in revolutionary politics, see McInnes (1967).

[21] See, for instance, Simon (1955), Winter (1964), March and Olsen (1976, 1989), March (1988).

Arguments that have parallel implications for the Enlightenment paradigm are to be found in reconceptualisations of professional practice. Thus, Schön (1983, 1987) has criticised the idea that professional work involves the application of scientific knowledge to practical problems. Rather, such work is characterised by a knowing-in-action that is different in character from scientific knowledge but which is rigorous in its own terms. Furthermore, it is modified by reflection-in-action, an ability to think about what one is doing while doing it. It is through such reflection-in-action that professional skill and wisdom are built up in the course of experience; and these capacities are essential because real world problems do not generally present themselves in ways which match the technical knowledge produced by research. Schön comments at one point: 'In recent years there has been a growing perception that researchers, who are supposed to feed the professional schools with useful knowledge, have less and less to say that practitioners find useful' (Schön 1987: 10).[22] Where, from the point of view of a crude positivism, the traditional practices of professionals are based on folk knowledge that must be eliminated in favour of sound, scientifically validated techniques produced by research, from this perspective they are seen as more or less skilful and principled adjustments to circumstance that it may not be possible to better, and which certainly cannot be bettered by the substitution of research-based techniques.

This questioning of the Enlightenment view of the relationship between theory and practice matches counter-Enlightenment ideas, and is reflected particularly clearly in the work of Michael Oakeshott. He draws a sharp distinction between theory and practice, treating the former as a product of the latter, rather than vice versa, and as having only very limited practical value. On this basis he criticises rationalists who, in his terms, are preoccupied with theoretical knowledge that can be codified as a set of rules for behaviour, and who downplay or entirely dismiss practical wisdom, which by its very nature resists codification:

> The conduct of affairs, for the Rationalist, is a matter of solving problems, and in this no man can hope to be successful whose reason has become inflexible by surrender to habit or is clouded by the fumes of tradition. In this activity the character which the Rationalist claims for himself is the character of the engineer, whose mind (it is supposed) is controlled throughout by the appropriate technique and whose first step is to dismiss from his attention everything not directly related to his specific intentions. This assimilation of politics to engineering is, indeed, what may be called the myth of rationalist politics. (Oakeshott 1962: 4)

[22] This view of the nature of practice is not entirely new, of course. It reflects the Greek distinction between *techne* and *praxis*, and in particular Aristotle's emphasis on the distinctiveness of the latter.

Oakeshott argues that 'the history of Rationalism' is 'the history of the invasion of every department of intellectual activity by the doctrine of the sovereignty of technique' (Oakeshott 1962: 17). But the most significant of these invasions is in the field of politics; and here his target is by no means only the conception of politics built into the engineering model: it applies equally to that characteristic of the critical model. What is central to rationalism, according to Oakeshott, is the project of transforming human social life on the basis of theory; and he argues not only that this is impossible, but that the attempt to achieve it has had, and inevitably will have, disastrous consequences. This is because it ignores the practical wisdom embodied in existing practices; and, in destroying traditional forms of life and wisdom, it leaves us more and more dependent on the very rationalism that is the source of our problems.

While Oakeshott's conservative politics may not be widely accepted, his insistence on the difference between theory and practice and the necessary independence of the latter from the former resonates with arguments in other fields.[23] Indeed, parallels are even to be found in debates within sociology:

> There is, then, a perverse cognitive emphasis involved: institutions and organisations are treated as though they were founded in and were primarily about theories, despite the fact that sociology generally thinks it has taken Marx's lesson that ideas and theories are relatively inconsequential in shaping and operating the institutions of society. The failings and short-comings of institutions, then, get attributed to the fact that they *possess the wrong ideas* and a principal means of social reform comes to be that old standby – argument. The effect of this is, of course, that the determination of what needs to be done to solve a problem comes to be equated with what needs to be done to win an argument against the positions that are attributed to the institution being criticised. That sociologists can show that some theory is faulty means they can suppose that they know what is wrong with an institution and that they also know what it would take to make it do the right things. They tend not to ask, then, whether the things they think right *would* work and how they could tell whether this is so. Making an argumentative case is not the same as designing a practice, organisation or institution but it is the capacity to do the latter which is required if one *is* to reconstruct social life. (Sharrock 1980: 122–3)

At the heart of the Enlightenment paradigm, then, it is suggested, is an intellectualist fallacy which treats ideas as the mainspring of human affairs, and seeks to transform those affairs on the basis of supposedly scientific theory. But practice cannot be governed by technique or by

[23] See, for example, Hirst's (1983) discussion of the role of disciplinary knowledge in educational practice.

theory, it is argued, so that the potential contribution of research to these activities is much more limited than the Enlightenment paradigm suggests.

## The nature of research

Enlightenment thinking about the relationship between research and practice generally assumes a close parallel between natural and social science, with the former acting as a model for the latter. And it was, of course, the success of natural science in technological terms, in large part, which stimulated hopes of a social science which would bring about the rational transformation of human social life. More recently, the natural science model has been the source both of disappointment at the failure of social research to have an equivalent practical impact, and of fear at what the result might be if it *did* ever have that impact. For these and other reasons, there has been sustained criticism of the natural science model, and increasing stress on the differences between natural and social scientific knowledge. These developments clearly have implications for ideas about the relationship between social research and practice, raising doubts about the capacity of social research to meet the requirements of the Enlightenment paradigm.

There have, of course, long been alternative conceptions of social research methodology. In the first half of the twentieth century these were generally promoted through appeals to conflicting views of how natural scientists went about their work, and they were typically framed in Enlightenment terms (Hammersley 1989: ch. 4). From the 1950s onwards, however, there has been a growing chorus of criticism, from various directions, which has largely denied the relevance of the natural science model (early examples include Hayek 1952; Strauss 1953; Dray 1957; Winch 1958; Taylor 1964; Louch 1966). Much of this criticism has been associated with what have come to be referred to as interpretive approaches to social research, and these form an alternative basis for conceptualising the relationship between research and practice. Interpretivism has shaped much ethnographic work in sociology and social anthropology, a lot of which has approximated to what I referred to earlier as the disciplinary model. Equally, though, it has been drawn on by those constructing more 'critical' approaches (see, for example, Habermas 1968b; Fay 1975, 1987; Taylor 1981).

Rather than providing practically relevant information about causal relationships, interpretive research is seen as making a contribution to practice by rendering explicit the presuppositions which constitute various forms of social life, and perhaps also by showing how these relate to wider cultural patterns. In more specific terms, such research provides knowledge of the perspectives and behaviour of actors who are the target for policy and practice. In this way it may allow practitioners to understand those actors in a deeper way than they currently do: to recognise their distinctive intentions and motives, and to see the logic of their perspectives on the world, including their views about practitioners. Equally important, though, an interpretive approach may focus on the beliefs and activities of practitioners themselves, perhaps revealing assumptions or patterns of behaviour of which they are not fully aware. And, in the process, this may uncover alternative possibilities that were not previously considered. As Fay (1975: 80) comments: 'the result of this sort of analysis is . . . a kind of enlightenment in which the meaning of actions, both of one's own as well as of others, are made transparent'. Here, then, we have a rather different basis to the natural science model for the idea that research may enlighten practitioners.

In recent years, however, this interpretive conception of the nature of social research and its contribution to practice has itself been criticised, on the grounds that it assigns an unwarranted superiority of epistemological status to the accounts produced by researchers. Those versions of the critical model which use an interpretive approach to 'raise the consciousness' of the oppressed have been criticised in this way. They have been challenged as at the very least patronising and as in practice oppressive (Gitlin et al. 1989). Similar criticisms have been directed against more conventional interpretive work. It has been argued, for example, that anthropological accounts represent a kind of imperialism, imposing Western views on other societies under cover of a false mantle of objectivity (Clifford 1988). Here, the epistemological warrant of social research, whether scientific or interpretative, is denied on the basis of relativistic and sceptical arguments which point to the reliance of all accounts on presuppositions that cannot be fully tested and which necessarily reflect the socio-historical backgrounds and circumstances of those who produce them. What is involved is the application to researchers themselves of social constructionist ideas which had previously been applied only to the people studied. This implies that researchers actively construct the phenomena they describe in their research reports, rather than simply representing them 'as they are'. The critics draw on a wide range of resources to support their argument, including Kuhn's proposal that scientific paradigms are incommensurable, Feyerabend's critique of scientific imperialism, Winch's extreme version of cultural relativism, and Gadamer's philosophical hermeneutics, not to mention the scepticism and pluralism of much poststructuralism and postmodernism (see Bernstein 1983, 1991; and Chapter 1).

In effect, these arguments seem to undercut all appeals to expertise and authority on the part of social researchers. Their accounts of the world become one possible view among many, with no special claim to validity. As a result, it is not clear what distinctive role is left for them to play (as researchers) in connection with social and political practice.

## Assessing the challenge to the Enlightenment paradigm

The arguments outlined in the previous section constitute a fundamental critique of the Enlightenment paradigm; they question every element of it. And if they were to be accepted *in toto*, and at full force, we would have to conclude not only that research can make no contribution to practice but also that there is little warrant for research in the conventional sense of that term. But, of course, what we have here is a motley collection of arguments, of varying degrees of cogency, and open to a range of interpretations. My own view is that they do not lead to the radical conclusions just mentioned, and indeed many of the writers whose work I have cited would not draw those conclusions either. While we should certainly recognise that policy interventions cannot be regarded as the equivalent of pulling a lever in a machine, this does not imply that they can never be effective or desirable. Nor does rejection of Enlightenment meta-narratives about progress mean that social improvement is impossible. And the fact that there is value conflict need not lead us to conclude that there can be no agreement about what is and is not desirable. Similarly, while practice is rarely, if ever, the mere application of theory or technique, this is not to say that it is not rational; or that theories and techniques are never of use to practitioners, as supplements to their practical wisdom and judgment. So we need not assume that all decision-making must be an anarchic process, in the sense that the outcome depends entirely on contingent factors. And, finally, the fact that social research may not be able to conform closely to the natural science model, and that it cannot provide knowledge whose validity is absolutely certain, does not mean that we must conclude that it is incapable of producing knowledge at all and therefore lacks all authority.

Care must be taken, then, not to exaggerate the force and implications of these criticisms. At the same time, it seems to me that they do have sufficient cogency and power to undermine the Enlightenment paradigm, and some of the models based on it of the relationship between research and practice. That paradigm greatly overestimates the ease and scope for successful policy intervention, and the role that research can play in providing a basis for it. The progressive meta-narrative which underlies it tends to encourage excessive ambition in the realm of both politics and research. We cannot be so sanguine about the prospects for intervention bringing about desirable social change (see Hindess 1987). And judgments about what is desirable are more open to question than the Enlightenment paradigm implies, very often involving trade-offs between one group's interests and another's, without benefit of any sort of calculus. Furthermore, I think we must recognise that the role of social research in relation to practice must be much more limited than the Enlightenment model assumes. The reason for this is that research findings rarely cover all the considerations relevant to decision-making processes, and are always fallible. Also, sensible judgments of the relevance and validity of information, and of what is the most appropriate course of action in particular circumstances, have to be made in the light of local knowledge.

This critique also means that, as social researchers, we must adopt a more modest evaluation of our capacities to produce knowledge than the Enlightenment paradigm encourages. One of the effects of that paradigm, in my view, has been the prevalence of exaggerated claims about what can be and has been produced by social research, in desperate attempts to bridge the chasm between what it can do and what the Enlightenment paradigm implies it should do. Indeed, even the following is probably not an unduly negative assessment of the current state of sociological knowledge:

> It seems reasonable to characterise the best sociological arguments as establishing in-principle possibilities. They can, that is, show that in principle a particular line of argument could be true, that there are no fatal, *a priori* objections to it and that it has a measure of empirical plausibility, i.e. one can see what things would be like if it were true, and there is some (usually only a little) evidence which shows that things are/might be more-or-less like that. (Sharrock 1980: 120)

Where does this leave us in thinking about the relationship between research and practice? The criticisms of the Enlightenment paradigm I have outlined apply most forcefully to the engineering and critical theory models, because both of these assume a solid base of research knowledge which carries strong implications for practice. In this way, they inherit the excessive ambition of that paradigm: they make claims about the potential contribution of research to practice which cannot be sustained. While the engineering model rules out research-based conclusions about legitimate goals, it assumes that research can lead to conclusions about what are appropriate means to achieve those goals. Yet, the distinction between goals and means is a contextual one, and the criteria for selecting means cannot but be value laden (Fay 1975: 50–3). And the problem here is not just value ladenness but the sheer range of considerations that have to be taken into account in deciding on means, a range which research cannot cover effectively at present or in the foreseeable future, and whose scope should not be decided by means of research because it requires practical wisdom and judgment based on local knowledge.

The critical approach also makes excessive claims about the potential practical contribution of research. In some versions, like the engineering model, it relies on the discovery of sociological laws or quasi-laws, this time as a basis for explaining oppression and showing how it can be overcome (Fay 1975, 1987). Furthermore, it requires a level of certainty about its validity sufficient to be able to reject people's perceptions of what their needs are, a certainty that relies on a teleological metaphysics whose own validity is at the very least open to reasonable doubt (see Chapter 2).

By comparison with its competitors, the disciplinary model escapes the critique relatively unscathed. It is only affected by that part of it which concerns the possibility of rational knowledge, and this is the weakest element. Historically, the concept of progress developed as a generalisation from the sphere of knowledge to other realms (Bury 1932). And to deny the validity of the meta-narrative of social progress is not necessarily to deny the idea of progress in science. While there have been arguments against the concept of scientific progress, it is simpler in character than that of social progress, which in fact depends on it, and these criticisms are far less compelling.[24]

Earlier in this chapter, I presented the disciplinary model as a weak version of the Enlightenment paradigm, but it need not be seen in this way. It could be viewed in a more positive light. As I noted, research inspired by it has been criticised because it makes only a small contribution to practice. But there are reasons why we should not accept such criticism at face value. One is that assessment of the size of its practical contribution has been based on the excessive ambition of the Enlightenment paradigm. That paradigm, in the shape of the engineering and critical models, assumes a fairly direct causal, or quasi-causal, relationship between the production of knowledge, the development of policy, and progressive social change. This is open to criticism not just on the grounds that it tends to over-emphasise the determinate effects of ideas on social phenomena, but also because it assumes too simple a form of causal relation in the context of the social world. This certainly holds if we adopt an interpretive or interactionist perspective (see, for example, Matza 1964, 1969), but is equally true if we adopt a more 'positivistic' approach (Hage and Meeker 1988). Once we recognise this, we are forced to accept that research will inevitably have a relatively weak (because highly mediated) impact on practice. Furthermore, this is not just a matter of the *degree* of impact; it also has implications for its nature. The practical consequences of research findings cannot be read off from what is taken to be their intrinsic

---

[24] For arguments supporting the concept of scientific progress, see Newton-Smith (1981).

nature. What effects they have, which may be judged as desirable or undesirable, are highly contingent, and therefore not entirely predictable, products of the mediation process. For this reason, we should not set high expectations for the practical control which research can provide, and we must be prepared to value the more modest contribution that disciplinary research makes.

However, there is another, deeper, reason to question criticism of the disciplinary model for the limited practical contribution of the research it inspires. This is that such criticism assumes an instrumentalist conception of the value of knowledge: it presupposes that knowledge is of value only to the degree that it makes a contribution to practice. It is such instrumentalism which leads to the dismissal of disciplinary research, even by some researchers, as based on a 'fantasy which society can no longer afford us to indulge in' (Elliott 1988: 193), or as constituting an 'academic luxury of detachment from the real world', which is socially irresponsible (Pollard 1984: 189, 194).

Instrumentalism underpins both the engineering and critical models. This does not need demonstrating in the case of the former, its instrumentalism is explicit. But instrumentalism is also characteristic of the critical tradition. In the eleventh *Thesis on Feuerbach* Marx declared that the point was not just to interpret the world but to change it; and, indeed, Marxism and critical theory adopt the view that all knowledge functions to preserve or change society. Research in this tradition is premissed on the idea that through social transformation the gap between theory and practice can be overcome (Prokopczyk 1980). This is at the core of Marx's work, being a reaction against the element in Hegelianism which sees theory as reconciling us with the world (see Plant 1973). Instrumentalism also informs Habermas's influential account of the three interests which underlie research. He adopts the Greek distinction between *techne* and *praxis,* but he rejects the associated concept of *theoria,* conventionally associated with the pursuit of knowledge for its own sake (see Lear 1988), replacing it with the notion of an emancipatory interest. For him, and other critical theorists, all forms of inquiry are constituted by interests other than the pursuit of knowledge itself (Habermas 1968a).[25]

While instrumentalism is part of the spirit of the age, it is not beyond

---

[25] His argument that natural science is constituted by a technical interest in control and that much social research has been constituted by a practical interest in enhancing communication is open to serious criticism. And his appeal to the concept of an emancipatory interest as the basis for both philosophical reflection and for social research is the weakest part of his argument. It rests on an ideal of uncoerced communication that is questionable and yet is supposed to be demonstrable *a priori* (see Lobkowicz 1972; McCarthy 1978).

question. It is true, of course, that we often use things, indeed even other people, as means to our ends; however, on occasion, we also treat them as of value in themselves. And, in fact, we cannot value *everything* instrumentally: in valuing one thing instrumentally we must, at least for the moment, value something else for itself. If everything were to be valued instrumentally, then nothing could be of any value, since nothing could give value to anything else. It would be foolish, then, to reject the idea that knowledge is of value in itself on the grounds that *nothing* can be of value in itself. Instrumentalism applied to knowledge must rely on the assumption that, while knowledge is not, something else *is,* valuable in itself.

The distinction between research and practice that I have relied on throughout this chapter may incline us to accept this more limited form of instrumentalism. Disciplinary research, like the theory it sometimes produces, may be seen as unworldly. Hence Elliott's (1988) deployment of the term 'fantasy', and Pollard's (1984) use of the contrast with 'the real world' in the quotations above. This was very much the Greek view of the character of *theoria*; though, ironically, it was regarded as of value in itself precisely because of its otherworldliness, on the grounds that it partook of the divine. Over time, value has come to be seen largely in human and practical terms, reversing the Greek view (Lobkowicz 1967). As a result, the idea that knowledge is valuable for its own sake has come to seem less and less plausible. It is important to remember, though, that this arises in large part from the original contrast between theory and practice: the one being above the world, the other within it. We need to recognise that research is itself a form of practice, in the sense that it is an activity pursued by human beings which takes place in the world, is directed towards a particular set of goals and uses social resources etc. Given this, we might consider why the value of research as a social practice must always be instrumental whereas, necessarily, at least some other practices are treated as having value in themselves.

What is typically involved in arguments about the instrumental value of research is its value in economic or political terms. So, we must ask why these forms of life are judged to be of value in themselves, whereas science and scholarship are not. Very often, such arguments amount to a deification of the market (on the Right) or of democracy (on the Left). Rather than constituting an institutional form which allocates resources and products in ways which can be judged to have advantages and disadvantages as regards convenience, fairness, efficiency, productivity etc., markets are sometimes treated as approximations to an ideal which embodies and/or gives access to all human values (Hayek 1967a). Similarly, democracy is viewed by many on the Left as an ideal form of life (see, for example, Carr 1991); rather than as an institutional form which can allow the expression of a range of views and interests, and resolve policy disagreements, to one degree or another. My point is not that market relations or democracy should themselves be judged in purely instrumental terms, simply that while they may be judged as valuable in their own right, as well as being of instrumental value, they do not and cannot encapsulate all human values.[26] To this extent the poststructuralists and *nouveaux philosophes* are correct to reject totalising theories (Dews 1986, 1987). Many things are found valuable in themselves by human beings, and we should reject monopolistic claims, not just for 'the life of the mind' but also for particular forms of economic and political life.

To claim that knowledge can be of value for its own sake is not to imply that *any* knowledge is of value, or that we should value knowledge according to its uselessness. It means that we should value knowledge about matters relevant to human life above ignorance about such matters. And such knowledge has value in terms of its relevance to our lives irrespective of whether it can be shown to have a direct and powerful influence on our practical activities. In other words, it is not to be judged, and the pursuit of knowledge does not need to be guided, by some sort of calculation of the degree of instrumental value it has. The fact that the practical benefit of disciplinary knowledge is not calculable does not make it worthless.

There are grounds, then, in the wake of the critique of the Enlightenment paradigm, for reconsidering the value of the disciplinary model of research. However, I do not believe that this model represents the only legitimate form of inquiry. There is also a clear role for research that is more closely related to forms of practice, whose value *would be* primarily instrumental. While the claims made for practice-orientated research by the engineering and critical models are excessive, there is no reason to deny the value of research which is concerned with producing knowledge that is directly useful to particular practitioner communities, whether national or local policy-makers, occupational groups, political parties, pressure and protest groups, gender or ethnic constituencies. While practical research may well draw on disciplinary knowledge, it will not in any straightforward sense simply apply that knowledge (and it may stimulate it). Furthermore, it must not be restricted by disciplinary boundaries: it should be geared to the informational needs of the practical activity which it is designed to serve.

[26] In fact, Hayek argues only that the free enterprise system provides the best means for the individual pursuit of other values. But, in my view he underestimates the effects of the market on the esteem in which various goals are held within a society. The phrase 'market values' is not without significance.

Disciplinary and practical research are distinct kinds of inquiry which have rather different goals and employ somewhat different procedures. They are both of value, each performing a function that the other cannot serve as effectively.

## Conclusion

Much of our thinking about the relationship between research and social and political practice is shaped by what I have called the Enlightenment paradigm, which sees research as providing a theoretical basis for social interventions which will transform social life in a rational manner that is in everyone's interests. In this chapter I have explored some of the problems surrounding this set of ideas. It seems clear that it involves excessive expectations about the practical payoff of research. This emerges from criticism of the concept of social progress it presupposes, and of its assumptions about the nature of policy-making and practice, the relationship of research to these, and the capacity of inquiry to produce reliable knowledge. Instead of seeing social and political practice as open to 'rationalisation' on the basis of scientific research founded on a method that guarantees valid results, we must recognise that politics and practice may be ontologically resistant to such 'rationalisation', and also that the knowledge produced by research is always fallible. Furthermore, what research offers is not a God's eye view but rather perspectives from particular angles, whose appropriateness can always be challenged.

At the same time, we must take care not to go from one extreme to another, from the excessive optimism of the Enlightenment to a renunciation of all belief in the practical value of research. While over-confident views about the capacity of theory to guide practice must certainly be abandoned, we should be careful not to celebrate irrationality, unthinking reliance on tradition, or spontaneous playfulness. Reactions against the Enlightenment paradigm carry the danger of leaving practice as a realm of mystery, and one where policy-makers and practitioners can always appeal to their own authority and wisdom, dismissing external criticism as misunderstanding.

Re-evaluating the three models that I considered earlier in the chapter, I have argued that we should not accept the currently fashionable dismissal of the disciplinary model. I have suggested that, once we abandon the Enlightenment paradigm, the contribution of disciplinary research to practice need not be seen as trivial or derisory. And I have shown how rejection of this model is based on an instrumentalism whose prevalence does not derive from its cogency. At the same time, I have argued that practical research, of a more modest kind than that sponsored by the engineering and critical models, is also of value. I conclude that we should value disciplinary and practical research each in its own terms, rather than make attempts to shape one in the image of the other or to integrate them in the form of some spurious unity of theory and practice.

# 8

# The Liberal University and its Critics

My starting point in this chapter is the fact that the organisation and practice of universities, and our ideas about them, have been and continue to be structured by conflicting ideals. A strong (though by no means exclusive) influence in the past has been what I will call the *liberal* model. Today, more than ever, that model is under attack, from a variety of directions, and in particular from advocates of what we might label the *economic* and the *ideological* models. While its infuence persists, not just in many aspects of the way in which higher education is organised but also in arguments about the role of universities, there is little doubt that the fortunes of the liberal model are in decline.[1] And, this is not just because economic and political forces are against it, but also because some of its key assumptions have come to be questioned. In other words, the attack on the liberal university has been as much theoretical as practical. And it is the theoretical side of that attack I will be primarily concerned with here. It seems to me that we need more clarification of our ideas about how universities ought to be before we can get a clear sense of what is happening to them and what, if anything, can be done about it.

So, in this chapter I want to look at the liberal concept of the university against the background of the challenge from its competitors, the economic and ideological models. Working with just three views about the nature and role of universities is, of course, an extreme simplification of a complex reality. But what I am presenting are ideal types which I hope will clarify some of the issues at stake. First, then, I need to spell out in more detail what I mean by the 'liberal university'.[2]

[1] For an interesting account of this decline in the case of the German university, see Lobkowicz (1987).

[2] The term 'liberalism' is not one that enjoys consensual usage. It has been interpreted in a wide variety of ways (Manning 1976; Gray 1986). Even those who call themselves liberals often differ substantially in their commitments. And critics sometimes use the term as little more than an expression of disapproval. There is also a rather specific ambiguity in the meaning of the term which is of significance here. It arises from the discrepancy between its meaning in the context of political philosophy and the sense implied by the phrase 'liberal education': a liberal education is not in any straightforward sense an education informed by the principles of liberal political philosophy. I will draw on both senses in my discussion. In this respect, and others, my account is not a straightforward description of liberal views of the university, but rather an attempt to formulate the liberal model in a way which makes its distinctiveness as clear as possible against the background of its main competitors.

## The liberal model of the university

From a liberal perspective, universities are primarily concerned with the pursuit and dissemination of knowledge that is of universal, or at least very general, value. It is assumed that knowledge of the natural world and of human culture is achievable by rational means, and that it has intrinsic and not just extrinsic value. These ideas about the possibility and desirability of knowledge have a long history. It would be a mistake, for instance, to designate them as stemming merely from the Enlightenment. They were influential in the founding of the European universities in the Middle Ages, and of course before that they are to be found in the writings of Plato and Aristotle. The notion of knowledge for its own sake was encapsulated in the Greek concept of *theoria*, variously translated as theory, philosophy or science.[3]

Of course, the questioning of these ideas has a similarly long history. Many of the criticisms directed against the founding assumptions of the liberal model today are foreshadowed in the writings of the Greek sophists, sceptics and stoics. And while the liberal model has been extremely influential in structuring universities from their origins to the present, that influence has always been tempered by the effects of other ideas. I am not suggesting that there was once a liberal golden age from which we are in decline, simply that the relative influence of the liberal conception of the university is declining at present.

Both research and education in universities are portrayed by liberals as consisting of participation in a continuing conversation which includes not just those presently active but scholars of the past as well, with the latter represented in a literature which has both substantive and methodological significance. The term 'liberal education' is often most strongly associated today with the humanities, indeed with the idea that the humanities should be the core of the university curriculum.[4] However, this is not implied in my use of the term. For me, liberal education includes science as much as the humanities and the social sciences. We find liberal views among many writers on science. Thus, despite their substantial differences about the actual and proper practice of science, both Karl Popper and Michael Polanyi regard science as concerned with the pursuit of knowledge for its own sake. They do not deny, indeed they welcome, its practical benefits, but the pursuit of

---

[3] See Ferruolo (1985) for the argument that the establishment of the European universities was not simply a response to the demand for occupational training but more importantly reflected a commitment to the pursuit of learning. As regards the Greek origins of these ideas, see for example Lear (1988) on Aristotle. On the Greek concept of theory, see Lobkowicz (1967) and Ball (1977).

[4] For a useful review see Conrad and Wyer (1980).

such benefits is not the goal or the rationale for science as far as they are concerned. That rationale lies in the intrinsic value for human beings of knowledge of themselves and their world.[5] My definition of the liberal model is broad, then, incorporating both the liberal arts and research-based interpretations of the university ideal, which have been in conflict for much of the nineteenth and twentieth centuries.

Of course, science and the humanities do vary considerably in the character of the teaching and research that they involve: they require different sorts of conversation. In natural science, concern with the cumulation of knowledge means that both research and teaching are largely present-orientated; the literature defined as relevant has little historical depth but great contemporary breadth, so much so that it involves a very extensive division of labour. Associated with this is a relatively sharp distinction between research and teaching, with the latter conceived in large part as the dissemination of research findings and of established research skills. In the humanities, by contrast, while progress may well take place, it does not take the form of a simple cumulation of knowledge. As a result, items from a long past are often included in a single canon of literature, sometimes taken to represent timelessly valuable exemplifications of perennial themes in human life and modes of thought. We find such canons, most explicitly, in philosophy and in English literature. There may also be relatively little distinction between research and education: the work of learners and experts may be regarded as varying only in the degree of skill they exercise and knowledge they deploy, with education consisting of exemplification by the teacher and practice by the learner (along with feedback from the teacher on that practice).

These contrasting versions of the liberal model are, of course, themselves ideal types, so that their relationship to actual practice in the sciences and humanities is variable and debatable. For instance, some recent work in the philosophy and sociology of natural science has questioned the idea that it involves the cumulation of knowledge in any simple sense.[6] At the same time, the trend in the nineteenth and twentieth centuries within the humanities has been away from the model I have discussed here and towards the scientific version. For this and other reasons established canons of literature, and indeed the very idea

[5] Popper does not state this explicitly, but it seems to me to inform his whole account of science, and is not incompatible either with his evolutionary epistemology or with his recommendation of piecemeal social engineering based on applied research. Furthermore, it is congruent with his political liberalism; see, for instance, Popper (1963: chs 17, 18). Polanyi is very explicit about this issue: see Polanyi (1961, 1962).

[6] The work of Kuhn (1970) has been the stimulus for much reconsideration of the notion of scientific progress. See also Newton-Smith (1981).

of a canon, have come under increasing attack (Searle 1990; Gorak 1991).

The social sciences are, of course, the major battleground between these conflicting views. But this battle is not of direct relevance to my concerns in this chapter. For present purposes, the contrast I have drawn between science and the humanities serves merely to indicate the range of forms of research and education, and of thinking about them, which I am including under the heading of the liberal model.

There are two other principles central to the liberal model besides the rational pursuit, and dissemination, of intrinsically valuable knowledge. While subordinate to the first, they are nevertheless important. These are academic autonomy and neutrality. Academic autonomy is often referred to, perhaps rather misleadingly, as 'academic freedom'. This is the requirement that the pursuit of knowledge be relatively unconstrained by extraneous demands, such as those deriving from the political interests of the state or of powerful religious or economic groups in society. This principle concerns both the relationship between universities and outside agencies *and* that between individual academics and those involved in the management and administration of universities. The core of academic autonomy is the right of the individual academic to teach and research as he or she judges appropriate, supported with some resources, and (within broad boundaries) to be accountable only on academic grounds and to academic authorities.[7]

We must be careful not to assume that the liberal model requires complete autonomy. It does not. *Complete* autonomy would involve giving academics an absolute right to ignore ethical considerations and to transgress civil and criminal law, and this would be unacceptable from a liberal point of view. Academic freedom is not an all or nothing matter, then, and for that (and other) reasons it will always be contested, as it has been in the past. We are certainly seeing a major contraction of the autonomy of universities in Britain today. And this is part of a wider trend across the Western world. But, as Guy Neave (1988) has pointed out, the patterns of academic autonomy have long varied substantially even among European societies.

We can get a sense of this by looking at the case of German universities in the nineteenth century. These were widely admired elsewhere in Europe and in the USA, yet German professors were state employees (as they still are), and professorial appointments were formally made by

---

[7] This may usefully be seen as an example of the licence and mandate granted to professionals, see Hughes (1971: 287–92). This definition of academic autonomy is narrower than that often employed, where it is identified with civil liberties in general. On the history and definition of the concept of academic freedom see Hofstadter and Metzger (1955) and the chapters by van Alystyne, Searle, Rorty and Schmitt in Pincoffs (1975).

the German state governments. The convention was that the relevant faculty submitted a list of candidates and the State Education Minister appointed someone from this list. Furthermore, this convention was sometimes broken. One such case led Max Weber to write several newspaper articles on the issue of academic freedom (Weber 1974). It is worth pointing out too that the academic freedom which existed within German universities in the nineteenth and early twentieth centuries was concentrated on a small professoriate who in many ways restricted the autonomy of junior staff. In these respects academic autonomy was more limited at that time in Germany than, say, in Britain.

Of course, Weber was not concerned only with preserving academic autonomy. Indeed, today his name is probably most closely associated with the third and final element of the liberal model I want to discuss: academic neutrality. His concern with neutrality emerges clearly in one of the newspaper articles I mentioned above. Having argued that the goal of the university is the pursuit and dissemination of rationally founded knowledge, he declares that: 'universities do not have it as their task to teach any outlook or standpoint which is either "hostile to the state" or "friendly to the state".' Research and teaching within them must be neutral in the sense that: 'they are not institutions for the inculcation of absolute or ultimate moral values' (Weber 1974: 21).[8]

There can be few concepts that have been subject to more misunderstanding than Weber's concept of value neutrality. In arguing that research and teaching within universities be value neutral, Weber was not suggesting that they can or should be concerned only with descriptive facts about the state of the world, free from all influence by values. He was only too well aware, as a proponent of the liberal model, that all scholarship is premissed on the value of truth. And he also emphasised, of course, that social scientists cannot understand human behaviour without taking account of the role of values in motivating it.

Beyond this, though, Weber argued that social scientists, like historians, are primarily interested in unique individual phenomena, and that these must be selected, indeed constructed, on the basis of values other than truth. This is the principle of value relevance, and it means that practical values play a key role for Weber, quite legitimately, in defining the phenomena on which research and teaching in the humanities and social sciences focus. Finally, and just as importantly, Weber

---

[8] Interestingly, elsewhere in the same article, Weber qualifies this position: 'The one element of any "genuine" ultimate outlook which they [universities] can legitimately offer their students to aid them in their path through life is the habit of accepting the obligation of intellectual integrity; this entails a relentless clarity about themselves. Everything else – the entire substance of his aspirations and goals – the individual must achieve for himself in confronting the tasks and problems of life' (1974: 21).

argues that social scientists can engage in the rational assessment of value judgments and the prescription of morally appropriate and technically effective means to given goals, *relative to ultimate values* (Bruun 1972; Keat and Urry 1975: ch. 9).

In short, neutrality towards values for Weber concerns only what he calls absolute or ultimate values, only the selection of these is excluded from the realm of rational inquiry. He believed that all particular value judgments, whether evaluations or prescriptions, can be traced back to some set of ultimate values beyond which justification cannot go. At that level one simply accepts or does not accept a particular value: there is no rational basis for choosing among ultimate values. Furthermore, he regarded those ultimate values as in conflict, so that one cannot choose to live by them all. Against this background, the principle of value neutrality was a device to prevent social scientists smuggling their own ultimate values into their research and teaching, and thereby presenting these as if they were rationally justified. It was, and is, a barrier against scientism or scientific imperialism.

Properly understood, Weber's position is a subtle and powerful one. Even so, in my view, it is not an entirely satisfactory interpretation of the concept of academic neutrality. It has been subjected to powerful criticisms by those in the natural law tradition, notably Strauss and Midgley, and also by Habermas (Strauss 1953; Habermas 1976; Midgley 1983). Habermas, for instance, has pointed out that Weber's position renders all ethical and political decisions irrational. The natural law theorists make an even more fundamental point: that Weber's position renders irrational the whole of science, and also his own arguments for value neutrality. This is because all of these are necessarily based on an irrational commitment to truth.

However, I think we can adopt most of Weber's account of the role of values in social science, and his recognition that value conflict seems endemic (in modern societies anyway), without accepting his Nietzschean view of the irrationality of value commitment. But in order to do so we must construct a somewhat different view of what academic neutrality entails. Rather than seeing liberal neutrality in heroic terms, it is better regarded as a pragmatic adaptation to the existence and intractability of disagreement about both factual and value matters. What it amounts to is an agreement to rely only on, or only to present as true without evidence, knowledge claims which other members of the relevant research community accept as true. It seems to me that this is an essential element of the operation of what Polanyi (1962) calls 'the republic of science'.

It is here that the meaning of the term 'liberal' as used in political philosophy becomes relevant to my argument. The origins of liberal political philosophy lie in the religious and political conflicts of the sixteenth and seventeenth centuries. It is no accident that at that time there was a revival of interest in the writings of the Greek sceptics (Popkin 1979). Where before there had been at least the hope of widespread acceptance of a comprehensive religious and philosophical view of the world, of the kind put forward by Thomas Aquinas, by the seventeenth century it had become clear that any such hope was ill founded. As a result, in political philosophy there was a gradual change from a conception of the state as promoting virtue among its citizens to one that saw it as simply preserving the minimum conditions for a tolerable life, for example avoiding conflicts between religious groups by allowing them freedom to live by their own ideals.

We can see a related change in ideas about knowledge and education at about the same time. There is a shift from the assumption that a rationally based comprehensive world view can be constructed, and should provide the framework for inquiry and teaching, to recognition that there is substantial and apparently endemic disagreement about many important matters. The medieval Scholastics gained a reputation for interminable dispute, and this was one of the factors leading to the subsequent influence of scepticism. What the scientific revolution of the seventeenth century made clear, however, was that complete scepticism about the possibility of knowledge was not necessary: some rational knowledge was possible. Yet that knowledge was only attainable if science was not restricted by theological and metaphysical dogma. At the same time, it became apparent that such knowledge was not immediately accessible in all areas. So, science did not presuppose a well-worked out and rationally established metaphysical framework, nor did it promise to produce such a framework in the foreseeable future (though some involved in the new science believed that it could, Descartes and Leibniz for example). Successful as the new science was in generating widespread agreement about some matters, it was spectacularly unsuccessful at producing such agreement in other areas, notably about ethical and political issues, and about human behaviour generally.

Arising from this background, what is central to the liberal model of the university, as of the polity, is that the existence of conflicting views, and our inability to resolve many of these conflicts, is recognised and accommodated, rather than being ignored or treated as something which can be transcended through the construction of some overarching system. We must not pretend that something has been rationally established when it has not. What neutrality means, then, is neutrality about those matters where rational agreement has not yet been reached. In neither research nor teaching, the liberal insists, must claims be presented as knowledge if they are subject to widespread rational disagreement. And implied in this is a relatively modest assessment of the current state of knowledge.

There are two main differences between this interpretation of the concept of neutrality and that of Weber. One is that neutrality is not restricted to ultimate values: it can include practical value judgments and even factual claims about which there is genuine disagreement. The other is that value judgments are treated as open in principle to rational agreement in much the same way as are factual matters: however, they require somewhat different sorts of evidence, and it is likely to be more difficult to reach agreement about them.

### The liberal university and its critics

I will identify two major sources of criticism of the liberal model deriving from alternative views of the social role of universities, what I referred to earlier as the economic and the ideological models. First, though, let me outline the nature of those two models.

### *The economic model*

The economic model sees the primary task of universities as the efficient provision of training for potential recruits to those occupations deemed to require a high level of knowledge and skills. From this point of view, education is a type of investment which has both an individual and a social (or a national) return. Similarly, research is regarded as of value only to the extent that it solves technical problems faced by government, industry and the professions. This is what is sometimes referred to as the engineering model of the research–practice relationship (see Chapter 7).[9] Knowledge is seen, then, as directed towards practical goals and its value is judged primarily if not solely in these terms. The economic model is often associated with an instrumentalist conception of knowledge, perhaps even with a rejection of any concern about the truth of knowledge over and above its usefulness. Indeed, 'truth' may be redefined as usefulness.

The current popularity of the economic model in British government circles is manifest, but this popularity extends more widely, across the political spectrum and also into the universities themselves. Substantial numbers of academics today probably see their role largely in terms of the economic model, though they may seek to combine this

[9] The growth of the economics of education indicates the increasing influence of the economic model. A key early text exemplifying this model of the university is Kerr (1964). The Robbins Report's arguments for coordination and expansion of higher education were also in large part premised on arguments deriving from this model (Robbins 1963). In relation to research, the growth of science policy studies is an equivalent indicator. It should be said, though, that many lay advocates of the economic model hold to doctrines now abandoned by most educational economists. On the second generation of studies in the economics of education, see Blaug (1983).

with adherence to other views. And, of course, the idea that universities are, and should be, engaged in vocational training is by no means new. Since their beginnings, European universities have been concerned, to one degree or another, with occupational preparation for those entering the Church, the state, and the professions. However, I think there has been a significant shift in the character and conceptualisation of such preparation in the twentieth century: from what we might call a professional to a market orientation. The professional orientation views the occupational task as a sacred calling which requires a cultured outlook, rather than mere technical expertise, and is accompanied by a sense of the responsibility and dignity of the office. The sacred element applied literally in the case of training for the Church, but it was extended metaphorically to other professions. Interestingly, the sense of sacredness seems to have stemmed in part from the cultural aura supplied by the knowledge produced in the universities. This provided the latter with some autonomy from the demands of practitioner communities. This version of occupational preparation was and is broadly compatible with the liberal model.

Market orientation, by contrast, implies a much more instrumental and specific attitude to the occupational task and to what is required for its performance. This seems to leave little room for academic autonomy: what is to be taught as well as judgments about how effectively it is being taught seem to lie with those who are to recruit university graduates, or with government authorities acting on their behalf. Similarly, the priorities for research are to be decided by customers or by government agencies. In Britain, the Rothschild Report's contract model of applied research is an influential model for this approach (Rothschild 1971; but see also Rothschild 1982: 9–15). In my view, it is very questionable whether there can be much compatibility between this version of the economic model and liberalism as I have defined it here. The goal is no longer the pursuit and dissemination of knowledge which has universal validity and relevance, but rather servicing the needs of a particular national economy. And it follows from this that autonomy is not required, indeed is not desirable. Nor is neutrality. What is to be discovered and taught is simply what meets national, organisational or occupational needs, and there may be proscription of anything judged to be inimical (or even irrelevant) to those needs.[10]

[10] In the case of national needs, what these are may be decided by the government or be left for resolution by market forces. Thus, there are both statist and free market versions of the economic model. There is an interesting question here about the relationship between what I have called the liberal model and economic liberalism, as developed by Hayek and Friedman. My view is close to that of Polanyi: the market is a different form of autonomous organisation from that characteristic of science, though they both come under the value of autonomy (see Polanyi 1968).

*The ideological model*

What I mean by the ideological model is the view that universities should promote a single, comprehensive view of the world in which is embedded a particular set of political or religious ideals.[11] While the pursuit and dissemination of knowledge (especially the latter) remain the goal of the university, advocates of this model reject the principle of neutrality, or minimise its scope, since in their judgment there are few major issues on which reasonable doubt remains: the general framework into which all knowledge fits is already known. Furthermore, what is taken to be known is defined by some central authority, not by members of the 'republic of science', and so only very limited autonomy is required and allowed.

The term 'ideological model' covers a very wide range of possible and actual cases. We can think of the European universities in some periods of the Middle Ages as coming close to this type. And when Protestants gained control over universities after the Reformation, a similar imposition of religious doctrine occurred (Hofstadter and Metzger 1955: ch. 1; Green 1969: ch. 3; McLaughlin 1990). Catholic universities today still bear some resemblance to this model, and even more so fundamentalist Protestant colleges. In these examples knowledge is explicitly founded on faith, but the ideological model comes in secular form as well. The German National Socialist universities of the 1930s and 1940s are examples, so are the Marxist–Leninist universities of Eastern Europe in the mid-twentieth century.[12]

Diverse philosophical resources have been drawn on to support institutions approximating to the ideological model. Relevant here are Heidegger's speeches when he was rector of Freiburg University under the Nazis, and it has been argued by some that his National Socialism derived directly from his philosophy (Löwith 1988). In the case of

---

[11] The term 'ideological model' can be read as derogatory, and indeed so it is from a liberal point of view, but I will endeavour to use it in a descriptive sense here. It corresponds broadly to what Kolakowski (1975b) refers to as the 'totalitarian conception of the university'. More than I do, he emphasises the duty of the liberal university to promote and defend its core values in society, though he also sees neutrality as a strategy designed to protect the university against outside pressures.

[12] On the problem of academic freedom in Catholic universities, see Curran (1990). For a detailed account of a fundamentalist Protestant college, see Peshkin (1986). On the National Socialist takeover of German universities, see Hartshorne (1937). Immediately after the 1917 Revolution, the Soviet reformers seem to have retained some commitment to liberal ideals, but these were soon casualties of their battles with the universities whose staff and students were generally anti-communist (see Fitzpatrick 1970: 68–88). (Pre-revolutionary Russian universities were, of course, not very liberal, see McClelland 1979.) For a useful overview of Soviet higher education, see Matthews (1982: ch. 4). In practice, Eastern European universities seem to have also operated under the influence of a version of the economic model.

Eastern Europe, Marx was of course the authority for claims that the universities there exercised positive intellectual freedom rather than the purely negative freedom of bourgeois institutions.[13] Much more recently, Alasdair MacIntyre (1990) has proposed a view of the university which seems to come close to the ideological model, drawing on Thomism. He argues that 'reason can only move toward being genuinely universal and impersonal insofar as it is neither neutral nor disinterested, that membership in a particular type of moral community, one from which fundamental dissent has been excluded, is a condition for genuinely rational enquiry' (MacIntyre 1990: 59–60).

The criticisms of the liberal university made by advocates of the economic and ideological models can be listed under two main headings: what I will call the political and the cognitive challenges.

*The political challenge*

A common criticism of what is produced and taught under the auspices of the liberal model is that a lot of it is of no practical relevance; and this usually means, of course, of no economic or political relevance. Even when the results of research or of what is taught relate to an important topic, it is argued, this knowledge is often merely theoretical – it does not address the practical problems that people face.[14] One way to formulate this criticism is by means of the concept of citizenship, concentrating on what is expected of individuals, groups and institutions that form part of a community. There are two ways in which the liberal university may stand condemned in these terms.

First, liberal political philosophy implies a very thin concept of citizenship, and the concept of liberal education I have outlined here conforms to this. Weber's restriction of the moral teaching of universities to intellectual integrity (see note 8) is not uncharacteristic; though, of course, for most of their history universities have in effect played a broader role than this, notably in preparing future members of governing elites. Similarly, research in the liberal university displays only a very limited concern with its political and practical payoffs.

Worse still, and this is the second point, in modern times the concept

---

[13] On Heidegger's justification for the National Socialist university, see Heidegger (1985, 1988); and for background, see Janicaud (1989), Sluga (1989), Wolin (1990) and Zuckert (1990). The concept of positive freedom is usefully discussed by Singer (1983: ch. 3). See Popper (1966) for the argument that Hegelianism and Marxism are inherently totalitarian.

[14] One of the most influential deployments of this argument in Britain in recent years has been against the teaching of 'educational theory', including the sociology of education, to trainee teachers. This was usually combined with another criticism which I will examine below: that the teaching of theory to teachers, and especially of sociology, has had undesirable effects.

of citizenship has become almost entirely associated with the nation state, whereas the liberal model of the university implies a conception of citizenship which relates in part to international communities of scholars. The scope for conflict between liberal universities and the demands of national states is obvious here (see Kerr 1990).

Criticism of the liberal university for making an inadequate contribution to national societies raises two issues. First, we must ask whether to be of value knowledge must always be of practical use. These days this may seem hardly in need of justification, the idea that knowledge is valuable for its own sake is so widely rejected. It is worth pointing out, though, that even if we deny knowledge intrinsic value, we must treat *something* as having intrinsic value. Otherwise everything is instrumental but all to no purpose. So, if it is the notion of intrinsic value we baulk at when faced with the idea of knowledge for knowledge's sake, we must recognise that, whatever our views, this is a hurdle which has to be jumped at some point. And the ground may be no more solid in other places.

At the root of this criticism of liberalism is a disagreement about values, about the nature of the good life. From the liberal point of view, there is no single or primary good to be enshrined in public policy. One may defend the intrinsic value of knowledge without denying that other things also have intrinsic value. For the critics, by contrast, there is usually only one good. In the economic model, it is the pursuit of economic success, individually and/or nationally. From the point of view of the ideological model, it may be the religious life, in one form or another, or it may be politics. An illustration of a privileging of the political life is what Carr (1991) calls the moral model of democracy, in which self-development is identified with participation in democratic politics.

The authoritarian potentiality of views that recognise only one form of good life need hardly be underlined; we are all familiar with the idea of paradises that end in infernos. But it needs to be emphasised that even participatory democracy does not eliminate this potentiality. Even if one believes that such a form of democracy can be implemented in large societies without its degeneration into manipulation by elites, one must still recognise that majorities may tyrannise minorities and individuals within such a democratic arrangement. And such treatment is especially likely of those for whom political participation is not the most important part of life. Recognition of multiple goods leads the liberal to insist that restrictions be placed even on democratic decision-making to preserve a large degree of individual autonomy. And the need for such autonomy applies to institutions, such as universities, too.

Another important implication of the idea of multiple goods is that the liberal model does not involve the claim that the knowledge produced and disseminated in universities has intrinsic value only. It is usually claimed to have instrumental value too. Here the second issue arises: the question of the different ways in which knowledge may be useful. What the critics of liberalism usually have in mind when they declare the knowledge produced under its auspices to be of little practical relevance is the sort of usefulness represented by the supply of a hammer when one needs to knock in a nail. When a problem is faced, what is most useful is a solution to it. This is characteristic of the engineering model, and is sometimes identified with positivism (Janowitz 1972; Bulmer 1982); but something very like it also lies at the root of 'critical theory'. Such theory is seen as enlightening the oppressed about their interests and circumstances in such a way as to at least set the stage for their emancipation. In both cases, to be useful knowledge must have a powerful and direct effect on action and its success (Fay 1987).

I certainly would not want to deny the value of this sort of usefulness. But I do question the assumption that it is the *only*, or the most common, form of usefulness that knowledge can have. This is not a novel argument of course. Often contrasted with the engineering model of the relationship between research and practice is the enlightenment model. What is involved here is the provision of general resources: ways of thinking and feeling that have potential relevance to many decisions but which in most cases do not provide a solution to a problem in any direct sense. Once again, then, it seems to me that the critics would have us value only one thing where more than one is of value: both solutions to practical problems and general resources for approaching a wide range of problems are useful.

Let me turn now to a different sort of political challenge to the liberal university, this time deriving primarily from the ideological model. This is the argument that, despite its claims to neutrality, the production and dissemination of knowledge under the liberal model *does* have a significant effect on the world, and that this is an undesirable effect. Here we often have ironic contrasts made between academic claims to neutrality and the role that universities are alleged to play in society, along with accusations of naivety on the part of liberals.

There are several directions from which this argument can come, but the one that has become most familiar arises from the radical Left. It is an argument that achieved particular prominence in the late 1960s and early 1970s, but which remains popular in some quarters today. Here the liberal university is accused of serving the needs of capitalism, and/or of reinforcing hierarchies and benefiting dominant groups in other ways (see, for example, Cockburn and Blackburn 1969; Cowley 1969; Gless and Smith 1990).[15]

---

[15] Ironically, the equivalent argument from the Right is that universities, and the education system generally, are anti-capitalist.

Whether or not this charge is true is an empirical matter, and one about which there is little evidence. I will say only that it would be extraordinary if universities had had a simply negative impact on the wider society. Even putting aside the problems of determining what is a good and a bad effect, one would expect to find a complex pattern of consequences varying between institutions and over time, so that drawing up a balance sheet and calculating the relative weight of desirable and undesirable effects would produce results of questionable value.

Of more interest, though, is the denial of the very possibility of neutrality which is often associated with this view. This criticism is generally based on a mistake about what the principle of neutrality involves, taking it to imply neutrality towards all value judgments. But it is not a mistake that should be blamed entirely on the critics. There is a tendency for liberals to see liberalism as neutral, in the sense of having no substantive implications about the good life. In other words, it is seen as a formal doctrine which concerns itself solely with procedural matters. This is the basis for the distinction between the right and the good to be found in the writing of some liberal political philosophers, like John Rawls and Ronald Dworkin, and which goes back at least to Kant. But, as I argued earlier, there is no need to see liberalism in this way, and there are good reasons for not doing so. Rather, we should see it as necessarily involving some prescriptions about the good: for instance, about the value of rational knowledge, and of tolerance and individual autonomy. Liberalism is not, and cannot be, completely neutral.[16] However, it is equally important to notice that what the liberal model is committed to is minimal by comparison with the economic and ideological models: it leaves open a great deal more space for tolerable disagreement, including neutrality towards competing forms of life, than the other models. So, to accuse liberals of not being neutral towards everything is true enough, but it does not represent an effective counter to their arguments for neutrality, nor a sound criticism of their achievements in living up to that ideal (though, of course, these may be criticised on other grounds).

What liberals object to in the ideological model is the presentation as true of ideas which are open to cogent criticism. This is rejected, not least, because it blocks the road of inquiry, making the production of knowledge more difficult. However, this objection raises fundamental questions about the nature and possibility of knowledge, and this is at the heart of the second challenge to the liberal model: the cognitive challenge.

---

[16] On the issue of whether liberalism can or should avoid judgments about the good, see the discussions in Larmore (1987), Flathman (1989) and Galston (1991).

*The cognitive challenge*
This is a more fundamental challenge than the political one, since it concerns the viability of the goal of the liberal university: the pursuit and dissemination of knowledge. There are two versions of this challenge. Both of them begin from a questioning of the correspondence theory of truth and the distinction between subject and object associated with it. We can find sources for these criticisms in, respectively, Hegel's criticism of Kant, and Nietzsche's reaction against Hegel. The first underpins Marxist criticisms of the liberal university, the second motivates poststructuralist attacks on conventional scholarship (and on Marxism).[17]

Kant himself was by no means an unambiguous exponent of the correspondence theory of truth, given his insistence on our inability to know anything of the noumenal world, of things-in-themselves. However, it seems clear that he did see knowledge as something gained by a subject about objects which are independent of that subject. Hegel's criticism raised the question of how such knowledge could be possible. After all, if subject and object are separate, how can the former ever gain knowledge of the latter? For this to be possible, the object would have to be of a kind which the subject could have knowledge of. Yet there is nothing in Kant (or for that matter in the assumptions of other modern proponents of the correspondence theory of truth) that can guarantee this. Hegel's solution to this problem, inherited by Marx, is that the subject/object split does indeed obstruct and distort our knowledge of the world, even humanity's knowledge of itself, but that this split is not a permanent feature of human life. Over the course of historical development, albeit in a dialectical rather than a simply incremental fashion, subject and object come to be unified, and at the end-point true knowledge is possible. Marx differs from Hegel primarily in his views of the motor and terminus of historical development. He retains Hegel's teleological view of history, certainly in his early work.

Equally significant for subsequent developments has been the radical sociology of knowledge built into Marx's position. This treats truth as selectively available according to social location: under capitalism the proletariat have privileged (though not automatic) access to the truth about society and history because they are the universal class whose interest it is to overthrow capitalism and thereby to emancipate themselves and everyone else. This emancipation overcomes the

---

[17] For Hegel on Kant, see Singer (1983: ch. 4) and Walsh (1987). As regards Nietzsche's reaction to Hegel, see Houlgate (1986). On the poststructuralists and Nietzsche, see Dews (1987). For an interesting argument that the poststructuralists have misinterpreted Nietzsche, neglecting his later views on truth, see Clark (1990).

historical split between humanity as subject and as object. And it is this which provides the basis for Marxists' claims for the validity of their comprehensive theory of social reality (see Chapter 2).[18]

In recent years, many of the radical Left have abandoned the teleological element of this position. However, some have retained the core idea of Marx's sociology of knowledge and extended it, a good example being feminist standpoint epistemology (for example, Hartsock 1983; Harding 1986: ch. 6). Rejection of the notion of teleological historical development seems sensible. It is very difficult to defend. However, the idea that some category of human being has privileged access to the truth about society, or anything else, is just as problematic. It is almost impossible to prevent it collapsing into relativism. And, indeed, in recent years increasing numbers of social scientists have embraced relativism in one way or another, more or less explicitly. Among the most influential sources have been poststructuralists like Foucault, with Nietzsche looming in the background. Here, all knowledge is treated as simply an expression of the will to power, and therefore not as a representation of anything.

Neither Nietzsche nor Foucault is an unequivocal relativist, but their positions leave little room for rational political commitment. Thus, while Foucault's political sympathies differ markedly from those of Nietzsche, neither is able logically to treat those sympathies as anything more than irrational commitments.[19] In this respect, they are in much the same position as Weber.

A common political orientation to be found among relativists today is a form of radical democracy that involves a reaction against the way in which some voices are privileged in current social arrangements and others not heard. The relativist assumption here, of course, is that all voices are valid in their own terms, though this is often qualified by standpoint epistemology. We find this view among feminists, among advocates of constructivist epistemology and among critics of Western anthropology (see, for instance, Clifford 1986; Gless and Smith 1990; Guba 1990). Looked at from one perspective, this amounts to using relativism to question and undermine privilege. However, it involves what Woolgar and Pawluch (1985) call ontological gerrymandering: the selective application of sceptical arguments. It constitutes a futile attempt to overcome by moral means the cognitive anarchy created by relativism. And it fails because, given relativism, belief in democracy is

---

[18] For an illuminating discussion of Hegel and Marx from this point of view, see Prokopczyk (1980).

[19] On Foucault's politics, see Walzer (1983). Nietzsche was not an anti-semite or a supporter of German nationalism, but he was no democrat (see Dannhauser 1982). On the relativism of both, see Dews (1987).

no more rationally defensible than, for example, Nietzsche's politics of the 'overman' or Heidegger's National Socialism.

I am not trying to suggest that the cognitive challenge is no challenge at all, merely that the conclusions sometimes drawn from it are not convincing. Of course, the question remains of what defensible notions of knowledge and rationality are available for use by liberals. I have sought to answer this question elsewhere, arguing that a fallibilist non-foundationalism is compatible with a moderate realism, and that much the same approach can be applied to both factual and value issues (Hammersley 1992a: ch. 4).[20] The point I want to make here is that this cognitive challenge also faces proponents of the economic model, and those representatives of the ideological model who are not prepared to abandon rational argument.

Furthermore, I think the relative strengths of the liberal position are clear. It is not necessarily committed to some kind of naive foundationalism; it is compatible with subtle forms of realism, of the kind to which (it seems to me) anybody with any sort of political or ethical concerns must also be committed. Nor does the liberal model necessarily imply that rational knowledge is only available to an intellectual elite located in the universities. All that it requires is that such knowledge be possible, and that academics in universities can play a significant role in producing it. At the same time, it avoids the problems I have identified with the economic and ideological models. It does not require us to live in a society where economic success is the only criterion of value, nor are we forced to be 'good' or to be 'free' to anything like the same extent as with the ideological model. It has also shown itself to be a most effective means of producing knowledge, and there are serious doubts about the capacity of the other models in this respect (Polanyi 1962).

## Conclusion

I have argued, then, that the liberal conception of the university is organised around three key ideas. First, that the primary goal is the production and dissemination of knowledge which is intrinsically valuable and which constitutes a general cultural resource. Second and third are the supporting notions of academic autonomy and neutrality. I underlined the fact that autonomy is always a matter of degree, and that neutrality implies not treating as settled anything about which there is not substantial rational consensus.

In the second half of the chapter I looked at criticisms of this conception of the university from advocates of the economic and

---

[20] For a different approach to the same issue, see Searle (1990: 40).

ideological models. I argued that, though they raise important problems, neither the political nor the cognitive challenge to liberalism undermines it, and that none of the alternatives, nor even some form of radical democracy, offers a more convincing basis for the social organisation of the university.

As I explained at the beginning of this chapter, I have been concerned here with ideas about universities, rather than with how they are currently organised and their changing contexts. It may be, of course, that though liberal universities are desirable, they cannot survive in present political and social circumstances. Even if this is true, however, we must recognise the fact and not drift into identifying the ideal with the real. But, in any case, I think we should be suspicious of arguments which promote ideals on the grounds that they alone are politically realistic.[21] Declaring that 'there is no other way' can be a convenient device for avoiding consideration of the most important issues. And it is a strategy to which academics should be the last to resort or to succumb.

[21] Kerr (1964: 6) provides the precedent here, claiming that the 'multiversity' 'has its reality rooted in the logic of history. It is an imperative rather than a reasoned choice among elegant alternatives.'

# References

Abercrombie, N., Hill, S. and Turner, B.S. (1980) *The Dominant Ideology Thesis*, London, Allen and Unwin.

Abrams, P. (1984) 'The uses of British sociology, 1831–1981', in Bulmer (ed.) 1984.

Achinstein, P. and Barker, S.F. (1969) *The Legacy of Logical Positivism*, Baltimore, Johns Hopkins.

Acker, J., Barry, K. and Esseveld, J. (1982) 'Objectivity and truth: problems in doing feminist research', *Women's Studies International Forum*, 6, 4, 423–35.

Adorno, T.W., Albert, H., Dahrendorf, R., Habermas, J., Pilot, H. and Popper, K.R. (1976) *The Positivist Dispute in German Sociology*, London, Heinemann.

Albert, H. (1985) *Treatise on Critical Reason*, Princeton, NJ, Princeton University Press.

Alcoff, L. (1988) 'Cultural feminism vs post-structuralism: the identity crisis in feminism', *Signs*, 13, 3: 405–36.

Anderson, P. (1976) *Considerations on Western Marxism*, London, New Left Books.

Ansell-Pearson, K. (1992) 'Who is the *Übermensch*? Time, truth, and woman in Nietzsche', *Journal of the History of Ideas*, 53, 2: 309–31.

Apple, M. (1991) Foreword to Lather 1991.

Asad, T. (1975) 'Anthropological texts and ideological problems: an analysis of Cohen on Arab villages in Israel', *Economy and Society*, 4: 251–82.

Ashmore, M. (1989) *The Reflexive Thesis*, Chicago, University of Chicago Press.

Atkinson, P.A. (1990) *The Ethnographic Imagination*, London, Routledge.

Atkinson, P.A. (1992) *Understanding Ethnographic Texts*, Newbury Park, Sage.

Ayer, A. (1956) 'The Vienna Circle', in A.J. Ayer, W.C. Kneale, G.A. Paul, D.F. Pears, P.F. Strawson, G.J. Warnock, and R.H. Wolheim (eds), *The Revolution in Philosophy*, London, Macmillan.

Ball, T. (1977) 'Plato and Aristotle: the unity versus the autonomy of theory and practice', in T. Ball (ed.), *Political Theory and Political Practice*, Minnesota, University of Minneapolis Press.

Barnes, B. (1974) *Scientific Knowledge and Sociological Theory*, London, Routledge and Kegan Paul.

Barnes, B. (1982) *T.S. Kuhn and Social Science*, London, Macmillan.

Barnes, J.A. (1979) *Who Should Know What? Social science, privacy and ethics*, Harmondsworth, Penguin.

Barthes, R. (1975) *S/Z*, London, Jonathan Cape.

Becker, H.S. (1964) 'Problems in the publication of field studies', in A. Vidich, J. Bensman, and M. Stein (eds), *Reflections on Community Studies*, New York, Wiley.

Becker, H.S. (1967) 'Whose side are we on?', *Social Problems*, 14: 239–47.

Becker, H.S. (1986) *Writing for Social Scientists*, Chicago, University of Chicago Press.

Bell, C. and Roberts, H. (eds) (1984) *Social Researching: politics, problems, practice*, London, Routledge and Kegan Paul.

Berger, P. and Luckmann, T. (1967) *The Social Construction of Reality*, Harmondsworth, Penguin.

Bernstein, R.J. (1983) *Beyond Objectivism and Relativism: science, hermeneutics and praxis*, Oxford, Blackwell.

Bernstein, R.J. (1991) *The New Constellation: the ethical-political horizons of modernity/postmodernity*, Cambridge, Polity Press.

Best, S. and Kellner, D. (1991) *Postmodern Theory: critical interrogations*, London, Macmillan.

Bhaskar, R. (1978) *A Realist Theory of Science*, 2nd edn, Brighton, Harvester Press.

Bird, G. (1986) *William James*, London, Routledge and Kegan Paul.

Blair, M. (1993) 'Review of Peter Foster: policy and practice in multicultural and antiracist education', *European Journal of Intercultural Studies*, 2, 3: 63–4.

Blaug, M. (1983) 'Where are we now in the economics of education?' London, University of London Institute of Education. Reprinted in M. Blaug, *The Economics of Education and the Education of an Economist*, Aldershot, Elgar, 1987.

Bloor, D. (1976) *Knowledge and Social Imagery*, London, Routledge and Kegan Paul.

Blumenberg, H. (1983) *The Legitimacy of the Modern Age*, Cambridge, Mass., MIT Press.

Blumer, H. (1966) 'Sociological implications of the thought of George Herbert Mead', *American Journal of Sociology*, 71: 535–44.

Blumer, H. (1969) 'The methodological position of symbolic interactionism', in H. Blumer, *Symbolic Interactionism*, Englewood Cliffs, Prentice Hall.

Boelen, W.A.M. (1992) 'Street corner society: Cornerville revisited', *Journal of Contemporary Ethnography*, 21, 1: 11–51.

Bogard, W. (1990) 'Closing down the social; Baudrillard's challenge to contemporary sociology', *Sociological Theory*, 8, 1: 1–15.

Bowles, G. and Duelli Klein, R. (eds) (1983) *Theories of Women's Studies*, London, Routledge and Kegan Paul.

Brinton, C. (1967a) 'Enlightenment', in Edwards (ed.) 1967.

Brinton, C. (1967b) 'Romanticism', in Edwards (ed.) 1967.

Brodkey, L. (1987) *Academic Writing as Social Practice*, Philadelphia, Temple University Press.

Bruun, H.H. (1972) *Science, Values, and Politics in Max Weber's Methodology*, Copenhagen, Munksgaard.

Bryant, C.G.A. (1985) *Positivism in Social Theory and Research*, London, Macmillan.

Bubner, R. (1982) 'Habermas's concept of critical theory', in Thompson and Held (eds) 1982.

Buck-Morss, S. (1977) *The Origin of Negative Dialectics*, Hassocks, Sussex, Harvester.

Bulmer, M. (1982) *The Uses of Social Research*, London, Allen and Unwin.

Bulmer, M. (ed.) (1984) *Essays on the History of British Sociological Research*, Cambridge, Cambridge University Press.

Bunge, M. (ed.) (1964) *The Critical Approach to Science and Philosophy*, New York, Free Press.

Burger, T. (1976) *Max Weber's Theory of Concept Formation: history, laws and ideal types*, Durham, NC, Duke University Press.

Burgess, R.G. (1984) *In the Field: an introduction to field research*, London, Allen and Unwin.

Burgess, R.G. (ed.) (1985) *Issues in Educational Research: qualitative methods*, Lewes, Falmer.

Bury, J.B. (1932) *The Idea of Progress*, London, Macmillan.

Carby, H. (1982) 'White woman listen! Black feminism and the boundaries of sisterhood', in Centre for Contemporary Cultural Studies (ed.), *The Empire Strikes Back: race and racism in 70s Britain*, London, Hutchinson.

Carr, W. (1987) 'What is an educational practice?' *Journal of Philosophy of Education*, 21, 2: 163–75.

Carr, W. (1991) 'Education for citizenship', *British Journal of Educational Studies*, 39, 4: 373–85.

Carr, W. and Kemmis, S. (1986) *Becoming Critical*, Lewes, Falmer Press.

Carspecken, P.F. and Apple, M. (1992) 'Critical qualitative research: theory, methodology and practice', in LeCompte et al. (eds) 1992.

Chisholm, L. (1990) 'Action research: some methodological and political considerations', *British Educational Research Journal*, 16, 3: 249–57.

Chisholm, R. (1941) 'Sextus Empiricus and modern empiricism', *Philosophy of Science*, 8: 341–84.

Churchland, P.M. and Hooker, C.A. (1985) *Images of Science: essays on realism and empiricism*, Chicago, University of Chicago Press.

Clark, M. (1990) *Nietzsche on Truth and Philosophy*, Cambridge, Cambridge University Press.

Clegg, S. (1975) 'Feminist methodology – fact or fiction', *Quality and Quantity*, 19: 83–97.

Clifford, J. (1981) 'On ethnographic surrealism', *Comparative Studies in Society and History*, 23, 4: 539–64.

Clifford, J. (1986) 'Introduction: partial truths', in Clifford and Marcus (eds) 1986.

Clifford, J. (1988) *The Predicament of Culture: twentieth century ethnography, literature, and art*, Cambridge, Mass., Harvard University Press.

Clifford, J. and Marcus, G. (eds) (1986) *Writing Culture: the poetics and politics of ethnography*, Berkeley, University of California Press.

Cockburn, A. and Blackburn, R. (1969) *Student Power*, Harmondsworth, Penguin.

Code, L. (1991) *What Can She Know? Feminist theory and the construction of knowledge*, Ithaca, Cornell University Press.

Cohen, G.A. (1978) *Karl Marx's Theory of History*, Oxford, Clarendon Press.

Cohen, P.S. (1980) 'Is positivism dead?', *Sociological Review*, 28: 141–76.

Cohen, R.S. (1967) 'Otto Neurath', in Edwards (ed.) 1967.

Coleman, J. (1972) *Policy Research in the Social Sciences*, Morristown, NJ, General Learning Press.

Collier, A. (1979) 'In defence of epistemology', in Mepham and Hillel-Ruben (eds) 1979.

Connerton, P. (ed.) (1976) *Critical Sociology*, Harmondsworth, Penguin.

Connolly, P. (1992) 'Playing it by the rules: the politics of research in "race" and education', *British Educational Research Journal*, 18, 2: 133–48.

Conrad, C. and Wyer J. (1980) *Liberal Education in Transition*, Washington, DC, American Association for Higher Education.

Cook, J.A. and Fonow, M.M. (1986) 'Knowledge and women's interests: issues of epistemology and methodology in feminist sociological research', *Sociological Inquiry*, 56, 1: 2–29.

Cowley, J. (1969) 'The strange death of the liberal university', *Socialist Register*, London, Merlin.

Crouch, C. and Heath, A. (eds) (1992) *Social Research and Social Reform: essays in honour of A.H. Halsey*, Oxford, Oxford University Press.

Culler, J. (1992) 'In defence of overinterpretation', in U. Eco (ed.) *Interpretation and Overinterpretation*, Cambridge, Cambridge University Press.

Curran, C. (1990) *Catholic Higher Education, Theology and Academic Freedom*, Notre Dame, University of Notre Dame Press.

Dannhauser, W.J. (1982) 'The trivialization of Friedrich Nietzsche', *American Spectator*, 15, 5: 7–13.

Davis, A. (1981) *Women, Race and Class*, New York, Random House.

Deem, R. (1990) 'Gender, work and leisure in the eighties: looking backwards, looking forwards', *Work, Employment and Society*, special issue: 103–23.

Demerath, N.J. and Peterson, R.A. (eds) (1967) *System, Change and Conflict*, New York, Free Press.

Dennis, N. and Halsey, A.H. (1988) *English Ethical Socialism*, Oxford, Oxford University Press.

Denzin, N.K. (1992) 'Whose Cornerville is it, anyway?', *Journal of Contemporary Ethnography*, 21, 1: 120–35.

Denzin, N.K. and Lincoln, Y.S. (eds) (1994) *Handbook of Qualitative Research*, Thousand Oaks, Sage.

Department of Science (1993) *Realising Our Potential: a strategy for science, engineering and technology*, London, HMSO.

Descombes, V. (1980) *Modern French Philosophy*, Cambridge, Cambridge University Press.

Dews, P. (1986) 'The *nouvelle philosophie* and Foucault', in M. Gane (ed.), *Towards a Critique of Foucault*, London, Routledge and Kegan Paul.

Dews, P. (1987) *Logics of Disintegration: post-structuralist thought and the claims of critical theory*, London, Verso.

Dijk, T. van (1993a) 'Editor's foreword', *Discourse and Society*, 4, 2: 131–2.

Dijk, T. van (1993b) 'Principles of critical discourse analysis', *Discourse and Society*, 4, 2: 249–84.

Dixon, P. (1971) *Rhetoric*, London, Methuen.

Docherty, T. (ed.) (1992) *Postmodernism: a reader*, New York, Harvester Wheatsheaf.

Dorst, J.D. (1989) *The Written Suburb: an ethnographic dilemma*, Philadelphia, University of Pennsylvania Press.

Douglas, J.D. (1976) *Investigative Social Research*, Beverly Hills, Sage.

Dray, W. (1957) *Laws and Explanation in History*, Oxford, Oxford University Press.

Dryzek, J. (1990) *Discursive Democracy: politics, policy, and political science*, Cambridge, Cambridge University Press.

Du Bois, B. (1983) 'Passionate scholarship: notes on values, knowing and method in feminist social science', in Bowles and Duelli Klein (eds) 1983.

Edmondson, R. (1984) *Rhetoric in Sociology*, London, Macmillan.

Edwards, P. (ed.) (1967) *The Encyclopedia of Philosophy*, New York, Macmillan.

Eisner, E. (1983) 'Anastasia may still be alive, but the monarchy is dead', *Educational Researcher*, 12, 5: 13–14, 23.

Eisner, E. and Peshkin, A. (eds) (1990) *Qualitative Inquiry: the continuing debate*, New York, Teachers College Press.

Elliott, J. (1988) 'Response to Patricia Broadfoot's Presidential Address', *British Educational Research Journal*, 14, 2: 191–4.

Erickson, K.T. (1967) 'A comment on disguised observation in sociology', *Social Problems*, 14: 366–73.

Fay, B. (1975) *Social Theory and Political Practice*, London, Allen and Unwin.

Fay, B. (1987) *Critical Social Science: liberation and its limits*, Cambridge, Polity.

Feigl, H. (1969) 'The origin and spirit of logical positivism', in Achinstein and Barker (eds) 1969.

Ferruolo, S.C. (1985) *The Origins of the University: the schools of Paris and their critics*, Stanford, Stanford University Press.

Finch, J. (1984) '"It's great to have someone to talk to": the ethics and politics of interviewing women', in Bell and Roberts (eds) 1984.

Finch, J. (1985) 'Social policy and education: problems and possibilities of using qualitative research', in Burgess (ed.) 1985.

Finch, J. (1986) *Research and Policy: the uses of qualitative methods in social and educational research*, Lewes, Falmer.

Fitzpatrick, S. (1970) *The Commissariat of Enlightenment: Soviet organisation of education and the arts under Lunarcharsky, October 1917–1921*, Cambridge, Cambridge University Press.

Flathman, R. (1989) *Towards a Liberalism*, Ithaca, Cornell University Press.

Flax, J. (1986) 'Gender as a problem: in and for feminist theory', *American Studies*, 31, 2: 193–213.

Flax, J. (1987) 'Postmodernism and gender relations in feminist theory', *Signs*, 12, 4: 621–43.

Fonow, M.M. and Cook, J.A. (eds) (1991) *Beyond Methodology: feminist scholarship as lived research*, Bloomington, Indiana, Indiana University Press.

Foster, P. (1989) 'Policy and practice in multicultural and anti-racist education'. Unpublished PhD thesis, Open University.

Foster, P. (1990a) *Policy and Practice in Multicultural and Anti-racist Education*, London, Routledge.

Foster, P. (1990b) 'Cases not proven: an evaluation of two studies of teacher racism', *British Educational Research Journal*, 16, 4: 335–48.

Foster, P. (1991) 'Cases still not proven: a reply to Cecile Wright', *British Educational Research Journal*, 17, 2: 165–70.

Foster, P. (1992) 'What are Connolly's rules? A reply to Paul Connolly', *British Educational Research Journal*, 18, 2: 149–54.

Foster, P. (1993a) 'Teacher attitudes and Afro-Caribbean achievement', *Oxford Review of Education*, 18, 3: 269–82.

Foster, P. (1993b) 'Some problems in identifying racial/ethnic equality or inequality in schools', *British Journal of Sociology*, 44, 3: 519–35.

Foster, P. (1993c) 'Equal treatment and cultural difference in multi-ethnic schools: a critique of teacher ethnocentrism theory', *International Studies in the Sociology of Education*, 2, 1: 89–103.

Foucault, M. (1977) *Language, Counter-Memory, Practice: selected essays and interviews*, Oxford, Blackwell.

van Fraassen, B. (1980) *The Scientific Image*, Oxford, Oxford University Press.

Fukuyama, F. (1989) 'The end of history', *The National Interest*, 16 (summer).

Fukuyama, F. (1992) *The End of History and the Last Man*, New York, Free Press.

Gage, N. (1989) 'The paradigm wars and their aftermath: a "historical" sketch of research on teaching since 1989', *Educational Researcher*, 18: 4–10.

Galston, W. (1991) *Liberal Purposes: goods, virtues and diversity in the liberal state*, Cambridge, Cambridge University Press.

Gane, M. (1992) 'Nietzsche's imaginary lovers', *Economy and Society*, 21, 2: 173–91.

Gelsthorpe, L. (1992) 'Response to Martyn Hammersley's paper "On feminist methodology"', *Sociology*, 26, 2: 213–8.

Geuss, R. (1981) *The Idea of Critical Theory*, Cambridge, Cambridge University Press.

Giddens, A. (1973) *Class Structure of the Advanced Societies*, London, Hutchinson.

Giddens, A. (1979) 'Positivism and its critics', in T. Bottomore and R. Nisbet (eds), *A History of Sociological Analysis*, London, Heinemann.

Gilbert, G.N. and Mulkay, M. (1984) *Opening Pandora's Box: a sociological analysis of scientists' discourse*, Cambridge, Cambridge University Press.

Gillborn, D. and Drew, D. (1992) '"Race", class and school effects', *New Community*, 18, 4: 551–65.

Gillborn, D. and Drew, D. (1993) 'The politics of research: some observations on "methodological purity"', *New Community*, 19, 2: 354–60.

Gillies, D. (1993) *Philosophy of Science in the Twentieth Century*, Oxford, Blackwell.

Gitlin, A.D., Siegel, M. and Boru, K. (1989) 'The politics of method: from leftist ethnography to educative research', *Qualitative Studies in Education*, 2, 3: 237–53.

Glass, D.V. (1950) 'The application of social research', *British Journal of Sociology*, 1: 17–30.

Glazer, N. (1988) *The Limits of Social Policy*, Cambridge, Mass., Harvard University Press.

Gless, D. and Smith, B.H. (eds) (1990) *The Politics of Liberal Education*, Durham, NC, Duke University Press.

Goldthorpe, J.H. (1967) 'Social stratification in industrial society', in R. Bendix and S.M. Lipset (eds), *Class, Status, and Power*, 2nd edn, London, Routledge and Kegan Paul.

Gomm, R. (1993) 'Issues of power in health and social welfare', in J. Walmsley, J. Reynolds, P. Shakespeare and R. Woolf (eds), *Health, Welfare, and Practice*, London, Sage.

Gorak, J. (1991) *The Making of the Modern Canon*, London, Athlone.

Gouldner, A. (1965) 'Explorations in applied social science', in A.W. Gouldner and S.M. Miller (eds), *Applied Sociology: opportunities and problems*, New York, Free Press.

Gouldner, A. (1970) *The Coming Crisis of Western Sociology*, New York, Basic Books.

Graham, (1983) 'Do her answers fit his questions? Women and the survey method', in E. Garmarnikow, D. Morgan, J. Purvis and D. Taylorson (eds), *The Public and the Private*, London, Heinemann.

Gray, J. (1986) *Liberalism*, Milton Keynes, Open University Press.

Green, V.H.H. (1969) *The Universities*, Harmondsworth, Penguin.

Gregory, R. (1989) 'Political rationality or "incrementalism"? Charles E. Lindblom's enduring contribution to public policy making theory', *Policy and Politics*, 17, 2: 139–53.

Guba, E. (ed.) (1990) *The Paradigm Dialog*, Newbury Park, Sage.

Guba, E. (1992) 'Relativism', *Curriculum Inquiry*, 22, 1: 17–23.

Gubrium, J. F. and Silverman, D. (eds) (1989) *The Politics of Fieldwork: sociology beyond enlightenment*, London, Sage.

Gustavsen, B. (1986) 'Social research as participative dialogue', in F. Heller (ed.), *The Use and Abuse of Social Science*, London, Sage.

Habermas, J. (1968a) 'Appendix: Knowledge and human interests, a general perspective', in Habermas 1968b.

Habermas, J. (1968b) *Knowledge and Interest*, English trans, Cambridge, Polity Press, 1987.

Habermas, J. (1971) *Theory and Practice*, English trans, Cambridge, Polity Press, 1988.

Habermas, J. (1976) 'The analytical theory of science and dialectics', in Adorno et al. (eds) (1976).

Habermas, J. (1993) 'Notes on the developmental history of Horkheimer's work', *Theory, Culture and Society*, 10, 2: 61–77.

Hacking, I. (ed.) (1981) *Scientific Revolutions*, Oxford, Oxford University Press.

Hage, J. and Meeker, B.F. (1988) *Social Causality*, London, Unwin Hyman.

Hahn, O., Neurath, O. and Carnap, R. (1929) 'The scientific conception of the world: the Vienna Circle', in O. Neurath, *Empiricism and Sociology*, Dordrecht, Reidel, 1973.

Halfpenny, P. (1982) *Positivism and Sociology: explaining social life*, London, Allen and Unwin.

Hall, B., Gillet, A. and Tandon, R. (eds) (1982) *Creating Knowledge: a monopoly?*, New Delhi, Society for Participatory Research in Asia.

Halsey, A.H. (1982) 'Provincials and professionals: the British post-war sociologists', *Archives Européennes de Sociologie*, 23, 1: 150–75.

Halsey, A.H., Floud, J. and Anderson, C.A. (eds) (1961) *Education, Economy and Society*, New York, Free Press.

Halsey, A.H., Heath, A.F. and Ridge, J.M. (1980) *Origins and Destinations*, Oxford, Oxford University Press.

Hamilton, D. (1980) 'Educational research and the shadow of John Stuart Mill', in Smith and Hamilton (eds) 1980.

Hammersley, M. (1989) *The Dilemma of Qualitative Method: Herbert Blumer and the Chicago tradition*, London, Routledge.

Hammersley, M. (1990) *Reading Ethnographic Research: a critical guide*, London, Longman.

Hammersley, M. (1992a) *What's Wrong with Ethnography?*, London, Routledge.

Hammersley, M. (1992b) 'The paradigm wars; reports from the front', *British Journal of Sociology of Education*, 13, 1: 131–43.

Hammersley, M. (1993a) 'On the teacher as researcher', *Educational Action Research*, 1, 3: 425–45.

Hammersley, M. (1993b) 'On methodological purism', *British Educational Research Journal*, 19, 4: 339–41.

Hammersley, M. (1994a) 'On feminist methodology: a response', *Sociology*, 28, 1: 293–300.

Hammersley, M. (1994b) 'Ethnographic writing', *Social Research Update*, 5, University of Surrey.

Hammersley, M. and Gomm, R. (1993) 'A response to Gillborn and Drew on "race", class and school effects', *New Community*, 19, 2: 348–53.

Hammersley, M. and Scarth, J. (1993) 'Beware of wise men bearing gifts: a case study in the misuse of educational research', *British Educational Research Journal*, 19, 5: 489–98.

Hammond, M., Howarth, R. and Keat, R. (1991) *Understanding Phenomenology*, Oxford, Blackwell.

Hanson, N.R. (1958) *Patterns of Discovery*, Cambridge, Cambridge University Press.

Harding, S. (1986) *The Science Question in Feminism*, Milton Keynes, Open University Press.

Harding, S. (ed.) (1987) *Feminism and Methodology*, Bloomington, Indiana University Press.

Harding, S. (1992) 'After the neutrality ideal: science, politics and "strong objectivity"', *Social Research*, 59, 3: 568–87.

Harding, S. and Hintikka, M.B. (eds) (1983) *Discovering Reality*, Dordrecht, Reidel.

Harré, R. (1986) *Varieties of Realism*, Oxford, Blackwell.

Hartshorne, E.Y. (1937) *The German Universities and National Socialism*, London, Allen and Unwin.

Hartsock, N. (1983) 'The feminist standpoint: developing the ground for a specifically feminist historical materialism', in S. Harding and Hintikka (eds) 1983.

Harvey, L. (1990) *Critical Social Research*, London, Allen and Unwin.

Haskell, T.L. (1990) 'Objectivity is not neutrality: rhetoric vs practice in Peter Novick's *That Noble Dream*', *History and Theory*, 29: 129–57.

Hawkesworth, M.E. (1989) 'Knowers, knowing and known: feminist theory and claims of truth', *Signs*, 14, 3: 533–57.

Hay, J.R. (1975) *The Origins of the Liberal Welfare Reforms, 1906–1914*, London, Macmillan.

Hayek, F.A. (1952) *The Counter-revolution of Science*, Glencoe, Ill., Free Press.

Hayek, F.A. (1967a) 'The moral element in free enterprise', in Hayek 1967b.

Hayek, F.A. (1967b) *Studies in Philosophy, Politics and Economics*, London, Routledge and Kegan Paul.

Hearn, J. and Morgan, D. (eds) (1990) *Men, Masculinities and Social Theory*, London, Unwin Hyman.

Heidegger, M. (1985) 'The self-assertion of the German university', *Review of Metaphysics*, 38: 467–80.

Heidegger, M. (1988) 'The university in the New Reich', *New German Critique*, 45: 99–101.

Hindess, B. (1987) *Freedom, Equality and the Market*, London, Tavistock.

Hirsch, E.D. (1967) *Validity in Interpretation*, New Haven, Yale University Press.

Hirst, P.H. (1983) 'Educational theory', in P.H. Hirst (ed.), *Educational Theory and its Foundation Disciplines*, London, Routledge and Kegan Paul.

Hofstadter, R. and Metzger, W. (1955) *The Development of Academic Freedom in the United States*, New York, Columbia University Press.

Hollway, W. (1989) *Subjectivity and Method in Psychology*, London, Sage.

Holstein, J.A. and Miller, G. (eds) (1993) *Reconsidering Social Constructionism: debates in social problems theory*, New York, Aldine de Gruyter.

Homan, R. (1991) *The Ethics of Social Research*, London, Longman.

Honneth, A. (1987) 'Critical theory', in A. Giddens and J.H. Turner (eds), *Social Theory Today*, Cambridge, Polity Press.

Horkheimer, M. (1972) 'Traditional and critical theory', in *Critical Theory: selected essays*, New York, Seabury Press.

Horkheimer, M. and Adorno, T. (1973) *The Dialectic of the Enlightenment*, London, Allen Lane.

Houlgate, S. (1986) *Hegel, Nietzsche and the Criticism of Metaphysics*, Cambridge, Cambridge University Press.

Huber, J. (1973) 'Symbolic interactionism as a pragmatic perspective: the bias of emergent theory', *American Sociological Review*, 38: 274–84.

Hughes, E.C. (1971) *The Sociological Eye*, Chicago, Aldine/Atherton.

Iggers, G.G. (1968) *The German Conception of History*, Middletown, Conn., Wesleyan University Press.

Jacob, M. (1992) 'Science and politics in the late twentieth century', *Social Research*, 59, 3: 487–503.

Janicaud, D. (1989) 'Heidegger's politics: determinable or not?', *Social Research*, 56, 4: 819–47.

Janowitz, M. (1972) *Sociological Models and Social Policy*, Morristown, NJ, General Learning Systems.

Jansen, S.C. (1990) 'Is science a man? New feminist epistemologies and reconstructions of knowledge', *Theory and Society*, 19: 235–46.

Jay, M. (1973) *The Dialectical Imagination*, London, Heinemann.

Jay, M. (1984) *Adorno*, London, Fontana.

Jayaratne, T. Epstein (1983) 'The value of quantitative methodology for feminist research', in Bowles and Duelli Klein (eds) 1983.

Kaufmann, F. (1958) *Methodology of the Social Sciences*, New York, Humanities Press (first published 1944).

Keat, R. (1981) *The Politics of Social Theory: Habermas, Freud and the critique of positivism*, Oxford, Blackwell.

Keat, R. and Urry, J. (1975) *Social Theory as Science*, London, Routledge and Kegan Paul.

Keeves, J.P. (ed.) (1988) *Educational Research, Methodology, and Measurement: an international handbook*, Oxford, Pergamon.

Kemmis, S. (1988) 'Action research', in Keeves (ed.) 1988.

Kerr, C. (1964) 'The idea of a multiversity', in *The Uses of the University*, Cambridge, Mass., Harvard University Press.

Kerr, C. (1990) 'The internationalisation of learning and the nationalisation of the purposes of higher education: two "laws of motion" in conflict?', *European Journal of Education*, 25, 1: 5–22.

Kincheloe, J.L. and McLaren, P.L. (1994) 'Rethinking critical theory and qualitative research', in Denzin and Lincoln (eds) 1994.

Kolakowski, L. (1972) *Positivist Philosophy*, Harmondsworth, Penguin.

Kolakowski, L. (1975a) *Husserl and the Search for Certitude*, New Haven, Yale University Press.

Kolakowski, L. (1975b) 'Neutrality and academic values', in A. Montefiore (ed.), *Neutrality and Impartiality: the university and political commitment*, Cambridge, Cambridge University Press.

Kolakowski, L. (1978) *Main Currents of Marxism*, vol. 3, Oxford, Oxford University Press.

Korsch, K. (1970) *Marxism and Philosophy*, London, New Left Books (first published in German in 1923).

Krieger, S. (1983) *The Mirror Dance: identity in a women's community*, Philadelphia, Temple University Press.

Kristeva, J. (1980) 'La femme, ce n'est pas jamais ça', in E. Marks and I. de Courtivron (eds) *New French Feminisms*, Amherst, University of Massachusetts Press.

Krupat, A. (1992) *Ethnocriticism: ethnography, history and literature*, Berkeley, University of California Press.

Kuhn, T.S. (1970) *The Structure of Scientific Revolutions*, 2nd edn, Chicago, University of Chicago Press.

Laclau, E. and Mouffe, C. (1985) *Hegemony and Socialist Strategy: towards a radical democratic politics*, London, Verso.

Lakatos, I. (1970) 'Falsification and the methodology of scientific research programmes', in I. Lakatos and A. Musgrave (eds), *Criticism and the Growth of Knowledge*, Cambridge, Cambridge University Press.

Lakatos, I. (1975) *Proofs and Refutations: the logic of mathematical discovery*, Cambridge, Cambridge University Press.

Larmore, C. (1987) *Patterns of Moral Complexity*, Cambridge, Cambridge University Press.

La Rue, L. (1970) 'The black movement and women's liberation', *The Black Scholar*, May: 36–42.

Latapi, P. (1988) 'Participatory research: a new research paradigm?', *Alberta Journal of Education*, 34, 1: 310–19.

Lather, P. (1986) 'Issues of validity in openly ideological research', *Interchange*, 17, 4: 63–84.

Lather, P. (1991) *Getting Smart: feminist research and pedagogy with/in the postmodern*, New York, Routledge.

Leach, E. (1957) 'The epistemological background to Malinowski's empiricism', in R. Firth (ed.), *Man and Culture: an evaluation of the work of Bronislaw Malinowski*, London, Routledge and Kegan Paul.

Lear, J. (1988) *Aristotle: the desire to understand*, Cambridge, Cambridge University Press.

LeCompte, M.D., Millroy, W.L. and Preissle, J. (eds) (1992) *The Handbook of Qualitative Research in Education*, San Diego, Academic Press.

Lehman, T. and Young, T.R. (1974) 'From conflict theory to conflict methodology', *Sociological Inquiry*, 44, 1: 15–28.

Lewis, I. (1987) 'Encouraging reflexive teacher research', *British Journal of the Sociology of Education*, 8, 1: 95–105.

Lindblom, C. and Cohen, D. (1979) *Usable Knowledge: social science and social problem solving*, New Haven, Yale University Press.

Lloyd, C. (ed.) (1983) *Social Theory and Political Practice*, Oxford, Oxford University Press.

Lobkowicz, N. (1967) *Theory and Practice: history of a concept from Aristotle to Marx*, Notre Dame, University of Notre Dame Press.

Lobkowicz, N. (1972) 'Interest and objectivity', *Philosophy of the Social Sciences*, 2: 193–210.

Lobkowicz, N. (1987) 'The German university since World War II', *History of European Ideas*, 8, 2: 147–54.

Louch, A.R. (1966) *Explanation and Human Action*, Oxford, Blackwell.

Löwith, K. (1949) *Meaning in History*, Chicago, University of Chicago Press.

Löwith, K. (1988) 'The political implications of Heidegger's existentialism', *New German Critique*, 45: 117–34.

Lugones, M.C. and Spelman, E.V. (1983) 'Have we got a theory for you! Feminist theory, cultural imperialism and the demand for "the woman's voice"', *Women's Studies International Forum*, 6, 6: 573–81.

Lukacs, G. (1971) *History and Class Consciousness*, Cambridge, Mass. (first published in German in 1923).

Lukes, S. (1982) 'Of gods and demons: Habermas and practical reason', in Thompson and Held (eds) 1982.

Lukes, S. (1985) *Marxism and Morality*, Oxford, Oxford University Press.

Lundman, R.J. and McFarlane, P.T. (1976) 'Conflict methodology: an introduction and preliminary assessment', *Sociological Quarterly*, 17: 503–12.

van Maanen, J. (1988) *Tales of the Field: writing ethnography*, Chicago, University of Chicago Press.

McCarney, J. (1990) *Social Theory and the Crisis of Marxism*, London, Verso.

McCarthy, T. (1978) *The Critical Theory of Jürgen Habermas*, London, Hutchinson.

McClelland, J.C. (1979) *Autocrats and Academics: education culture and society in Tsarist Russia*, Chicago, University of Chicago Press.

McCloskey, D.N. (1985) *The Rhetoric of Economics*, Madison, University of Wisconsin Press.

McInnes, N. (1967) 'Georges Sorel', in Edwards (ed.) 1967.

MacIntyre, A. (1990) *Three Rival Versions of Moral Enquiry*, London, Duckworth.

McLaughlin, R.E. (1990) 'Universities, scholasticism and the origins of the German Reformation', *History of Universities*, Vol. 9, Oxford, Oxford University Press.

Mannheim, K. (1936) *Ideology and Utopia*, New York, Harcourt, Brace and World.

Manning, D.J. (1976) *Liberalism*, London, Dent.

March, J.G. (1988) *Decisions and Organizations*, Oxford, Blackwell.

March, J.G. and Olsen, J.P. (1976) *Ambiguity and Choice in Organizations*, Bergen, Universitetsforlaget.

March, J.G. and Olsen, J.P. (1989) *Rediscovering Institutions: the organisational basis of politics*, New York, Free Press.

Marcus, G. and Fischer, M. (1986) *Anthropology as Cultural Critique*, Chicago, Ill., University of Chicago Press.

Marquand, D. (1983) 'The collapse of consensus: ideology in British politics', in Lloyd (ed.) 1983.

Marsh, C. (1982) *The Survey Method*, London, Allen and Unwin.

Matthews, M. (1982) *Education in the Soviet Union*, London, Allen and Unwin.

Matza, D. (1964) *Delinquency and Drift*, New York, Wiley.

Matza, D. (1969) *Becoming Deviant*, Englewood Cliffs, NJ, Prentice-Hall.

Maynard, M. (1990) 'The reshaping of sociology: trends in the study of gender', *Sociology*, 24, 2: 269–90.

Mepham, J. and Hillel-Ruben, D. (eds) (1979) *Issues in Marxist Philosophy*, Vol. 3, Brighton, Harvester.

Merquior, J.G. (1985) *Foucault*, London, Fontana.

Merton, R.K. (1972) 'Insiders and outsiders', *American Journal of Sociology*, 78: 9–47.

Merton, R.K. (1973) *The Sociology of Science: theoretical and empirical investigations*, Chicago, University of Chicago Press.

Midgley, E.B.F. (1983) *The Ideology of Max Weber: a Thomist critique*, Aldershot, Gower.

Mies, M. (1983) 'Towards a methodology for feminist research', in Bowles and Duelli Klein (eds) 1983.

Mies, M. (1991) 'Women's research or feminist research? The debate surrounding feminist science and methodology', in Fonow and Cook (eds) 1991.

Miller, C. and Treitel, C. (1991) *Feminist Research Methods: an annotated bibliography*, New York, Greenwood Press.

Modood, T. (1992) *Not Easy being British*, Stoke on Trent, Trentham Books.

Moon, D. (1983) 'Political ethics and critical theory', in Sabia and Wallulis (eds) 1983.

Morris, C. (1946) *Signs, Language and Behavior*, New York, Braziller.

Myrdal, G. (1970) *Objectivity in Social Research*, London, Duckworth.

Neave, G. (1988) 'On being economical with university autonomy: being an account of the retrospective joys of a written constitution', in Tight (ed.) 1988.

Nelson, J.S., Megill, A. and McCloskey, D.N. (eds) (1987) *The Rhetoric of the Human Sciences*, Madison, University of Wisconsin Press.

Newton, K. (1990) *Interpreting the Text: a critical introduction to the theory and practice of literary interpretation*, New York, Harvester Wheatsheaf.

Newton-Smith, W.H. (1981) *The Rationality of Science*, London, Routledge and Kegan Paul.

Nicolaus, M. (1972) 'The professional organization of sociology: a view from below', in R. Blackburn (ed.), *Ideology in Social Science*, London, Fontana/Collins.

Nozick, R. (1974) *Anarchy, State and Utopia*, New York, Basic Books.

Oakes, G. (1988) *Weber and Rickert: concept formation in the cultural sciences*, Cambridge, Mass., MIT Press.

Oakeshott, M. (1962) *Rationalism in Politics*, London, Methuen.

Oakley, A. (1981) 'Interviewing women: a contradiction in terms', in Roberts (ed.) 1981.

Papadakis, E. (1989) 'Interventions in new social movements', in Gubrium and Silverman (eds) 1989.

Parijs, P. van (1981) *Evolutionary Explanation in the Social Sciences*, London, Tavistock.

Peshkin, A. (1986) *God's Choice: the total world of a fundamentalist Christian school and community*, Chicago, University of Chicago Press.

Pettigrew, M. (1993) 'Coming to terms with research: the contract business'. Paper given at ESRC sponsored seminar on Methodological and Ethical Issues Associated with Research into the Education Reform Act, University of Warwick.

Pfohl, S. (1993) 'Revenge of the parasites: feeding off the ruins of sociological (de)construction', in Holstein and Miller (eds) 1993.

Phillips, D.C. (1983) 'After the wake: postpositivistic educational thought', *Educational Researcher*, 12, 5: 4–12.

Phillips, D.C. (1987) *Philosophy, Science and Social Inquiry*, New York, Pergamon.

Phillips, D.C. (1990a) 'Subjectivity and objectivity: an objective inquiry', in Eisner and Peshkin (eds) 1990.

Phillips, D.C. (1990b) 'Postpositivistic science: myths and realities', in Guba (ed.) 1990.

Pincoffs, E. (ed.) (1975) *The Concept of Academic Freedom*, Austin, University of Texas.

Plant, R. (1973) *Hegel*, London, Allen and Unwin.

Polanyi, M. (1958) *Personal Knowledge*, Chicago, University of Chicago Press.

Polanyi, M. (1961) 'Science: academic and industrial', *Journal of the Institute of Metals*, 89: 401–6.

Polanyi, M. (1962) 'The republic of science', *Minerva*, 1, 1: 54–73.

Polanyi, M. (1964) *Science, Faith, and Society*, 2nd edn, Chicago, University of Chicago Press.

Polanyi, M. (1968) 'The republic of science: its political and economic theory', in E. Shils (ed.), *Criteria for Scientific Development, Public Policy, and National Goals*, Cambridge, Mass., MIT Press.

Pollard, A. (1984) 'Ethnography and social policy for classroom practice', in L. Barton and S. Walker (eds), *Social Crisis and Educational Research*, London, Croom Helm.

Popkin, R.H. (1979) *The History of Scepticism: from Erasmus to Spinoza*, Berkeley, University of California Press.

Popkin, R.H. and Schmidt, C. (eds) (1987) *Scepticism from the Renaissance to the Enlightenment*, Wiesbaden, Otto Harrassowitz.

Popper, K.R. (1963) *Conjectures and Refutations*, London, Routledge and Kegan Paul.

Popper, K.R. (1966) *The Open Society and its Enemies*, Vol. 2: *Hegel and Marx*, London, Routledge and Kegan Paul.

Popper, K.R. (1972) *Objective Knowledge*, Oxford, Oxford University Press.

Popper, K.R. (1976) 'Reason or revolution', in Adorno et al. (eds) 1976.

Popper, K.R. (1992) *Unended Quest: an intellectual autobiography*, London, Routledge.

Proctor, R.N. (1991) *Value Free Science?*, Cambridge, Mass., Harvard University Press.

Prokopczyk, C. (1980) *Truth and Reality in Marx and Hegel: a reassessment*, Amherst, Mass., University of Massachusetts Press.

Punch, M. (1986) *The Politics and Ethics of Fieldwork*, Beverly Hills, Sage.

Punch, M. (1994) 'Politics and ethics in qualitative research', in Denzin and Lincoln (eds) 1994.

Quantz, R.A. (1992) 'On critical ethnography (with some postmodern considerations)', in LeCompte et al. (eds) 1992.

Quine, W.V. (1953) *From a Logical Point of View*, Cambridge, Mass., Harvard University Press.

Quine, W.V. (1960) *Word and Object*, Cambridge, Mass., MIT Press.

Quine, W.V. (1984) 'Relativism and absolutism', *The Monist*, 67, 3: 293–6.

Quine, W.V. and Ullian, J.S. (1970) *The Web of Belief*, New York, Random House.

Radcliffe-Richards, J. (1980) *The Sceptical Feminist*, London, Routledge and Kegan Paul.

Rainwater, L. and Yancey, W.L. (1967) *The Moynihan Report and the Politics of Controversy*, Cambridge, Mass., MIT Press.

Ramazanoglu, C. (1992) 'On feminist methodology: male reason versus female empowerment', *Sociology*, 26, 2: 207–12.

Reilly, F.E. (1970) *Charles Peirce's Theory of Scientific Method*, New York, Fordham University Press.

Reinharz, S. (1979) *On Becoming a Social Scientist*, San Francisco, Jossey Bass.

Reinharz, S. (1983) 'Experiential analysis: a contribution to feminist research', in Bowles and Duelli Klein (eds) 1983.

Reinharz, S. (1992) *Social Research Methods: feminist perspectives*, New York, Oxford University Press.

Rescher, N. (1978) *Peirce's Philosophy of Science: critical studies in his theory of induction and scientific method*, South Bend, Ind., University of Notre Dame Press.

Richardson, L. (1990) *Writing Strategies: reaching diverse audiences*, Newbury Park, Sage.

Rist, R.C. (1994) 'Influencing the policy process with qualitative research', in Denzin and Lincoln (eds) 1994.

Robbins, Lord (1963) *Higher Education*, London, HMSO, Cmnd 2154.

Roberts, H. (ed.) (1981) *Doing Feminist Research*, London, Routledge and Kegan Paul.

Roman, L. and Apple, M. (1990) 'Is naturalism a move away from positivism? Materialist and feminist approaches to subjectivity in ethnographic research', in Eisner and Peshkin (eds) 1990.

Rooney, P. (1994) 'Recent work in feminist discussions of reason', *American Philosophical Quarterly*, 31, 1: 1–21.

Rose, G. (1978) *The Melancholy Science: an introduction to the thought of Theodor W. Adorno*, London, Macmillan.

Rose, G. (1979) 'Review of Buck-Morss *The Origin of Negative Dialectics* and of Tar *The Frankfurt School*', *History and Theory*, 8, 1: 126–35.

Rothschild, Lord (1971) 'The organisation and management of government R and D', in *A Framework for Government Research and Development*, Cmnd 4184, London, HMSO.

Rothschild, Lord (1982) *An Enquiry into the Social Science Research Council*, Cmnd 8554, London, HMSO.

Rouse, J. (1987) *Knowledge and Power: towards a political philosophy of science*, Ithaca, Cornell University Press.

Sabia, D.R. and Wallulis, J. (eds) (1983) *Changing Social Science*, Albany, State University of New York Press.

Saward, M. (1994) 'Postmodernists, pragmatists and the justification of democracy', *Economy and Society*, 23, 2: 201–16.

Sayer, D. (1979) 'Science as critique: Marx *vs*. Althusser', in Mepham and Hillel-Ruben (eds) 1979.

Schatzman, L. and Strauss, A. (1973) *Field Research*, Englewood Cliffs, NJ, Prentice Hall.

Scheffler, I. (1967) *Science and Subjectivity*, New York, Bobbs-Merrill.

Scheper-Hughes, B. (1992) 'Hungry bodies, medicine, and the state: towards a critical psychological anthropology' in T. Schwartz, G.M. White and C.A. Lutz (eds), *New Directions in Psychological Anthropology*, Cambridge, Cambridge University Press.

Schmitt, C. (1932) *The Concept of the Political*, English trans, New Brunswick, Rutgers University Press, 1976.

Scholem, G. (1982) *Walter Benjamin: the story of a friendship*, London, Faber and Faber.

Schön, D. (1983) *The Reflective Practitioner*, London, Temple Smith.

Schön, D. (1987) *Educating the Reflective Practitioner*, San Francisco, Jossey Bass.

Scriven, M. (1969) 'Logical positivism and the behavioral sciences', in Achinstein and Barker (eds) 1969.

Searle, J. (1990) 'The storm over the university', *New York Review of Books*, 37, 19: 34–42.

Sedgwick, P. (1982) *Psycho-Politics*, London, Pluto Press.

Sextus Empiricus (1985) *Selections from the Major Writings on Scepticism, Man, and God*, Indianapolis, Hackett.

Sharrock, W.W. (1980) 'The possibility of social change', in D.C. Anderson (ed.), *The Ignorance of Social Intervention*, London, Croom Helm.

Shaw, M. (1975) *Marxism and Social Science*, London, Pluto Press.

Sheridan, A. (1980) *Michel Foucault: the will to truth*, London, Tavistock.

Shklar, J. (1957) *After Utopia: the decline of political faith*, Princeton, NJ, Princeton University Press.

Sieber, S.D. (1981) *Fatal Remedies: the ironies of social intervention*, New York, Plenum Press.

Siegel, H. (1987) *Relativism Refuted: a critique of contemporary epistemological relativism*, Dordrecht, Reidel.

Silverman, D. (1989) 'Telling convincing stories: a plea for cautious positivism in case studies', in B. Glassner and J. Moreno (eds), *The Quantitative–Qualitative Distinction in the Social Sciences*, Dordrecht, Kluwer.

Simon, H. (1955) 'A behavioral model of rational choice', *Quarterly Journal of Economics*, 69: 99–118.

Simon, R. and Dippo, D. (1986) 'On critical ethnographic work', *Anthropology and Education Quarterly*, 17: 195–202.

Simons, H.W. (ed.) (1988) *Rhetoric in the Human Sciences*, London, Sage.

Singer, P. (1983) *Hegel*, Cambridge, Cambridge University Press.

Skagestad, P. (1981) *The Road of Inquiry*, New York, Columbia University Press.

Sluga, H. (1989) 'Metadiscourse: German philosophy and National Socialism', *Social Research*, 56, 4: 795–818.

Smart, C. (1984) *The Ties that Bind: law, marriage and the reproduction of patriarchal relations*, London, Routledge and Kegan Paul.

Smith, D.E. (1987) *The Everyday World as Problematic: a feminist sociology*, Milton Keynes, Open University Press.

Smith, D.J. and Tomlinson, S. (1989) *The School Effect: a study of multi-racial comprehensives*, London, Policy Studies Institute.

Smith, J.K. (1989) *The Nature of Social and Educational Inquiry*, Norwood, NJ, Ablex.

Smith, J.K. and Heshusius, L. (1986) 'Closing down the conversation: the end of the quantitative-qualitative debate among educational inquirers', *Educational Researcher*, 15, 1: 4–12.

Smith, J.V. and Hamilton, D. (eds) (1980) *The Meritocratic Intellect: studies in the history of educational research*, Aberdeen, Aberdeen University Press.

Spencer, H. (1946) *The Man versus the State*, New York, Appleton (first published 1892).

Sperber, D. and Wilson, D. (1986) *Relevance: communication and cognition*, Oxford, Blackwell.

Stacey, J. (1988) 'Can there be a feminist ethnography?', *Women's Studies International Forum*, 11, 1: 21–7.

Stanley, L. (1992) *The Auto/Biographical I: the theory and practice of feminist auto/biography*, Manchester, Manchester University Press.

Stanley, L. and Wise, S. (1983a) ' "Back into the personal" or: our attempt to construct "feminist research" ', in Bowles and Duelli Klein (eds) 1983.

Stanley, L. and Wise, S. (1983b) *Breaking Out: feminist consciousness and feminist research*, London, Routledge and Kegan Paul.

Stanley, L. and Wise, S. (1990) 'Method, methodology and epistemology in feminist research processes', in L. Stanley (ed.), *Feminist Praxis*, London, Routledge.

Stenhouse, L. (1975) *An Introduction to Curriculum Research and Development*, London, Heinemann.

Storing, H. (ed.) (1962) *Essays on the Scientific Study of Politics*, New York, Holt Rinehart and Winston.

Strathern, M. (1987) 'An awkward relationship: the case of feminism and anthropology', *Signs*, 12, 2: 276–92.

Strauss, L. (1953) *Natural Right and History*, Chicago, University of Chicago Press.

Sturrock, J. (ed.) (1979) *Structuralism and Since: from Levi-Strauss to Derrida*, Oxford, Oxford University Press.

Suppe, F. (ed.) (1974) *The Structure of Scientific Theories*, Chicago, University of Chicago Press.

Taylor, A.J. (1972) *Laissez-faire and State Intervention in Nineteenth-century Britain*, London, Macmillan.

Taylor, C. (1964) *The Explanation of Behaviour*, London, Routledge and Kegan Paul.

Taylor, C. (1981) *Social Theory and Practice*, Delhi, Oxford University Press.

Thomas, J. (1993) *Doing Critical Ethnography*, Newbury Park, Sage.

Thompson, J.B. (1982) 'Universal pragmatics', in Thompson and Held (eds) 1982.

Thompson, J.B. and Held, D. (eds) (1982) *Habermas: critical debates*, London, Macmillan.

Tight, M. (ed.) (1988) *Academic Freedom and Responsibility*, Milton Keynes, Open University Press.

Tiles, J. (1989) *John Dewey*, London, Routledge and Kegan Paul.

Toulmin, S. (1969) 'From logical analysis to conceptual history', in Achinstein and Barker (eds) 1969.

Trigg, R. (1980) *Reality at Risk: a defence of realism in philosophy and the sciences*, Brighton, Harvester.

Troyna, B. (1991) 'Under-achievers or under-rated? The experiences of pupils of South Asian origin in a secondary school', *British Educational Research Journal*, 17, 4: 361–76.

Troyna, B. (1992) 'Ethnicity and the organization of learning groups: a case study', *Educational Research*, 34, 1: 45–55.

Troyna, B. (1993) 'Underachiever or misunderstood: a reply to Roger Gomm', *British Educational Research Journal*, 19, 2: 167–74.

Troyna, B. and Carrington, B. (1989) 'Whose side are we on? Ethical dilemmas in research on "race" and education', in R.G. Burgess (ed.), *The Ethics of Educational Research*, Lewes, Falmer.

Vickers, G. (1990) 'The recovery of rhetoric: Petrarch, Erasmus, Perelman', *History of the Human Sciences*, 3, 3: 415–41.

Vision, G. (1988) *Modern Anti-realism and Manufactured Truth*, London, Routledge.

Walsh, W.H. (1987) 'Kant as seen by Hegel', in S. Priest (ed.), *Hegel's Critique of Kant*, Oxford, Oxford University Press.

Walzer, M. (1983) 'The politics of Michel Foucault', *Dissent*, 481–90.

Warnke, G. (1987) *Gadamer: hermeneutics, tradition and reason*, Cambridge, Polity Press.

Warren, C.B. (1988) *Gender Issues in Field Research*, Newbury Park, Sage.

Warren, C.B. (1993) 'The 1960s state as a social problem: an analysis of Radical Right and New Left claims-making rhetorics', in Holstein and Miller (eds) 1993.

Watson, G. (1962) *The Literary Critics*, Harmondsworth, Penguin.

Weber, M. (1949) *The Methodology of the Social Sciences*, New York, Free Press.

Weber, M. (1974) *Max Weber on Universities: the power of the state and the dignity of the academic calling in Imperial Germany* (translated with an introduction by E. Shils), Chicago, University of Chicago Press.

Weiner, G. (1989) 'Professional self-knowledge versus social justice: a critical analysis of the teacher-researcher movement', *British Educational Research Journal*, 15, 1: 41–51.

Weiss, C. with Bucuvalas, M. (1980) *Social Science Research and Decision Making*, New York, Columbia University Press.

Westergaard, J. (1979) 'In memory of David Glass', *Sociology*, 13, 2: 173–7.

Westkott, M. (1979) 'Feminist criticism of the social sciences', *Harvard Education Review*, 49, 4: 422–30.

Whyte, W.F. (1955) *Street Corner Society*, 2nd edn, Chicago, University of Chicago Press.

Whyte, W.F. (1992) 'In defense of *Street Corner Society*', *Journal of Contemporary Ethnography*, 21, 1: 52–68.

Wick, W.A. (1951) 'The "political" philosophy of logical empiricism', *Philosophical Studies*, 2, 4: 49–57.

Williams, A. (1993) 'Diversity and agreement in feminist ethnography', *Sociology*, 27, 4, 575–89.

Williams, M. (1991) *Unnatural Doubts: epistemological realism and the philosophical basis of scepticism*, Oxford, Blackwell.

Winch, P. (1958) *The Idea of a Social Science and its Relation to Philosophy*, London, Routledge and Kegan Paul.

Winch, P. (1964) 'Understanding a primitive society', *American Philosophical Quarterly*, 1: 307–24.

Winter, S.G. (1964) 'Economic "natural selection" and the theory of the firm', *Yale Economic Essays*, 4: 225–72.

Wirth, L. (1936) Preface to Mannheim (1936).

Wittgenstein, L. (1969) *On Certainty*, Oxford, Blackwell.

Wolcott, H.F. (1990) *Writing up Qualitative Research*, Newbury Park, Sage.

Wolin, R. (1990) *The Politics of Being: the political thought of Martin Heidegger*, New York, Columbia University Press.

Wolin, R. (ed.) (1991) *The Heidegger Controversy: a critical reader*, New York, Columbia University Press.

Woods, P. (1985) 'New songs played skillfully: creativity and technique in writing up qualitative research', in Burgess (ed.) 1985.

Woolgar, S. (ed.) (1988) *Knowledge and Reflexivity*, London, Sage.

Woolgar, S. and Pawluch, D. (1985) 'Ontological gerrymandering: the anatomy of social problems explanations', *Social Problems*, 32, 3: 214–27.

Wright, C. (1991) 'Comments in reply to the article by P. Foster', *British Educational Research Journal*, 16, 4: 351–5.

Zetterberg, H. (1962) *Social Theory and Social Practice*, New York, Bedminster.

Zuckert, C.H. (1990) 'Martin Heidegger: his philosophy and politics', *Political Theory*, 18, 1: 51–79.

# Name Index

# Subject Index